Shalom: God's Ultimate Purpose for the World

Shalom: God's Ultimate Purpose for the World

Modern Medical Mission in the Islamic Context

Dae-Young Lee

Preface by Jerry M. Ireland

WIPF & STOCK · Eugene, Oregon

SHALOM: GOD'S ULTIMATE PURPOSE FOR THE WORLD
Modern Medical Mission in the Islamic Context

Copyright © 2021 Dae-Young Lee. All rights reserved. Except for brief quotations in critical publications or reviews, no part of this book may be reproduced in any manner without prior written permission from the publisher. Write: Permissions, Wipf and Stock Publishers, 199 W. 8th Ave., Suite 3, Eugene, OR 97401.

Wipf & Stock
An Imprint of Wipf and Stock Publishers
199 W. 8th Ave., Suite 3
Eugene, OR 97401

www.wipfandstock.com

PAPERBACK ISBN: 978-1-6667-1441-8
HARDCOVER ISBN: 978-1-6667-1442-5
EBOOK ISBN: 978-1-6667-1443-2

06/16/21

Scripture quotations marked (NASB) are taken from the (NASB®) New American Standard Bible®, Copyright © 1960, 1971, 1977, 1995, 2020 by The Lockman Foundation. Used by permission. All rights reserved. www.lockman.org

Scripture quotations marked (NIV) are taken from the Holy Bible, New International Version®, NIV®. Copyright © 1973, 1978, 1984, 2011 by Biblica, Inc.™ Used by permission of Zondervan. All rights reserved worldwide. www.zondervan.comThe "NIV" and "New International Version" are trademarks registered in the United States Patent and Trademark Office by Biblica, Inc.™

Scripture quotations marked (KJV) are taken from The Authorized (King James) Version. Rights in the Authorized Version in the United Kingdom are vested in the Crown. Reproduced by permission of the Crown's patentee, Cambridge University Press

Dedicated to my beloved wife, Hyun-Jung Seo, and sons, Ji-Woo and Ji-Min, who are always with me for the mission of God.

For thus says the LORD, "Behold, I extend peace to her like a river, And the glory of the nations like an overflowing stream; And you will be nursed, you will be carried on the hip and fondled on the knees."

—ISAIAH 66:12 NASB

Contents

Preface by Jerry M. Ireland | ix
Acknowledgments | xi
Abbreviations | xiii
Introduction | xv

1. Biblical Concept of *Shalom* in Comparison to the Concept of Peace in Islam | 1
2. Healing in Islam and the Biblical Approach | 41
3. Christian Medical Mission | 82
4. Principles and Strategies of Christian Medical Mission in the Arab world | 120

Conclusion | 167
Bibliography | 171

Preface

IN THE WORLD OF Christian compassionate missions, and, more precisely, the world of Christian medical missions to the Arab world, pitfalls abound. There exists the ever-present danger of doing medical missions merely as a "platform," and thereby disingenuously. Or, more palatably to the non-Christian world, one might engage in medical work in a foreign land that has no genuine Christian content because there exists no explicit link to the gospel. Additionally, medical mission efforts have too often subverted, ignored, or dismissed local medical professionals, guidelines, and government regulations, putting the missionaries at odds with civil authorities in ways incompatible with the gospel and with truth. Paternalistic tendencies, especially among western mission workers have at times resulted in the sending of so-called "medical teams" that lacked even basic medical and missionary training.

These far-too-common shortcomings in medical mission work have minimally left a dark stain on the church but also raised (further) questions as to the legitimacy of the entire mission enterprise. If Christians cannot show compassion to the most needy and vulnerable, especially the sick, in ways that are Christ-honoring, culturally considerate, and carried out with honesty and integrity, then is there any hope at all for Christian cross-cultural efforts?

A large part of the problem when it comes to Christian medical missions is that these mission efforts seldom are carried out by those who have the multiple levels of expertise needed—that is, legitimate medical credentials, solid biblical-theological training including an understanding of biblical languages, and a more than rudimentary grasp of the complex issues that make up the discipline of missiology. This is precisely why this text you now hold proves so crucial. Dae Young Lee meets (and excels) in all of these disciplines and thereby not only provides sound biblical guidance on medical missions but does so in a way that keeps the church's evangelistic efforts central.

By focusing on and unpacking the deep theological concept of *shalom* and noting both its bridges to and divergence from Muslim concepts of peace, Lee offers an insightful take on what is sure to be a major focus of Christian mission in the twenty-first century. He calls on Christian medical mission organizations and personnel to acknowledge and repent of their sometime wayward efforts, such as "having built kingdoms of individual mission agencies which disempowered local indigenous churches and their leadership." The question of what medical mission work might look like viewed through a lens of indigeneity has rarely been asked and seldom answered to a satisfactory degree. This, though, is where this text shines brightest. Dae Young is unafraid to point to areas of neglect and shortcoming in medical missions because he is convinced by Scripture that there must be a better, more Christ-honoring way.

I heartily recommend this book for all whose Christian faith intersects in any way with medical missions. Church leaders, pastors, and mission boards who support medical missionaries should read this book to gain better insight into what kinds of activities are worthy of support and what kind need reconsideration or revision. Mission leaders who appoint, oversee, and send missionaries should read this book to gain clarity about what medical mission to the Arab world might look like when done in line with sound missiological principles. Missionaries who engage in medical missions of any kind should read this book for its biblical grounding, its missional principles, and its practical application. And students considering medical missions should read this book in order to better understand before they begin how to engage in this important need and to do it with excellence.

Jerry M. Ireland, PhD

Acknowledgments

My deepest gratitude goes to my mentor, Dr. Jerry M. Ireland, Dr. Edward L. Smither, Dr. David G. Cashin, and Dr. Roy King. This book would not have come together without their thoughtful advice. I am greatly indebted to them.

Abbreviations

ABCD	Asset-Based Community Development
CANs	Creative Access Nations
CHE	Community Health Evangelism
HOME	Health Outreach to the Middle East
MDGs	Millennium Development Goals
NASB	New American Standard Bible
NGOs	Non-Governmental Organizations
NIV	New International Version
SDGs	Sustainable Development Goals
STMs	Short-Term Missions
UNHCR	United Nations High Commissioner for Refugees
WHO	World Health Organization
YWAM	Youth With A Mission

Introduction

SHALOM[1] IS GOD'S ULTIMATE purpose toward the world that he created. The message of *shalom* is a great blessing promised by God and is realized through the reconciling ministry of Christ Jesus. The main theme of the biblical narrative is God's mission, the *missio Dei*. That is, God sends his people to invite the lost to his Kingdom, as Christopher J. H. Wright indicates:

> So the phrase originally meant "the sending of God"—in the sense of the Father's sending of the Son and their sending of the Holy Spirit. All human mission, in this perspective, is seen as a participation in and extension of this divine sending.[2]

Christian mission[3] will enable those suffering from despair and fear in the current situation of the Arab world[4] to experience *shalom* by opening

---

1. Strong, "*shalom*," in *New Strong's Concise Dictionary*. "Peace" refers to freedom from disturbance, mentally or emotionally calm and state of tranquility for individuals, and, state or period in which there is no war or a war has ended for communities (*English Oxford Living Dictionaries*).

2. Wright, *Mission of God*, 62–63.

3. Christian mission is the overarching term for various organized efforts to accomplish the Great Commission of making all nations disciples of Jesus Christ with proclaiming the gospel across the geographical and cultural boundaries. Manser, Bible reference editor, defines mission as "specific actions that bear witness to the good news of what God has done for his people. Israel, Jesus Christ and the church all in their different ways bear witness to the saving acts of God in history." Christian mission is empowered by the Holy Spirit (Manser, *Dictionary of Bible Themes*). *Missio Dei* is a Latin term which can be translated as the "mission of God," or "the sending of God," based on the Abrahamic covenant (Gen 12:1–3) and the Great Commissions in the Gospel (Matt 28:18–20; John 20:21) (Longman III, *The Baker Illustrated Bible Dictionary*, 1164).

4. The Arab world can be defined as the Arabic-speaking countries of the Middle East and North Africa regarded collectively, especially with reference to their political or cultural values. Zaharna, "An Associative Approach," 181. The twenty-two countries in the Arab World are: Mauritania, Western Sahara, Morocco, Tunisia, Algeria, Libya, and

their eyes to see Jesus breaking the bondage of hopelessness and hatred. Christian medical mission is a well-established means of both sharing the Gospel with unreached people and providing health care to those in need. Despite its long history of service in Christian mission, there is a lack of evaluation concerning the current medical mission principles and strategies. Collaboration between long-term and short-term medical missions should be well-established, as they complement each other for more effective impact on local individuals and communities.

Christian medical mission[5] has a long history in the Arab world, as it does in the whole world, and has been playing a crucial role in sharing the gospel with people in the region. Although current political and religious situations put considerable pressure on Christian mission in the Arab world, it opens doors for the gospel and provides numerous opportunities for Christian mission to reach out to the unreached people in the Arab world through professional medical ministries. The current situation in this region urges Christian mission to bring the biblical concept of *shalom* as so many people and communities have been suffering from unceasing violence resulting in a massive refugee crisis. Through a deeper understanding of *shalom*, this book demonstrates how Christian medical mission in the Arab world can be manifested in more biblical ways and can serve people who have been physically injured and emotionally broken by the situation more effectively.

Although missiologists consider Christian medical mission an effective tool to share the gospel as an essential part of Christian mission, it has been facing considerable challenges, like sustainability, relationship with national leadership, security and safety, and restrictions on locally unlicensed medical practices by national authorities. Advantages and disadvantages of different types of Christian medical ministry must be carefully evaluated, and thus provide a better conception from which to develop principles and strategies. In addition, studies addressing the role of medical mission in the relationship with overall Christian mission have developed

---

Egypt in North Africa; Sudan, Eritrea, Djibouti, and Somalia along the Horn of Africa; Palestine, Jordan, Lebanon, and Syria in the Fertile Crescent of the Middle East (often referred to as bilad as-sham, greater Syria, or the Levant); and Iraq and the Arabian peninsula, including Oman, Yemen, Saudi Arabia, Kuwait, Bahrain, Qatar, and the United Arab Emirates (often referred to as the khaleej al-Arabi or the Arab Gulf).

5. "Medical ministry" or "missions" refers to the spiritual work or service of a Christian or a group of Christians in cross-cultural contexts, through professional medical work related to the treatment of illness and injuries (Greenall, "What is the Future").

Introduction

throughout the nineteenth and twentieth centuries. These studies teach how Christian medical missions will play a better role in the advance of the Kingdom of God in the near future. Considering this careful evaluation and study, Christian medical mission will be able to overcome challenges and grow increasingly to effectively bring the transformational message of the gospel to the world's unreached.

It will also assist professional Christian medical workers as they seek a deeper understanding of the biblical concept of *shalom* to better care for patients with physical illnesses and injuries. Since the World Health Organization (WHO) has defined health in its broader sense in their 1948 constitution as "a state of complete physical, mental, and social well-being and not merely the absence of disease or infirmity,"[6] medicine itself has pursued not only physical wellness, but also the restoration of the wholeness to human beings. This ultimately requires human beings to be reconciled with God through Christ's redemptive ministry on the cross, and God has chosen Christian medical mission to be part of carrying out his comprehensive plan to restore the world to that wholeness.

God's mission is wholistic and church-centered; therefore, Christian medical mission should pursue Jesus' way in its endeavor of missions. Throughout this book, I suggest principles and strategies for Christian medical mission to consider so that the global church may move forward in Christian medical mission by missiological reflection. I want this book to identify areas of strength and weakness of Christian medical missions and help develop strategies in their contexts. I anticipate that this book may improve the quality of health care provided by Christian medical missions and stimulate scholarly reflection among missions.

6. WHO, "Constitution."

1

Biblical Concept of *Shalom* in Comparison to the Concept of Peace in Islam

THE HISTORY OF HUMANITY is full of violence. Despite the fact that human beings are eager to maintain peace and felicity in their daily lives, violent crimes that promote fear and anger fill mass media almost every day. Although the wondrous development of science and technology has contributed to mankind's material comfort and physical well-being, many of human problems like crime, war, genocide, racism, terrorism, unequal distribution and degradation of resources, and threat of nuclear weapons remain serious. In many parts of the world, material development in recent history seems unsuccessful in bringing peace. In the world's complicated situations, everyone wants peace, yet few seem to find and experience it. While natural disasters and calamities cannot be avoided, many problems the world faces can be corrected, as they are of all humans' own decision making, created by misunderstandings and differences of religions, ideologies, and socio-political systems.

Christian mission plays an important role in sharing the biblical message of *shalom* to these complex troubles in the world. In the circumstances of fighting against each other for petty ends and losing face of fundamental humanity, Christian mission should share the gospel, which ultimately provides the realization of *shalom* in the communities where it serves. Particularly speaking, *shalom* can be manifested in every act of practicing medicine by caring for patients individually and restoring the communities to which they belong collectively, because medicine respects every single life and its dignity. As God promises to restore people's lives through Jesus

Shalom: God's Ultimate Purpose for the World

Christ, Christian medical professionals should continue to offer the message of *shalom* to those who are broken and injured in the region. This book fills the gaps in our understanding of God's reconciliation ministry for people suffering in the current situation by demonstrating the biblical concept of *shalom*. In addition, it is beneficial to approach Muslims in the Arab world by sharing the biblical *shalom* in comparison to the concepts of peace in Islam on the basis of the Qur'an.

Shalom in the Old Testament

It is invaluable to study the concept of *shalom* thoroughly through examining its usage in the Scripture. Various forms of the word "*shalom*" and "peace" are found in the Old Testament. This topic has been well studied by James A. Swanson who introduced the meanings of *shalom* in his *Dictionary of Biblical Languages with Semantic Domain: Hebrews* (Old Testament):

> *Shalom* in the Old Testament is שָׁלוֹם [Strong's 3073, 7965], and means
>
> 1. peace, prosperity, i.e., an intact state of favorable circumstance;
> 2. completeness, i.e., the state of a totality of a collection;
> 3. safeness, salvation, i.e., a state of being free from danger;
> 4. health, i.e., a state of lack of disease and a wholeness or well-being;
> 5. satisfaction, contentment, i.e., the state of having one's basic needs or more being met and so being content;
> 6. friend, companion, i.e., one who has an association with another with affection or regard;
> 7. blessing, i.e., the content of the act. of giving kindness to another;
> 8. unit: יהוה שָׁלוֹם (YHWH) Yahweh is Peace, i.e., the name of an altar;
> 9. unit: שַׂר שָׁלוֹם, Prince of Peace, i.e., the name of messiah.[1]

Terry McGonigal suggests *shalom* theology as a way of understanding God's message of the whole.[2] He describes that *shalom* is the expression of God's kingdom which displays his glory in all creation. God's divine act for *shalom* in his creation is expressed throughout history and will continue

---

1. Swanson, "Shalom," *Languages with Semantic Domain*.
2. McGonigal, "If You Only Knew."

to be manifested in diverse humanity. Even if there are many conflicts surrounding the differences of humanity such as genders, tribes, nationalities, ethnicities, and so forth, the message of *shalom* brings mankind together in restoration to a relationship with God through his redemptive ministry of Jesus Christ. McGonigal confidently states God's desire for his creation:

> God's design for and delight in diversity are embedded in the creation narratives, which describe order, relationships, stewardship, beauty and rhythm as the essential foundations for *shalom*, "the way God designed the universe to be."[3]

God's character and actions displayed throughout the Old Testament are the exemplary model of how human beings can experience *shalom* in his sovereign rule over creation.

Shalom as Completeness, Soundness, and Welfare

Shalom in Hebrew can simply be translated as "peace" and is frequently used as both a greeting and farewell. Gerhard Kittel and Gerhard Friedrich indicate: "*Shalom* is a common term in rabbinic works. It occurs in greetings in the general sense of well-being."[4] When the LORD meets with Gideon, the LORD tells him in Judges 6:23, "Peace to you, do not fear; you shall not die." This greeting is also found in Judges 19:20, so it can be considered as a common greeting among the Israelites. Moreover, in Ezra 4:17–18, the king, Artaxerxes, sends a letter answering Rehum, the commander, and starts with the greeting "peace (שְׁלָם)."[5] Similar usage of "peace" is found in Daniel 4:1, when King Nebuchadnezzar begins his announcement with the greeting, "May your peace abound!" These prove that the word of peace for greetings was used far and wide beyond Israel, even Babylon and Persia. Another typical usage of *shalom* for the meaning of peace is demonstrated in Exodus 4:18. Jethro says to Moses, "Go in peace," when Moses wants to return to his brethren who were in Egypt. 1 Samuel 1:17 also shows the same usage when Eli asks Hannah to "go in peace." It can be found more in the verses of Judges 18:6, 1 Samuel 20:42, 1 Samuel 25:35, and 2 Kings 5:19. These show that *shalom* was used as a standard

---

3. McGonigal, "If You Only Knew."
4. Kittel and Friedrich, ed., *Theological Dictionary*, 209.
5. Swanson, "Peace," *Languages with Semantic Domain*.

greeting in the Israelite community for a long period of time when people were both meeting and parting.

This usage of *shalom* as a greeting is also found many places in the New Testament. Luke 8:48 is a good example: when a woman having a hemorrhage for twelve years got healed by touching Jesus' cloak, Jesus blessed the woman by saying, "Go in peace." Here, it is evident that *shalom* is a common phrase of greeting in the Jewish society in Jesus' time as well, and is still used in many societies and cultures today. When a person greets another person by saying *shalom* (שָׁלוֹם לְךָ, "Peace to you"), the other person responds with a phrase *Aleikhem shalom* (עֲלֵיכֶם שָׁלוֹם; "To you, peace").[6] This sounds quite similar to the greetings of the Arab Muslim community in which a person greets with the Arabic saying, "*As[t]-Salaam-Alaikum* (اَلسَّلامُ عَلَيْكُم)," meaning "Peace be unto you," and the other person responds with "*Wa-Alaikum-As[t]-Salaam* (وَعَلَيْكُمُ ٱلسَّلَام)," meaning "And unto you, peace."

Perry B. Yoder sees *shalom* as welfare in the interpretation of Psalm 35:27.[7] In Genesis 43:27, when Joseph inquires about his brothers' welfare, he uses the same term of *shalom*. In addition, 2 Samuel 11:7 describes that David asks Uriah, concerning the peace of Joab, the peace of the people, and the peace of the battle with the Ammonites. In this context, "peace" does not refer to the absence of hostilities but the welfare of those involved and the progression of the fighting. This concept includes basic physical, material, and emotional well-being of people in need. The concept of *shalom* is not only related to the physical welfare, but also the emotional and spiritual state. In addition, as author David Andrew indicates, the word *shalom* is most used in the Old Testament to represent this integrated vision of God for his kingdom. Thus Andrew concludes that the biblical concept of *shalom* is closely related to the spiritual reality that comes from the intimate relationship with God.[8] He also defines that *shalom* indicated not merely the absence of strife or conflict, but the presence of pervading, profoundly saving well-being that has brought life to people, groups, and nations.[9]

---

6. "Shalom Aleikhem," *Encyclopaedia Judaica*.

7. Yoder, *Shalom*, 15. *Shalom* also means completeness, soundness, and welfare (Carpenter and Comfort, *Holman Treasury*, 135).

8. Andrews, *Integral Mission*.

9. Andrews, *Integral Mission*.

Shalom in Relationship

In the Old Testament, the primary meaning of *shalom* is closely related to relationships and relies on the basis of reciprocity and complementarity as a practice of exchanging valuable things for mutual benefits. Yoder emphasizes *shalom* in the relationship with covenant made between two parties:

> The use of a covenant in order to regulate relationships and bring about *shalom*, as in the covenants mentioned, makes clear that relationships involve responsibility.[10]

This intimate relationship improves each other's qualities, and implies an external peace between two entities, such as individuals or nations, and to an internal sense of peace within the individual. It consists of a relationship system with different levels of complexity that affect and are affected by each other, and, furthermore, a relationship to the socio-cultural structure and physical environment surrounding the relationship. God's purpose in the creation of man and woman is to demonstrate his desire of *shalom* in their relationship. God's diversity in creation and community is essential for the biblical concept of *shalom* just as the way that God designed the universe. McGonigal explains in his article: "In Creator's design, as the man and woman respond to each other in love, they reflect God's own nature in *shalom* relationships."[11] The essential condition in which people experience *shalom* is to follow God's laws and principles. In this regard, those who love God's law have great peace, as Psalms 119:165 says. Personal peace is promised to those who obey God's law, and this goes further to the relationship between people and nations.

Hamor and his son, Shechem, mention *shalom* in consideration of the relationship with Jacob's family in Genesis 34:21. Genesis 37:4 also uses *shalom* when Joseph's brothers hate him and can not speak to him in a way that is friendly ("peaceably," KJV). The nature of a mutual relationship depends on individuals and their demonstrated behavior in each interaction. Furthermore, *shalom* is used for the relationship between King Solomon of Israel and King Hiram of Tyre in 1 Kings 5:12, and there is obviously more than a personal relationship between Solomon and Hiram. From this perspective, the characteristics of this relationship point to the covenant between nations,

---

10. Yoder, *Shalom*, 76. Greever defines *shalom*: "A pervasive concept in the Bible that most commonly relates to a relationship of love and loyalty with God and one another" (Greever, *The Lexham Bible Dictionary*).

11. McGonigal, "If You Only Knew."

Shalom: God's Ultimate Purpose for the World

a relationship well beyond the individuals. Interpersonal relationships occur within a structural and cultural context, and the nature of the relationship is strongly influenced by the type of group to which it relates.

The Fall broke this relationship reflecting *shalom*, which has affected the entirety of God's creation, and no one on earth can restore it. McGonigal describes four categories reflecting this pervasive influence of the Fall to the nature of *shalom* relationship:

> Humanity's relationship with God, with each other, and with all creation has been permanently diminished. Evil sends waves of destruction crashing over all creation. Creation's *shalom* is torn asunder as the questioning-disobeying process ruptures every divinely created relationship;
>
> 1. Between Man and Woman ([Gen]3:7, 12, 16)
> 2. Between Humanity and God the Creator-Protector (3:8–13, 21–23)
> 3. Between Humanity and Animals (3:14–15)
> 4. Between Humanity and Nature (3:16–20)[12]

This broken relationship needs God's divine intervention to counteract evil and restore *shalom*. Although the enemy is powerful, its power will never be eternal. McGonigal continues to highlight the importance of reconciliation with explanation about two cognates of the word *shalom*: *shalem* as "to make right" and "to restore," and *shelem* as "peace offering." The former is used for the horizontal relationship between people, and the latter for the right relationship with God. This concept is illuminated in the commandments from God after Exodus (Exod 19–40, Leviticus, Numbers, and Deuteronomy), and clearly demonstrates that God initiated restoration of the broken relationship with human beings.[13] Yoder explains the *shalom* relationship between God and the Israelites:

> Another way to understand this point is to remember that God's love for the people was channeled through acts of liberation which expressed *shalom* justice. These initial acts of love by God set the basis for the relationship between Yahweh and Israel. The law, within the context of covenant and grace, now expresses how

---

12. McGonigal, "If You Only Knew."
13. McGonigal, "If You Only Knew."

Israel channels its love toward God; how Israel enters into and maintains this *shalom* relationship established by God.[14]

The Apostle Paul precisely expounds *shalom* made through Christ that in 2 Corinthians 5:18–19, "God reconciled us to himself," and in Colossians 1:20–22, "God reconciles all things to himself." God calls all believers to the ministry of reconciliation: He always desires to reconcile humanity to himself by breaking the bondage that the enemy has brought in, and by restoring the relationship through Jesus Christ, which will ultimately bring *shalom* to all creation.

People's volitional disobeying God's commandment has lost *shalom* between God and humanity, which brought hostility to the whole relationships between individuals and nations. The experience of evil shattered the beauty of *shalom*, and *shalom* has been lost because of mankind's willful violation of God's decrees. "Hostility" implies a hostile disposition and animosity which results in a real action in the relationship. In other words, hostility can be defined as a specific action and its results through which distress has been brought on human beings and societies by rebellion against God. McGonigal mentions that evil is the antonym of *shalom*, and it ruptures every divinely-created relationship, which was found in Genesis chapter 3. This broken relationship continues to affect every aspect of people's lives, and hostility to one another is a serious manifestation of evil in these fallen relationships. The disruption of peace at every level among all peoples is indisputable, and all of humankind is subject to the suffering coming from this disruption.

Shalom is used as "the removal of hostility between the believers and God,"[15] and the Apostle Paul indicates in Ephesians 2:14 that Jesus Christ destroyed the barrier of hostility between Jews and Gentiles for a new social structure in the early church. Yoder states:

> The new nature which comes from our transformation, from the love of Christ controlling us, automatically results in a new way in human relations. Again, the old social divisions cannot any longer count among us. The New Testament does not here separate the personal aspects of the atonement—putting on the new nature

---

14. Yoder, *Shalom*, 76–77.

15. Gruenler, "Romans." Merriam-Webster dictionary also explains: "a state of tranquility or quiet: as a: freedom from civil disturbance, and b: a state of security or order within a community provided for by law or custom." (Mish, "Peace," 911).

and laying off the old—from the corporate aspects—the reconciliation of old enemies into one new society.[16]

Ecclesiastes 3:8 puts war and peace in direct contrast: "There is a time for war and a time for peace." Greever indicates that the absence of hostility is a good thing, given that Solomon's name derives from the term for peace, שָׁלוֹם, *shalom*, and he was allowed to build the temple while David was not because of the wars which surrounded him (1 Kgs 5:3).[17] Therefore, hostility resulting in destructive relationship will be taken away by the reconciling ministry of Christ Jesus, and *shalom* will be experienced under his righteous reign.

Swanson defines *shalom* as a condition or sense of harmony and tranquility,[18] which stretches beyond the mere absence of hostility. The biblical concept of *shalom* in the Old Testament involves wholeness and completeness as one of the most prominent theological concepts related to the relationship with God. The creation story in Genesis discloses a good and perfect world and the centrality of the Creator. It is about the harmony that existed between God and his creation and between creation itself. Malachi 2:5 describes God's covenant with Levi, a covenant of life and peace, as an object of reverence. Verse six explains more about the reasons that God gave him the covenant of life and peace: "True instruction was in his mouth and unrighteousness was not found on his lips; he walked with Me in peace and uprightness, and he turned many back from iniquity" (Mal 2:6).

Walking with God in peace and uprightness has a meaning of remaining harmony with God by faith and obedience. The covenant of life and peace is found in the intimate relationship with God. The background of the covenant of life and peace is from an allusion to the covenant with Phinehas, Aaron's grandson, in Numbers 25:10–13. There, Phinehas defended God's honor by killing two offenders involved in the idolatry and immorality connected with the Ba'al of Peor. The zeal of Phinehas for God's honor became the occasion for God's covenanting with him and his descendants as God's true priests.[19] Psalm 106:29–31 praises the intervention of Phinehas as righteousness as God honors his people who are zealous against sin. The term "harmony" is used most frequently in the field of music, meaning "the combining of contrasting elements for far better sound." Similarly,

16. Yoder, *Shalom*, 68.
17. Greever, "Peace."
18. Swanson, *Dictionary: Hebrew*, "εἰρήνη (*eirēnē*)."
19. Brand, et al., "Peace," 1261–62.

God's people who used to be alienated from God now enjoy harmony of *shalom* in the reconciled relationship through Christ Jesus.

Peace Offering

In Leviticus chapters one to seven, there is a detailed description of Israel's five sacrifices: the Burnt Offering, the Grain Offering, the Peace Offering, the Sin Offering, and the Guilt Offering.[20] The Peace Offering is also called "fellowship offering" (NIV) in the Old Testament, and the name is closely related to *shalom*—שְׁלָמִים.[21] It is primarily a communion between God and the Israelites, and is the only offering in which worshippers partook of the meat of the animal, as the fat of the animal was consumed on the altar of the Lord. The meat of this offering was shared with people in a meal before God as a celebration, according to Leviticus 3, 7:11–21, and 7:29–34, while most of the scarifies in the Old Testament were not eaten by people.[22] This illustrates the meaning of peace offering: "This offering most likely indicated that the worshiper was at peace with God and others; all the worshiper's relationships were whole."[23] This peace offering needed a sacrifice of animal which required slaughter and bleeding, symbolizing "the brokenness of the proper relationship between sinful humans and the holy God."[24] Therefore, this peace offering symbolizes the complete sacrifice of Jesus Christ that brings the reconciled relationship of God to every individual who believes in Jesus Christ. Moreover, the reconciled relationship through the peace offering given by Jesus Christ does not remain only between individuals and God, but extends to the communities and the whole of creation. When the Apostle Paul talks about the new identity between the Israelites and the Gentiles in the church, he associates Jesus Christ with peace offering in Ephesians 2:14–19 by saying that he "broke down the barrier of the dividing wall (NASB)," and "made the two into one new man, thus establishing peace (NASB)."

---

20. Langston and Clendenen, "Sacrifice and Offering," 1428.
21. Longman, et al., ed., "Sacrifice and Offering," 1461.
22. Dockery, "Peace Offering."
23. Longman, et al., ed., "Sacrifice and Offering," 1461.
24. Longman, et al., ed., "Sacrifice and Offering," 1461.

Shalom: God's Ultimate Purpose for the World

Shalom in the New Testament

Shalom in Greek

The term *shalom* in Greek is εἰρήνη, which literally means "one, peace, quietness, rest,"[25] in the New Testament. This Greek word εἰρήνη has a broader meaning in *Theological Dictionary of the New Testament: Abridged in One Volume*:

> This is even more true when *shalom* has nothing to do with peace as the opposite of war but implies well-being as distinct from every form of evil, as in salutations, or in relation to the work of physicians, or in the problem posed by the good fortune of the wicked. In such contexts *ěirēnē* has to denote, not merely rest, but a state of well-being or wholeness, so that one can even be said to die in peace (as distinct from suffering violence). Nor is this well-being restricted to material welfare.[26]

This condition is absolutely based on what Christ has done on the cross for human beings to have ultimate peace with God by breaking the bondage of sin and its consequences. Its usage in the Septuagint is broader compared to the extrabiblical usage, which is merely the meaning of the opposite of war.[27] The Apostle Paul clearly describes that Christ himself is our peace, who has made the two one and has destroyed the barrier, the dividing wall of hostility (Eph 2:15).

Shalom in the Gospel

In Luke 2:14, a great company of the heavenly host appears with the angel praises God: "Glory to God in the highest, and on earth peace to men on whom his favor rest." Peace is assured to those who please God. It was a message of peace to the world that had known so much war and violence. Warren W. Wiersbe states: "The famous *Pax Romana* (Roman Peace) had been in effect since 27 BC, but the absence of war does not guarantee the

---

25. Strong, *Concise Dictionary*, "1515. εἰρήνη (ěirēnē)."

26. Kittel and Friedrich, ed., *Theological Dictionary*, 208. Walker explains: "This word, εἰρήνη, does not have only a meaning of the absence of hostility, strife, and disorder, but also refers to the condition of being silent and secure, and furthermore, to the spiritual sense with "the expectation of peace through the coming of the Christ" (Walker, *International Standard Bible Encyclopaedia*, 2293).

27. Kittel and Friedrich, ed., *Theological Dictionary*, 208.

presence of peace."[28] The Roman world was experiencing the *Pax Romana* which was marked by external prosperity and tranquility when Jesus was born, but the angels proclaimed a deeper and more lasting peace by the Savior. Willard M. Swartley rightly points out:

> The *Pax Romana* was celebrated as an ideal state of affairs, a time of one worldwide Greco-Roman language and culture, a time of prosperity and order. These latter features accord with the Hebrew notion of *shalom*. But the *Pax Romana* was also a situation in which many subjugated peoples suffered oppression from Rome's "golden age" of prosperity—features that oppose and mock *shalom*.[29]

This requires further examination of *shalom* in the relationship between Jesus Christ and the earthly empire. Even if believers live under earthly authority, they would resolutely follow Jesus Christ as Lord, which expects fierce persecution in certain religious–political situations like the Roman Empire during the first two centuries.

It is worth examining how the New Testament writers portray *shalom* related to Jesus and his ministry on earth. In various settings, doves have a great symbolism in the Bible.[30] They have been a symbol of peace in the Bible as in broader human history, and also represent the Holy Spirit in the New Testament.[31] The story of Noah's dove in the Old Testament (Gen 8) signifies that God declared peace with humanity after the Flood had purged the earth because of its absolute wickedness. Relating this symbolic message to the New Testament, the dove represented the Holy Spirit bringing ultimate peace of the reconciliation between God and man. When Jesus sent out the twelve disciples, he asked them to be as "shrewd as snakes and as innocent as doves" (Matt 10:16, NIV), because they were expected to be hated and persecuted in the world. The followers of Christ should bring peace, as doves do, in the world that is full of violence and hatred under the rule of a malicious enemy. In addition, it is significant that, in all the four Gospel accounts, the Holy Spirit is pictured as a dove at Jesus' baptism, symbolizing peace with God. The Savior who is holy and innocent as another picture of dove has brought peace to all mankind through his life and sacrifice on the cross.

---

28. Wiersbe, *Bible Exposition Commentary*, Vol. 1, 176.
29. Swartley, *Covenant of Peace*, 30.
30. Hart, *The Animals Mentioned in the Bible*.
31. Freeman, *The New Manners and Customs of the Bible*, "Raven" and "Dove."

Shalom: God's Ultimate Purpose for the World

In the world where conflict and tension are expected, people have become relationally fatigued, and many isolated from their own communities. The world needs a better way of handling relationships, which would come from a personal, deep, reflective relationship with God through Christ Jesus. Jesus uses a term of "the peacemaker" (Matt 5:9, Greek: ειρηνοποιός) in the Sermon on the Mount, and Douglas W. Kennard defines peacemaker as "one who demonstrates that he is a son of the Father by generously loving and praying for his enemies that persecute him (Matt 5:39–45)."[32] Swartley also emphasizes the importance of reconciliation in the active work of peacemaking according to the will of the God of peace for men.[33] Jesus calls his disciples to be peacemakers who have purposefully chosen to engage in relational disputes and with the biblical perspective which reflects God's moral character. As peacemakers, God's work of redemption would be engaged in the very deepest level of people. *Shalom* is the state in which God created all things to exist and flourish, as well as the state for which God is reconciling the world to enjoy. Among the entire Bible, this word "peacemaker" appears only here in Matthew 5, and Kenneth E. Bailey distinguishes "peacemakers" from peacekeepers and pacifists, as they "work for healed relationships on all levels."[34] There is a similarity in Luke 6:35 known as the Sermon of the Plain, and Jesus says, "love your enemies, and do good, and lend, expecting nothing in return; and your reward will be great, and you will be sons of the Most High; for he himself is kind to ungrateful and evil men" (NASB). Peacemakers love their enemies and do good to them, and furthermore they are supposed to lend what they possess to those in need with an expectation of nothing in return, only being rewarded in God's kingdom as his sons and daughters. As Swartley states that "peacemaking is rooted in God's moral character,"[35] God's children should reflect his character in their everyday lives by loving their neighbors. Sometimes peacemakers may bring momentary warfare to the present world for the sake of peace, but the millennial reign of the Messiah where peace and righteousness reigns throughout the earth is certainly promised and anticipated.

---

32. Kennard, *The Gospel*, 40. *Holman Illustrated Bible Dictionary* defines "peacemakers" as "those who actively work to bring about peace and reconciliation where there is hatred and enmity" (Brand at el., *Holman Illustrated Bible Dictionary*, 1262).

33. Swartley, *Covenant of Peace*, 56.

34. Bailey, *Jesus Through Middle Eastern Eyes*, 87.

35. Swartley, *Covenant of Peace*, 56.

There is a different emphasis regarding peace in Matthew 10:34–36. Jesus said that he came to bring peace between believers and God as well as peace among humans. However, the inevitable result of Jesus' coming is conflict—between Jesus Christ and the anti-Christ. This can happen even between members of the same family, according to verses 35–36. Jesus brought a sword symbolizing conflict, as peace with God involves opposition to Satan and his work. Swartley observes that many instances of violence and conflict in the New Testament are metaphorically related to spiritual warfare.[36] The followers of Christ must press on in the battle against all that is false and destructive until the God of peace finally crushes the one of all lies and destruction. This is a glorious promise about the triumph of the church over Satan, and Jesus Christ is the One who has brought the way into the world. Paul's letters consistently teach that Jesus Christ has decisively defeated the malicious enemy in his death and resurrection and is now through his Church which proclaims the gospel. He will eventually vanquish evil and throw the evil one into the lake of fire in his second coming, through which the world will experience the ultimate peace that God has promised. All the believers must have faith that God's peace overwhelms Satan with his authority and shatters his lies.

When Jesus promised his disciples the Holy Spirit, he also promised peace which the world cannot give. This peace is a gift given through Jesus' redemptive work, and the promise of the Holy Spirit brings ultimate inner rest of spirit to his disciples. This is why his followers are neither to let our hearts be troubled and nor to be afraid even in troubles (John 14:27). Furthermore, Jesus encouraged his disciples that they might have peace in him when he awaited the final completion. Even if they have troubles in the world, they would be strengthened by Jesus' proclamation that he had overcome the world (John 16:33). The goal of Jesus' ministry on earth is to bring the ultimate message of *shalom* to the world, which comes from the culmination of his crucifixion and resurrection.

Shalom in the Pauline Letters

The Apostle Paul clearly explains that *shalom* comes only from God through the life and work of Christ. In Romans 5:1–3, he said, "having been justified by faith, we have peace with God through our Lord Jesus Christ, through whom also we have obtained our introduction by faith into this grace in

---

36. Swartley, *Covenant of Peace*, 50.

Shalom: God's Ultimate Purpose for the World

which we stand; and we exult in hope of the glory of God." God has made peace with us through the blood of Christ, so we are no longer God's enemy. Paul's point in these passages is that justification by faith leads human beings to peace with God and peace betwixt people who used to be enemies. In this sense, the most important concept of peace in the Pauline letters is reconciliation. As mentioned in Philippians 1:2, grace and *shalom* are inextricably linked together throughout the Bible. All mankind must personally respond to God's grace manifested in the cross in order to fully experience *shalom* from God. Without God's gracious extension of mercy shown on the cross, there can be no *shalom*, as reconciliation of broken relationships is never possible apart from God's intervention. Furthermore, mankind is not only saved, but also sanctified by the God of peace to grow in the deeper relationship with him (1 Thess 5:23–24). Paul assures Christians that eventually the God of peace will crush Satan (Rom 16:20), and the victory over him is certainly promised for the eternal experience of *shalom*.

The Apostle Paul decisively illuminates the Holy Spirit, who brings peace into the life of believers throughout his letters. The Holy Spirit indwells every believer after they have repented and trusted in Christ. Peace is the essential nature of the Holy Spirit, and one of the fruits of the Spirit (Gal 5:22–25). Romans 14:17 describes that the kingdom of God is a matter of righteousness, peace and joy in the Holy Spirit. When believers seek the will of God, they experience supernatural peace granted by the presence of the Holy Spirit. Manser observes that "peace is an indication of the Holy Spirit's presence,"[37] and "the result of the Spirit's work is contrasted with fear, the opposite emotion of peace,"[38] as a part of understanding Romans 8:14–17. He also sees that in Acts 9:31 the church throughout Judea, Galilee, and Samaria enjoyed a time of peace as the Holy Spirit strengthened and encouraged the believers.[39] Instead of anxiety, confusion, anger, or depression in the midst of dreadful circumstances, the peace of God becomes the default state of mind for the believers who have the Holy Spirit. Paul uses a unique expression of "the gospel of peace" in Ephesians as an important part of the full armor of God (Eph 6:15) necessary for believers to stand firm against the schemes of the devil. Harold W. Hoehner explains that believers can stand firm in the battle by the gospel which gives them

---

37. Manser, *Dictionary of Bible Themes*, "Holy Spirit" and "Peace."
38. Manser, *Dictionary of Bible Themes*, "Holy Spirit" and "Peace."
39. Manser, *Dictionary of Bible Themes*, "Holy Spirit" and "Peace."

peace.⁴⁰ In other words, Paul talks about the stability or surefootedness that the gospel of peace would provide for believers.

Although the church was established on the new covenant relationship with God through Jesus for both the Jews and the Gentiles, there was a serious tension between these two groups in the early church. God broke down the middle wall of partition between the Jews and the Gentiles (Eph 2:11–22) by the blood of Christ, and made it clear that the new church would comprise of both Jews and the Gentiles who had formerly been alienated from each other. Swartley summarizes God's willful plan of bringing the Gentiles to his church through two main persons in early church history, the Apostles Peter and Paul, as portrayed in the book of Acts:

> From here forward in the history of this early church, the incorporation of Gentiles into the new faith community will occupy center stage in the unfolding drama. While Saul(Paul) is first converted—transformed from a man of violence to a messianic peacemaker—and called to head a mission to the Gentiles, it is Peter who welcomes the first Gentile into the hitherto all Jewish Christian faith community and proclaims the theological rationale for it. That Paul and Peter share together in this momentous paradigm shift—two historic episodes—is of no small significance.⁴¹

As Isaiah prophesied that the Messiah would end hostility and establish an era of wholeness, Christ offers this peace to all people regardless of their race. Just like Jesus brings harmony and wholeness to people's relationships with God and one another, the Apostle Paul urges the Jews and the Gentiles to be unified in Christ. Jesus enables all to have peace with God and grants a state of spiritual restoration just as he resurrected from the dead.⁴² McGonigal also observes the full dimension of *shalom*, which are realized by Christ's work on the cross destroying down the vertical wall between God and human beings as well as the horizontal wall separating people from each other.⁴³ The message of *shalom* that the Apostle Paul's letters continue to emphasize for the early church is to build up the unity of all people who now have access to the same God through the work of Christ in the same Spirit. Throughout the Pauline letters, Paul describes peace as an essential quality of God as found in "God of Peace" (Rom 15:33).

40. Hoehner, "Ephesians."
41. Swartley, *Covenant of Peace*, 162–63.
42. Clendenen, *Holman Illustrated Bible Dictionary*, 1261–62.
43. McGonigal, "If You Only Knew."

Shalom: God's Ultimate Purpose for the World

Shalom with the Year of Jubilee

Augustine Calmet explains: "The Jubilee year was the fiftieth year which occurred after seven weeks of years, or seven times seven years."[44] John D. Barry states: "During this year, economic debts were to be forgiven, land restored to families who sold in order to repay debt, and slaves sold to repay debt were to be liberated."[45] The year of *jubilee* is also called as "the favorable year of the Lord" (Isa 61:2, NASB) and "the year of liberty" (Eze 46:17). According to Leviticus 25:10–15, the Israelites must consecrate the fiftieth year as the Sabbath rest at the end of seven sabbatical annual cycles. In the year of *jubilee*, the declaration has two essential components that the original land allotments have to be restored, and that each person must return to his family property and to his own clan, which demonstrates the message that God's people should never forget that both masters and servants belong to God's kingdom together.[46]

The year of *jubilee* proclaims the full restitution of all property, so its primary object is to "prevent the accumulation of land on the part of a few to the detriment of the community at large," and to "render it impossible for anyone to be born to absolute poverty, since everyone had his hereditary land."[47] The year of *jubilee* tries to bring equality to the community and rejects slavery. In addition, the year of *jubilee* is a time to leave the fields that people must neither sow nor reap what grows of itself or harvest the untended vines. Furthermore, God's people are expected to live faithfully with the surpassing promise that God is the Provider, *Yahweh Yireh or Jehovah Jireh* (Gen 22:13–14). God's people must have a faith that God provides all that they need and he is the One who faithfully meets the needs of his people. John E. Anderson explains:

> The concept of *Jubilee* was an important institution by which Israel understood their theological identity and by which God provided protection against economic calamity.[48]

---

44. Calmet, *Great Dictionary*, "Jubilee." He indicates that it is *Jobel* in Hebrew, and Barry et al. explain the origin of the word *jubilee* that could be "from the Phoenician *ybl*, meaning ram, as the year of *jubilee* was announced with blowing of a ram's horn trumpet" (Barry et al., "Year of *Jubilee*.").

45. Barry et al., "Peace."

46. DeYoung and Gilbert, *What Is the Mission of the Church?* 147–48.

47. Easton, "Jubilee," Barry et al., "Peace."

48. Anderson, "A Biblical and Economic Analysis," 27. Brand also states: "This year also reflected God's provision for the soil's conservation (Lev 25:11–12, 18–21). During

He continues explaining:

> This conclusion provides a solid foundation for a serious economic analysis of *Jubilee* provisions, not merely as an unrealized and highly idealized method of wealth redistribution in ancient Israel, but rather as the foundation for right relationships between God's people and the land.[49]

The fundamental theological basis of the year of *jubilee* regarding land is God's ownership over his creation and mankind's stewardship to cultivate his creatures. God says in Leviticus 25:23 clearly: "The land, moreover, shall not be sold permanently, for the land is Mine; for you are but aliens and sojourners with Me" (NASB). Ronald J. Sider precisely explains:

> God, the landowner, permits his people to sojourn on his good earth, cultivate it, eat its produce, and enjoy its beauty. But we are only stewards. Stewardship is one of the central theological categories of any biblical understanding of our relationship to the land and economic resources.[50]

In addition, the year of *jubilee* is closely related to God's divine plan of restoring his broken relationship with human beings through Jesus Christ. God proclaims restoration by forgiveness of man's sinful nature, which breaks all the bondages of human depravity. The Israelites must forgive debts and free slaves on account of debt, which brought restoration of both personal and social conditions to a peaceful order. It was a time that the community experienced justice, redemption, and peace that *Yahweh* had provided with his grace and mercy. In this sense, the year of *jubilee* reminded the Israelites of God's divine deliverance from their slavery in Egypt. Isaiah proclaims "the favorable year of the Lord" (Isa 61:2) as the acceptable year, "the year of *jubilee* on which liberty was proclaimed to the captives."[51] The church is called to celebrate the gift of liberation from slavery of our sinful nature and to share the good news with those who are still in this captivity of sin. Jesus Christ has eliminated the wall of estrangement which alienated human beings from God and separated from each other. Teague relates *shalom* to Edenic imagery for reconciliation with God, saying that Jesus Christ

---

the year of *jubilee*, the Israelites were once again taught that they were to live in faith, that the Lord would satisfy their needs." (Brand et al., "Year of *Jubilee*," 1695.)

49. Anderson, "A Biblical and Economic Analysis," 29.
50. Sider, *Rich Christians in an Age of Hunger*, 74.
51. Jamieson, Fausset, and Brown, *Commentary Critical and Explanatory*.

provides the way of returning to Eden, enabling mankind to regain the lost knowledge of God.[52] His emphasis on the concept of integral mission draws attention to the whole restoration of the relationship with God the Creator, an emphasis which definitely supersedes the idea of mission as a simple integration of verbal proclamation and social action.

When Jesus announced his ministry in Luke's Gospel (Luke 4:18–19), the message of *jubilee* was embedded in his proclamation quoted from Isaiah 61:1–2, which portrays the year of *jubilee* as good news. Jesus' earthly ministry demonstrates visible signs of God's grace and mercy, which will eventually restore peace and wholeness to God's creation. "The year of the Lord's favor (Luke 4:19)" turns into a metaphor of salvation through Jesus Christ who forgives sin completely. Ireland indicates that Jesus' sermon at the inauguration of his ministry emphasizes physical deliverance as well as spiritual deliverance that the righteous King will bring to human beings.[53] Salvation that Jesus proclaims should be understood as transformation of all aspects of all persons. God's proclamation of peace for his people is not only freedom from sin, but also a challenge to seek his compassion and social justice for the oppressed and marginalized. Mark R. Gornik shares his experience and vision for Baltimore's New Song Community Church, which witnesses the gospel to the neighboring communities and makes some pertinent observations regarding the sociopolitical manifestations of the *jubilee* that Luke portrays in his Gospel:

> Under the *Jubilee* reign of God, the gospel means all things are made right—the poor are lifted up, the prisoners are released, sins are forgiven, the curse of sin is reversed. We should not forget that in the time of Jesus, "gospel" bore political and social meaning. It was a salvation much different from the world's political order and was not interiorized or spiritualized. Christ's proclamation of the gospel was both personally and socially transforming.[54]

Swartley clarifies that Luke's description of Jesus' messianic mission uses a specific textual arrangement and various social terms in this passage, for the emphasis on the word of *gospelize* (*euangelizomai*) in the relationship with the theme of "release," which expresses his special stress on the peaceful freedom that the gospel proclaims through the person of Jesus Christ.[55] He

52. Teague, "Integral Mission," 18.
53. Ireland, *For the Love of God*.
54. Gornik, *To Live in Peace*, 28.
55. Swartley, *Covenant of Peace*, 135–36.

quotes Yoder's expression for the year of *jubilee* as "a visible socio-political, economic restructuring of relations among the people of God."[56]

A church's priority on the peacemaking effort to its neighbors depends on its foundational message of the gospel, and the biblical perspective of the year of *jubilee*, "the year of the Lord's favor" (Luke 4:19) can make transformational changes in the community. Christian mission is called to proclaim the year of *jubilee* as a way of building up the people of peace. The message of *jubilee* is meant to be lived out not only for individual disciples, but also for the church and the communities that it serves. It opens a new beginning of life under the laws and principles of God's kingdom. The year of *jubilee* is certainly more than simple social justice, and Christian mission should acknowledge that the principle requires practices of alleviation of poverty and compassionate care for the marginalized. As the global church and Christian mission commit to live toward and work for *shalom*, the principle message of the year of *jubilee* should be practiced for the world much empowered by violence, hostility, envy, and rivalry in order for people to grasp the eternal hope through the encounter of Jesus Christ.

Covenant of Peace:
The Kingdom of God, Gospel, and Shalom

The phrase "the Covenant of Peace" occurs only four times in the Old Testament (Num 25:12–13; Isa 54:9–10; Ezek 34:25, 37:26). The Covenant of Peace was first given to Phinehas, son of Eleazar, who was a Levitical priest. He was faithful in serving the Lord and turned God's anger away from the Israelites. He secured the priesthood in his family and was "zealous for the honor of his God and made atonement for the Israelites" (Num 25:12–13). God's covenant of life and peace with Levi is associated with the Davidic covenant and the prophetic promises of the coming messianic kingdom. The Psalmist confirms that God rewarded Phinehas' zeal and intercession with the endless covenant to all generations (Ps 106). God looks for people like Phinehas who followed God wholeheartedly and removed the unrighteousness in Israel as a peacemaker before God.

Isaiah chapter 9 is written about the birth and the reign of "the Prince of Peace" who will reign on David's throne and over his kingdom. The promise of "the Prince of Peace" displays his establishment of peace on earth which will be the hope that the Israelites could hold onto throughout

---

56. Swartley, *Covenant of Peace*, 136.

Shalom: God's Ultimate Purpose for the World

sufferings and afflictions. The Messiah would be a descendant of David and rule in righteousness forever. The ultimate peace that God promised throughout Old Testament history would become realized by the Messiah's coming and ruling in righteousness.[57] There are usages of *shalom* in the title or name of God in the Old Testament. Gideon gave a name of יהוה שָׁלוֹם (*yhwh-shalom*) which literally means *Yahweh is Peace (The Lord of peace)* to the altar that he built at Ophra (Judges 6:24).[58] שַׂר שָׁלוֹם is found in Isaiah 9:6, and it translates to "Prince of Peace" (NASB) as a title of the Messiah. David S. Dockery states: "The Messiah's royal titles attest to his close relationship to God and depict him as a mighty warrior capable of establishing peace in his realm."[59] He continues explaining that the Messiah's title "Prince of Peace" closely refers to the characteristics of justice and peace which will be realized in the kingdom of God. This was fulfilled by judgment of the Northern Kingdom (Isa 9:8—10:4), judgment of the Assyrians (Isaiah 10:5–34), and restoration of God's exiled people (Isa 11:11—12:6). Ultimately, the Prince of Peace will reign over all nations at the end of time.[60]

The Covenant of Peace is that peace with God and one another is fundamental to the promises of Israel's restoration and the new creation. The foundation of God's reign over his kingdom is directly linked to the nature of righteousness. The King's reign of righteousness is described in Isaiah chapter 32, and the King will create righteousness and peace when his Spirit is poured out onto his people (Isa 32:15–18). Yoder also states, "Literally, this passage (Isa 32:16–17) speaks of *shalom* as the wages or work of righteousness."[61] Although the immediate future was not quite optimistic,[62] Isaiah prophesized that restoration would follow the judgment, and justice would then return to the land. The foundation of the ultimate peace is righteousness.

Shalom should be realized in people's lives through transformation by the gospel message and, furthermore, will be found in their societies by the multiplication of people's righteous acts. The Covenant of Peace is God's promise of granting peace to his people in the new temple and Jerusalem

---

57. Brand, et al., "Peace."
58. Barry, et al., "Peace."
59. Dockery, "Isaiah 9:1–7."
60. Dockery, "Isaiah 9:1–7."
61. Yoder, *Shalom*, 14.
62. Dockery, "Isaiah 9:1–7."

Biblical Concept of Shalom in Comparison to the Concept of Peace in Islam

as the realization of his reign over his people. God's promise of peace is described in Leviticus 26:6 (NASB):

> I shall also grant peace in the land, so that you may lie down with no one making you tremble I shall also eliminate harmful beasts from the land, and no sword will pass through your land.

Dockery interprets the meaning of peace as God's covenant:

> God's covenant of peace with his people would involve the assurance of an enduring relationship with the One who is our peace and a pledge to protect their welfare and to abundantly bless them by his divine grace, wisdom, and power.[63]

However, in the Old Testament period, this promise of peace to the Israelites was not fulfilled because of the Israelites' failure to obey and carrying out God's commandments. God gave his commandments to the Israelites in the Sinai covenant after the Exodus, but they willfully went astray. In addition, Solomon's prayer for peace with God was not fulfilled because of Solomon's own failure to be faithful to God.

The prophet Isaiah addresses the ultimate fulfillment of God's promise of peace through Jesus Christ. His prophesies lead up to the peaceful government of God and, finally, to "new heavens and a new earth" (Isa 65:17). Isaiah describes the Messiah as the peaceful ruler with righteousness and justice over his kingdom (Isa 11:3–5). This suggests that *shalom* can ultimately come true through just and righteous rule. In Isaiah 11:6–9, he continues to rhetorically describe the prophetic meaning of ultimate peace as the whole picture of peace and safety in the Messianic age. This illustrates the conditions of the future consummation of the Messianic kingdom. The prophesy proclaims that Christ is the only one who can complete righteousness on earth through his messianic ministry on the cross. The Prince of Peace would bring peace and tranquility under his government when he restores his kingdom. However, the fact that there has been an inclination to interpret this scripture as the manifestation of the final consummation of this world in the evangelical church communities is not deniable.[64]

---

63. Dockery, "Isaiah 9:1–7."

64. Because this passage alludes that *shalom* is an observable quality, it is also important not to neglect the responsibility of the church to take care of this world, because the world is a beautiful creation by the Creator. Broker explains the complete picture of *shalom* in the kingdom of God through the vision that human beings experience peace among peoples and with other creatures on Earth as well (Brocker, *Coming Home to Earth*, 68–69). He criticizes a tendency of too much emphasis on individual soul saving

Shalom: God's Ultimate Purpose for the World

Isaiah 53 is the most important chapter pertaining to mankind's salvation, and this prophecy explains how much the Messiah as the Suffering Servant would suffer during his sacrifice for man's sins.[65] Isaiah 53:5 states that the Messiah would bring ultimate peace to human beings through his punishment as "an end to the cycle of one society punishing another for the evils it commits in its rebellion against God."[66] Human beings and their societies can possibly cease a vicious cycle of sin's consequences, and experience the restoration of broken relationships with God, people, and nature by believing in the Messiah's sacrifice. The substitute punishment of the Messiah breaks the wall which separates people from God, and brings *shalom* to the relationship with each other and with nature. Following the prophesy of Jesus' suffering in Isaiah 53, Isaiah foretells the culmination of God's covenant through Jesus Christ, with the announcement of Israel's restoration from the Babylonian exile in Isaiah 54. Walter A. Elwell commented: "The Lord swears that he will never remove his covenantal blessings of peace, mercy, and kindness from his people."[67] Greever also concludes:

> It is only in the inauguration of the new covenant that this lasting peace with God and one another is achieved, and thus this new covenant is called a covenant of peace, a covenant that assuages divine wrath (Isa 54:10; Ezek 34:25; 37:26).[68]

The coming of Christ, his life, suffering, death, and resurrection are the cornerstones of God's redemptive process. All human beings who believe in the covenant of peace through Jesus Christ and his atonement on the cross will be beneficiaries of his blessings of peace and enjoy the reconciled relationship under his righteous reign over all of creation.

The Covenant of Peace is promised as "the rebuilding of God's temple as a visible reminder of his presence," in Ezekiel 37:26, and earlier in Ezekiel 34:25, a beautiful land of God's kingdom by God's care and protection is portrayed.[69] In the context of Ezekiel chapter 34, God condemns irresponsible, corrupted leadership of the Israelites, and then he promises

---

and raises a voice that church has been neglecting its role to take good care of God's creation on earth. This prophesy enables human beings as well as all creatures in suffering to envision the righteous reign of the Messiah in his kingdom.

65. Martin, "Isaiah."
66. Snodderly, "Shalom," 196.
67. Elwell, *Evangelical Commentary, Vol. 3*.
68. Greever, "Peace."
69. Dyer, "Ezekiel."

to establish his righteous leadership upon his people by placing "one shepherd, his servant David" who is the Messiah (Ezek 34:23–24). In the sentence of Ezekiel 34:25, the subject, the prime mover, is God, who is always the ultimate leader and king of his people, and the fulfilment of his merciful promise is fundamentally realized by the Messiah. The peace promised in this passage is that of a restored relationship with God and the secure enjoyment of a life made full and rich through God's blessings. There will never be any threats to life under God's righteous reign. Isaiah 54:9–10 is an amazing promise that God will never punish the world, like he did in the the days of Noah. He swore that he would neither be angry at his people, nor rebuke his nations. His "Covenant of Peace" will never be shaken because his lovingkindness overwhelms over his people. The "Covenant of Peace" promised through Isaiah is placed just after the prophesy of the suffering Messiah, the Lord's righteous servant, and it is followed by the promise of the abundant life of joy and peace as the covenant of blessings in Isaiah 55. Swartley pertinently states:

> Out of the crisis of the exile Second Isaiah forged new visions and understandings of *shalom*. Not only is God's order of *shalom* now seen in cosmic proportion, but Israel's vocation is defined as one of agent and witness through which *shalom* extends to the whole world.[70]

The "Covenant of Peace" consistently promised throughout the Old Testament became fulfilled by the birth of the Messiah who is the cornerstone extending his promise of peace to the whole world.

The core characteristics of God's kingdom are ultimately found in *shalom*, the state of complete restoration of relationship between God and his creation. Jesus' redemptive work on the cross and his victory over Satan by his resurrection has brought *shalom* to his people. The key feature of the kingdom of God is revealed on its Greek word of *basileia* (βασιλεία) which means "rule," "reign," or "a realm."[71] When God, who has a perfect attribute of love and righteousness, rules over his people in his kingdom, there must no doubt be *shalom* in every aspect of people's lives and their communities as well as in all creation. The kingdom of God always exists partially in this present age, never in full. This is what we call inaugurated eschatology. Swartley summarizes the whole gospel message with three definitions:

---

70. Swartley, *Covenant of Peace*, 31.
71. Strong, *Concise Dictionary*, "932. βασιλεία."

Shalom: God's Ultimate Purpose for the World

"the reign (kingdom) of God," "gospel," and "peace."[72] This foundational concept develops into the Pauline letters, which completes the New Testament theology. He introduces a conceptual diagram which enlightens the biblical concept of *shalom*. The root of *shalom* is absolutely founded on the attributes of God, *Yahweh*, that are "righteousness and justice," "*chesed*; *emunah*; grace," and "covenant (*berith*)," and *shalom* becomes a reality in the "God-people relationship" through salvation, which will be fully established in the kingdom of God eschatologically at the end of this age.[73] In the New Testament, ειρήνη, the gospel of peace, is definitely from the reconciled relationship with God and with fellow humans through Jesus Christ by the grace of God. This peace will be manifested as the fruit of peace—"love of God, love of neighbor, love of enemy, not returning evil for evil, and overcoming evil with good," and these manifestations in Christians' lives will bring faith, hope, holiness, and harmony in the body both in personal life and in communities corporately, which is the splendid blessing and wholeness of the promised world.[74]

Interestingly, this realization of *shalom* in the kingdom of God is manifested in healing, as Jesus replied to John the Baptist that "the blind receive sight, the lame walk, the lepers are cleansed, the deaf hear, and even the dead are raised" (Matt 11:5). As previously studied, *shalom* has a meaning of physical, emotional, and spiritual health and well-being. Many miracles in Jesus' ministry are inseparably connected to healing and physical restoration as the essential manifestations of God's kingdom. Physical healing and forgiveness of sins come together to announce the breaking in of God's reign through Jesus' earthly ministry. As Swartley studies the Gospel of Matthew, he points out the importance of healing in Jesus' ministry in terms of the message of peace in the kingdom of God:

> In light of this prominent association between healing and Jesus' messianic proclamation of the dawning kingdom, Matthew's use of the 'Son of David' title in healing narratives qualifies, even subverts, the dominant meta-narrative of a messianic 'Son of David' who destroys enemies to gain peace.[75]

---

72. Swartley, *Covenant of Peace*, 11–26.
73. Swartley, *Covenant of Peace*, 30.
74. Swartley, *Covenant of Peace*, 41.
75. Swartley, *Covenant of Peace*, 78.

However, there is always an unescapable tension between Jesus' first coming, bringing the kingdom of God to earth and his second coming, which will eventually fulfill the full scope of *shalom*. Until the final fulfillment of his covenant in Jesus' second coming, God's people are to live a godly life according to kingdom principles in the fallen world. *Shalom* can not only be experienced in the time of God's complete reign at the end of this age, but also must be experienced on earth through the church, which exercises this principle as God's people. In the Lord's prayer, imminent realization of God's kingdom seems expected. Throughout human history, however, people have constantly faced sickness, diseases, injustice, oppression, and hatred. Even just after Jesus conquered death by his resurrection, the early church had to experience unspeakable suffering and persecution. These illustrate that "the Covenant of Peace" always has two different dimensions in human history, an "already, but not yet" message to God's people who live in the fallen world.

"The Covenant of Peace" is portrayed in the Sermon on the Mount and Beatitudes (Matt 5—7) as well as in the Sermon on the Plain (Luke 6:17–49). Sharp comparison between the earthly kingdom and God's kingdom is made through the passages. When God truly reigns the kingdom, his people would hold onto heavenly values of life, and the two kingdoms are not dissimilar in definition. If God's people live in an intimate relationship with God who loves them unconditionally, even in this transient earthly life, they would taste the ultimate peace through this loving relationship. The "Covenant of Peace" is fundamentally based on God's loving and righteous attributes, all of which will be fulfilled through the work of Christ according to Apostle Peter who writes the nature of the new heavens and new earth as the place "in which righteousness dwells" (2 Peter 3:13). Kevin DeYoung and Greg D. Gilbert assert that the subject of the new heaven and new earth is always God, and although God's people are invited to build it as his vice-regents in the world, the new heaven and new earth manifested as *shalom* absolutely is "a gift from God to his people."[76] Even if the manifestation of the kingdom of God varies in different contexts, Swartley explains a vision that universal church has to grasp:

> But within this diversity arising from contextual demands, opportunities, and challenges, a common horizon of vision emerges: the establishment on earth of God's will for peace, the reconciliation of former enemies, and the bringing together of many peoples in

---

76. DeYoung and Gilbert, *What Is the Mission of the Church?*, 203–5.

Shalom: God's Ultimate Purpose for the World

one new creation that fulfills the ancient vision of making sacred the name of God in the world.[77]

A main theme of the Old Testament is the kingship and lordship of God, *Yahweh*, over all creatures and universe as well as his chosen people, the Israelites, although there is no direct mention of the kingdom of God in the Old Testament. The central theme of the New Testament is certainly the kingdom of God, which is demonstrated in the inauguration of Jesus' ministry in Galilee with the proclamation, "Repent, for the kingdom of heaven is at hand" (Matt 4:17; Mark 1:14–15), and his many teachings directly or indirectly related to the message of the kingdom of God.[78]

The Beatitudes illuminate the blessings of God's kingdom which are for both individuals and communities experiencing God's presence. David L. Turner divides the Beatitudes into two categories: the first four are related to "the disciple's vertical relationship to God," and the rest is to "the disciple's horizontal relationship to people." The personal qualities as the source of peace are "spiritual poverty," "repentance," "unassuming humility with total dependence on God," "ethical rightness and the upright lifestyle," while the social qualities as the sources of social rest are "mercifulness toward others," "integrity, transparency, and freedom from corruption," "peacemaking for others and cessation of hostilities with people," "desire for righteousness."[79] Peacemakers are one of the second group for the community. Regarding the seventh Beatitude of being peacemakers, Swartley asserts:

> The Beatitude is thus an identity-forming declaration. It assumes the gift of the gospel's grace and it also calls forth *blessedness* for those who receive the gospel of the kingdom. Becoming and being a peacemaker draws God's gift of grace. Within this context peacemaking is also a virtue for God's kingdom people, a value which believers cultivate and practice.[80]

He continues to put an emphasis on being peacemakers by loving enemies (Matt 5:44) as the moral virtue of God's people living in the kingdom of God.[81] The "Covenant of Peace" is promised to his people who faithfully

---

77. Swartley, *Covenant of Peace*, 14.
78. Carpenter and Comfort, "Kingdom."
79. Turner, "Whom Does God Approve," 33–41.
80. Swartley, *Covenant of Peace*, 401.
81. Swartley, *Covenant of Peace*, 401.

live their lives under his commandments and moral characteristics that Christ has demonstrated throughout his earthly life.

Shalom related to Christian Mission

In the last two decades, conflicts in the Arab world have not subsided despite the efforts of so many who endeavor to achieve peace worldwide. According to the Global Peace Index 2017, the last decade has seen a 2.14 percent decline in global peacefulness, but, surprisingly enough, a 247 percent increase in deaths from terrorism since 2008.[82] Mark Brocker insightfully puts this unavoidable violence into two categories:

1. killing, consumption, and destruction essential for the flourishing of life, and
2. exploitive killing, indulgent consumption, and wanton destruction that diminishes life.[83]

In many places in the Arab world, people suffer from this destructive sort of violence. It is necessary to discern the felt needs of today's Arab culture because the Christian message should speak to the basic felt needs of human beings. All human beings, including Muslims, long for *shalom* in their lives, and need to deal with the situations of common life such as sickness, pain, fear, poverty, and death in their daily lives. Christian cross-cultural workers should be ready to respond toward questions arising from these situations on the basis of clearly understanding the biblical concept of *shalom*. Dean S. Gilliland explicates the synthetic model of appropriate theologies as components of the totality of life through the incarnation of Jesus:

> The lifestyle God expected of the Jews can be gathered up in one word—"*Shalom*." Spiritual issues cannot be treated as though they are unconnected to other compartments of life. Jesus' teachings had authority because personal piety, politics, social relationships, religious habits and ethics were critical to his message. The synthesis, therefore, embraces all aspects of life.[84]

---

82. Institute for Economics & Peace, "Global Peace Index 2017."
83. Brocker, *Coming Home to Earth*, 69.
84. Gilliland, "Ch. 28: The Incarnation as Matrix for Appropriate Theologies," 511. In his footnote, *shalom* is the harmony intended between people and God and involves all facets of human relationships. Even while living in an alien culture during the exile, God commanded his people to "seek the *shalom* of the city (Babylon)," Jeremiah 29:7.

Shalom: God's Ultimate Purpose for the World

Regarding Jeremiah 29:7, DeYoung and Gilbert explain further that *shalom* is not only a status related to "ultimate, eternal peace," in heaven, but also to peace in the secular or even pagan cities that Christian mission has to seek for.[85] However, they continue to clarify that what God asked of the Israelites was not simply to bring God's blessings through their faithful presence, but to reflect the full characteristics of God as his chosen people in order for the Babylonians to know God and to repent of their sins to be saved from God's wrath and punishment.[86] In this context, *shalom* has a more active sense of practicing the kingdom values through Christian missions toward those who do not live with them.

The incarnation of Jesus urges Christian cross-cultural mission to become a bridge between Christians and people who are alienated from the truth. God demonstrates his ultimate desire to reconcile with human beings by sending his Beloved Son into the fallen world, which will eventually bring restoration and the wholeness in their relationship with God. This restored relationship through a personal encounter with Jesus enriches the interpersonal relationship with the neighbors who Christian mission serves. When positive, life-enriching traits are exhibited in close relationships in Christian mission, people are more likely to have faith in them, and place their trust in the words and actions shown through the missions. Robert Linthicum, an urban pastor and community organizer, clearly explains the scriptural definition of *shalom* on the basis of his understanding of Jewish history. He indicates that the biblical *shalom* deals with public relations more than personal morality. God ultimately wants the world to be in full realization of *shalom* through God's sovereign rule over his people.[87] He agrees with Walter Brueggemann who distinguishes the meaning of *shalom* in two distinct contexts which are related to the "haves" and the "have-nots." For those who face oppression and exploitation by the society, *shalom* means an action of liberation. On the contrast, for the "haves," *shalom* has a nuance of management as well as of celebration for the resources that God has granted.[88] This observation can be found in almost all societies, because people have an inclination to interpret their social and economic positions for their own benefit. According to Brueggemann, the "haves" who exercise power in the society hold a greater responsibility for *shalom* in their society even if the

---

85. DeYoung and Gilbert, *What Is the Mission of the Church?* 201.
86. DeYoung and Gilbert, *What Is the Mission of the Church?* 203.
87. Linthicum, "Why Build a Justice Interpretation Around *Shalom*?" 1–2.
88. Brueggemann, *Peace*, 25–53.

"haves-nots" are also accountable for it. When both political and spiritual leaders of society morally collapse and become exploiters of each other, people in their society tend to become like those leaders, finding reasons to justify their own exploitation based on their leaders. As a result, the whole society does not experience *shalom* any more. This phenomenon is exactly the reason why leaders have a much bigger responsibility for their society. Regardless of people's social and economic status in the society, all absolutely need *shalom*. The unfortunate reality of life is that *shalom* for the "haves" can be earned or maintained in different ways, sometimes in opposite ways, than the "have-nots" can get it from the society. The complicated tension between two groups for *shalom* seems inescapable. The only way that both the "haves" and the "have-nots" can experience *shalom* and be satisfied more equally is to practice justice and righteousness in the society, and to show compassion and love to one another. In this perspective, the church should play an important role, and Robert Linthicum thoughtfully suggests:

> One of the essential tasks of the church is to bring together through Christ those searching for liberation or salvation with those who are the managers of society and seek security, so that they might work together to build a *shalom* that is truly just and equitable for all, that brings people into an ever-deepening relationship with God and each other and consequently contributes to the formation of society as God intended it to be lived.[89]

It is obvious that a restored personal relationship with God through Jesus Christ must be exhibited in both personal and community lives in economic, political, and social/spiritual systems. These primary indicators mentioned by Linthicum manifest the biblical message of *shalom* completely among people by building up the social system of practicing justice and righteousness (Isa 32:17–18). How both individual believers and church communities care for their neighbors, especially with the marginalized in their society, is the fundamental indicator of personal relationship with God.

In addition to the socio-economic issues that the church has been facing for making *shalom* come to fruition through its ministry, there are other important issues that Christian mission should not neglect in the Arab world. Although many Arab countries enjoyed prosperity long ago, for much of history, the Arab world has been suffering from ongoing violence, and many countries in the region are held back by despotism and

---

89. Linthicum, "Why Build a Justice Interpretation Around *Shalom*?" 3.

Shalom: God's Ultimate Purpose for the World

absolutism governed by Islamic religious authority and power. In addition, serious tension constantly exists between different religious groups in the region. To understand the root of this problem in the region in terms of expressions of *shalom*, Clinton Stockwell studied three main fundamentalist groups—Christianity, Judaism, and Islam—derived from the major Abrahamic religions in the contemporary era of the history.[90] According to Stockwell, every fundamentalist follows their own philosophical belief that leads all to exclusion, hatred, and revenge among these people groups. Muslims consider themselves to be the true worshippers of Allah with the belief that the Bible is corrupted and the Qur'an is the final revelation from Allah. Jews claim that they are God's only chosen people, and they must own the promised land with the belief that God has intentionally purposefully given it to them. The biblical message of *shalom* that brings harmony among people who have different religious beliefs will provide ways of Christian mission to approach the other fundamental religious groups. Conservative Islamic countries and their rulers adhere to isolationism to protect their own political power, and many are believed to abuse the Islamic conservative tradition and belief for their own benefits. Religious extremism can often be a conduit for misery and tragedy; therefore, Christian mission to the Arab world also has a lot of issues to consider when bringing the biblical *shalom* through biblical contextualization of the gospel. Christian cross-cultural workers have to seek *shalom* in any way possible by looking at Jeremiah's letter to the Exiles in Babylon (Jer 29:7). In the letter, the Israelites in Babylon were commanded to seek *shalom* of the city and to pray for it, not only for their oppressors, but also for their own personal *shalom*. Linthicum observes Babylon as "a virtual synonym for depravity" at that time,[91] and Revelation 17 and 18 use the name of Babylon for indicating the city against God's just and righteous reign, which Warren W. Wiersbe describes as "a political and economic system that sought

---

90. Stockwell, "Fundamentalisms and the Shalom of God," 266–79. Fundamentalism is defined as "the belief that there is one set of religious teachings that clearly contains the fundamental, basic, intrinsic, essential, inerrant truth about humanity and deity; that this essential truth is fundamentally opposed by the forces of evil which must be vigorously fought; that this truth must be followed today according to the fundamental, unchangeable practices of the past; and that those who believe and follow these fundamental teachings have a special relationship with the deity." (Altemeyer and Hunsberger, "Authoritarianism, Religious Fundamentalism, Quest, and Prejudice," 118).

91. Linthicum, "Why Build a Justice Interpretation Around *Shalom*?" 6.

to control people's minds and destinies."[92] Yet, God commands the exiles through Jeremiah that his people should be messengers of *shalom* to the depraved city of Babylon. Today's evangelical church community should carefully seek God's will in this context when reaching out to those who are against the gospel, including Muslims. In recent decades, on the basis of Islamophobia, hate-crimes against Muslims have immensely increased, especially in western countries, and Muslim women became particularly vulnerable to this violent action. Fear and hatred against Muslims, which is present even among the evangelical church community, does not at all contribute to sharing the love of God.

God is present to those whose lives are enslaved by evil. In such communities, people suffer from violent conditions. In contrast, health and healing are visible signs of *shalom*. Christian medical mission communities should approach these circumstances with the message of *shalom* that would convert despair to hope by the power of the Holy Spirit. Beth Snodderly explains the background of unrestrained violence and corruption in societies where she served, and demonstrates what God desires human life to be—individuals and societies experiencing *shalom*. She describes the holistic aspects of *shalom*:

> Rather, God's will demonstrated by another observable sign of *shalom*: health and healing. To a formerly wicked city and the people in it, God says through the prophet Jeremiah, "I will bring health and healing to [the city]; I will heal my people and will let them enjoy abundant peace/*eirene* and security (Greek *pistin*—the root word for faithfulness)" (Jer. 33:6). This passage demonstrates that there is no dichotomy between social and spiritual healing or between physical and spiritual healing. *Shalom* is holistic.[93]

She has great insight concerning how Christian missionaries should engage better in the places where *shalom* is not being experienced. Her scholarly studies help churches prioritize their mission in the world marked by political instability and injustice. Snodderly gives a strong biblical foundation for understanding the church's mission and practical solutions to tangible concerns. When the underlying reasons that people do not experience *shalom* in the places where Christian medical missions serve are acknowledged, it will help one understand how Christian missionaries can better engage in

---

92. Wiersbe, *Bible Exposition Commentary*, Vol. 1, 176.
93. Snodderly, "Shalom," 194.

each context. She explicitly states the importance of a holistic approach to the communities that battle for *shalom*:

> The body of Christ contains people with the gifts to "do" or "make" *shalom* in many different areas: justice, peace-keeping, skill-building for economic independence, health, fighting and eradicating disease, etc. All of these peace-making activities can potentially demonstrate the values of the kingdom and bring *shalom* into the lives of troubled people and societies.[94]

Recognizing that people of different cultural backgrounds perceive the definition of peace differently, Christian workers should be able to approach ministry in biblically-contextualized ways. Some Arab Muslims believe that sickness can be caused by the evil eye, spirits, the devil, and *jinn*, which bring so much fear to individuals and their families. Many animistic practices are designed to protect themselves from sickness caused by such sources. Interestingly, some Muslims who hold to these folk practices are not even aware that their practices are distinctive from Islamic teaching. All gospel laborers should be aware of folk beliefs and practices, and should be well-prepared to present the gospel in a way that will bring people freedom from their animistic belief and practices.

Interview Analysis: Peace in Islamic Teaching and in the Context of the Arab World

This analysis is based on interviews with twelve Syrian Muslim participants living in Lebanon. The interviewees were contacted personally and wrote their answers on paper. These brief interviews have exposed interviewees' thoughts about the concept of peace based on Islamic teaching and their perception of the current unstable situation in the region. This interview analysis will provide Christian missionaries a grasp of a viewpoint from which ordinary people living in the Arab world think.

All twelve interviewees indicated that Islam is basically a religion of peace, tolerance, and love according to the Qur'an, and this is always presented in the greeting, "Peace be with you." They believe other religions should be tolerated and exist with Islam without any serious conflicts, as the nature of Allah is believed to be peace. One interviewee particularly stated that all religions are revealed by Allah, so they should complement

---

94. Snodderly, "Shalom," 197.

each other. Two interviewees mentioned that one of Allah's names is peace, and, interestingly, one of them blamed the media that distorts the message of Allah as a reason of the unrest in Islam.

Five interviewees regarded the external forces beyond the Arab world plundering natural resources, including oil, as the reason for the current turmoil in the region. One interviewee stated that Muslims in the Arab world are being persecuted and robbed of their rights. Three interviewees blamed Muslims who do not live according to Muslim teaching accordingly as a reason of the current turmoil among Islamic countries. One thought that the unrest in the region is a part of Allah's test and trial and that all Muslims have to return to the genuine Islamic teaching to experience true peace. A way of resolution to bring peace in the region is to follow closely the Islamic teaching. One interviewee said that political disparities and divisions have caused deterioration in the social system such as unemployment, inequality, a poor education system, and so on. Two interviewees mentioned *zakat* (زكاة, a form of alms-giving to the poor and needy as one of five pillars of Islam)[95] as a way of bringing peace to Muslim communities.

Peace in Islam[96]

The Arabic word *salām* (سَلاَم) is used in a variety of expressions in Arabic to mean peace. The Arabic *salam* (سَلاَم) and Hebrew *shalom* (שָׁלוֹם) are cognate Semitic terms. Peace is certainly valued in Islam, as the name of Islam is closely related to peace. The root of the word of Islam, which is "s-l-m," refers to the English word "peace." Islamic scholars, and indeed most Muslims, believe all the teachings of Islam are closely related to the goal of peace. The Qur'an teaches either directly or indirectly about the spirit of peace which is considered to be the ultimate destination of Islam. Maulana Wahiduddin Khan states that many verses of the Qur'an deal with the objects and events of the universe as signs of nature which project the universe as a model of peace and harmony.[97] However, the concept of peace in Islamic theology is very different from the biblical concept of *shalom*,

---

95. Snodderly, "Shalom," 175.

96. Swartley, *Encountering the World of Islam*, 506. Islam is the religion of Muslims, a monotheistic faith regarded as revealed in the Qur'an through Muhammad, the Prophet of Allah, and the ritual observances and moral code of Islam given as a series of revelations, which were codified in the Qur'an.

97. Khan, "Concept of Peace."

Shalom: God's Ultimate Purpose for the World

and this book explores their differences in the literature of Islamic theology and common cultural practices in the Arab world. The concept of peace permeates Islamic theology and its culture.[98] Islam means living in a peaceful environment that emerges as a result of submission to Allah, according to the Qur'an's teaching that all humanity should embrace peace. *Al-Salam* is one of the ninety-nine names of Allah in Islam, which has a meaning of "the peace of Allah."[99] The Qur'an presents the universe as the model to follow, characterized by harmony and peace. When Allah created heaven and earth, he ordered things in such a way that each part might perform its function peacefully without clashing with any other, according to Huseyin Algul's study of Islamic theology. He interprets the concept of peace in Islam by stating that Muslims can reach peace and safety by submitting their selves to Allah. In addition, his study shows that Muslims can willingly place themselves in a peaceful environment through submitting themselves to justice and righteousness. Algul states that the Qur'an emphasizes peace and reconciliation as basic to all social and even international relations.[100]

In contrast to the strong emphasis on peace in Islam, many verses of the Qur'an (Surahs 2:191, 193; 3:118; 4:75, 76; 5:33; 8:12; 8:65; 9:73, 123; 33:60, 62) command Muslims to kill and go to war to fight for Islam. In addition, Surah 5:33 states that Islam's enemies would be brutally killed, and Surah 9:5 urges readers to slay non-Muslims. Joshua Gillum defines religious terrorism as "the act/attempt to induce fear, panic, hatred, and disruption in the pursuit of a religious and political goal."[101] He has tried to defend Islam against the accusation of religiously motivated terrorism and violence of Islam by saying that those individuals are not true Muslims, and Islam is a religion based on peaceful principles.[102] This position concurs with the opinion that all terror attacks in the Arab world cannot simply be considered religiously motivated, but have complex historical, cultural, economic, and political issues underneath the phenomenon. However, Muslims cannot deny the fact that there are Islamic extremists in the Arab world who use terrorism as a means to meet their ends. Although many Muslims do not agree that these extremists practice the true Muslim faith, they still use a version of Islam derived from Qur'anic teachings to justify their terrorism.

98. Swing, "The Etymology of Salam."
99. Muhaiyaddeen, *Islam and World Peace: Explanations of a SUFI*, 160.
100. Algul, "Islam is a Religion of Love and Peace."
101. Gillum, "Is Islam Peaceful or Violent."
102. Gillum, "Is Islam Peaceful or Violent."

Niaz A. Shah claims that the Qur'an supports violence against non-Muslims in many verses and regards Muslims who do not join the fight as hypocrites.[103] The problem of Islamic terrorism may cast blame on the bad ideology of Islam, not bad people, as the reason for its violence. While Muslims try to be the peaceful and tolerant minority, when they become dominant in the society, they tend to exercise persecution against religious minorities through the political power and authority. Moreover, there are serious terror threats with religious justification when Muslims' demands are not met in the society, which is an observed phenomenon in many places all over the world. Many ordinary Muslims try to remain peaceful and live harmoniously with adherents of other religions, but in various situations the political and religious leaders instigate these ordinary Muslims, for their own benefit, by making use of the Islamic teachings from the Qur'an that support violence. In terms of the key role of the Qur'an that encourages and justifies violence, Islamic religious ideology provoking deadly violence are to be blamed and censured. John Kaltner states:

> The modern Arabic term for suicide (*intihar*) is not found in the Qur'an, and neither are the words that are commonly used today for violence (*'unf*) and terrorism (*irhab*). Despite this lack of explicit use of key terminology related to present-day manifestations of religiously motivated aggression, the Qur'an remains the central source for those seeking to justify or denounce violent acts done in the name of Islam.[104]

However, John L. Esposito's observation is certainly important to understand the violence related to Islam, which provides insightful perspectives in the relationship with politics in the Arab world. He asserts the importance of political background as a principal factor of violence related to Islam in recent history:

> Violence and terrorism in the name of Islam by a host of militant Muslim movements in recent decades is a product of historical and political factors, not simply religion or a militant Islamic theology/ideology. Focusing on reading the Quran or violent passages in the

---

103. Shah, "Use of Force," 347.

104. Kaltner, *Introducing the Qur'an*, 195. The Religion of Peace also indicates the Qur'an encourages and justifies violence (The Religion of Peace, "What Makes Islam So Different").

Quran can obscure the importance of the policies of authoritarian and oppressive regimes and their Western allies.[105]

The political and religious leaders in the Islamic countries in the Arab world with their allies tend to take advantage of the Islamic teaching by requesting people to fight against their enemies with religious justification. On the contrary some Islamic scholars criticize extremists' supplication of violence and terror attack by claiming extremists' exploitative urges for violence.

As salvation in Islam is based upon works, no Muslims can guarantee their salvation (Surah 101:6–9), but fighting in *jihad* is believed as "the guaranteed entrance to paradise."[106] This is one of the reasons that *jihadists* are eager to die for the cause of their religion. The Qur'an also justifies war and violence when Muslims are oppressed and experience injustice because of their faith. The Islamic Supreme Council of America defines the Arabic word *jihad* as struggling or striving in a purely linguistic sense, even if it is often translated as holy war. The Dictionary of Islam defines *jihad*:

> Lit. An effort, or a striving: A religious war with those who are unbelievers in the mission of Muhammad. It is an incumbent religious duty, established in the Qur'an and in the Traditions as a divine institution, and enjoined specially for the purpose of advancing Islam and of repelling evil from Muslims.[107]

A devoted Muslim must make genuine internal and external efforts for *jihad*, and to try to share the Islamic faith with people. Although *jihad* does not require violence, it can be justified when there is no peaceful alternative to protect their faith and people. In any situation of threat and violence, a proper religious authority will declare *jihad* for the religious military campaign to be activated as a concept of just war.[108] Abdullah Saeed provides helpful insights about violence justified in the Qur'an in his work *Jihad and Violence: Changing Understandings of Jihad Among Muslims*:

> In Islamic law, *jihad* as war is permitted mainly for the following: to defend one's homeland against invasion and aggression, for the propagation of religion (not conversion), and to punish those who violate peace treaties. Where there is no threat of invasion, where

---

105. Esposito, "Islam and Political Violence," 1079.
106. Gabriel, *Islam and Terrorism*, 28.
107. Kabbani and Hendricks, "Jihad, A Misunderstood Concept."
108. Shah, "Use of Force," 345.

there is freedom to propagate Islam, and there is peace between the Muslim state and others, *jihad* cannot be used.[109]

Esposito also states that Surah 9:5 is misinterpreted to justify extremists' unconditional violence against those who do neither believe in Islam, nor accept their militant actions with ignoring the request of stopping violence when the enemy stops its aggression.[110]

The Qur'an can chronologically be divided into two parts: the Meccan Surahs and the Medinan Surahs. In the earlier Meccan portion, taking a violent act is only commended against those who fight Muslims, and the aggressive commandments only after about 631 CE. While Muhammad initially emphasized peaceable relationships with people, he came to use harsher words in the Medinan Surahs, because he and his followers lived quite difficult lives during this period of time. The more serious conflicts with the Jews in Medina who rejected the teaching of Muhammad escalated the usage of violent words in the Medina Qur'an. This is one of the main reasons that his Qur'anic teaching in the later period of his life uses more violent words.[111] Therefore, the classical doctrine of *jihad* is considered to develop during the later stage of Muhammad's life, and further develop in the first two centuries of Islam, which is the seventh and eighth centuries CE.

Almost all Muslims except some extremist groups agree that *jihad* is essentially a doctrine of self-defense for the situation of imminent aggression by enemies, and it cannot be applied simply against people or communities who have different religions. In other words, as Saeed observes, the proper interpretation of *jihad* in modern days is a doctrine of war between the Muslim state and belligerent non-Muslims, who obviously oppress the Muslim state unjustifiably. However, in recent centuries there have been considerable reinterpretations of *jihad* amidst extremist groups that call for militant activities against exploitation and injustice in terms of economic and sociopolitical views.[112] Even though the Qur'an emphasizes peace as the basic virtue to all social relations, throughout history the Arab world has been experiencing unstoppable violence and hatred even within itself. Though Muslims have made every effort to establish and maintain peace, dreadful war and brute forces are inevitable in many places of the Arab world. Bassam M. Chedid expertly summarizes modern-day Islamic

109. Saeed, "Jihad and Violence," 74–75.
110. Esposito, "Islam and Political Violence," 1070.
111. Shah, "Use of Force," 345.
112. Saeed, "Jihad and Violence," 84–86.

Shalom: God's Ultimate Purpose for the World

fundamentalism, which commands all Muslims to go back to "a system of beliefs based on the Islamic *Shariah* law," and through "a true *jihad* based on total religious commitment and sacrifice, including martyrdom, Islam will recapture the lost power.[113]

Although both Christianity and Islam pursue peace, there are fundamental differences about its concept between the two faiths. Phil Parshall observes that the Muslim view of peace in the contemporary cultural context is broader and more all-inclusive compared to the Western Christian's view which pursues more individualistic inner peace based on a postmodern cultural context.[114] Because Muslims value the sense of community more deeply, the concept of peace is perceived as harmony and integration. Yet from a deeper level of theological understanding, there is a huge gap in the definition of peace. The fundamental difference is that Islam does not require a divine act of reconciliation for Muslims to experience *shalom* because sin is neither a problem that affects human nature before God, nor the root of life that has lost *shalom*.[115] The impression of peace in Islam is more about absence of violence and hostility, which can be granted by Allah through people's submission to him. However, true peace in Christianity will only be experienced when God's righteousness is established and the broken relationship with God due to sin is restored through Jesus Christ.

Rick Love regards peace as one of the most important aspects of kingdom ethics related to a Christian's moral encounter for Muslims.[116] Peacemaking is a powerful witness of God's love and forgiveness to Muslims because it brings resolution of conflict and harmony to the community. Especially in the Arab culture based on honor and shame, peacemaking through restoring relationship is critically important. Love emphasizes peacemaking for church-planting that because the church is community

---

113. Chedid, *Islam*, 73. *Shariah* (Arabic: شريعة, literally meaning "the path leading to the watering place") law, formed during the second and third centuries of the Muslim era (eighth to ninth centuries CE), is a constitution of duties based on Islamic religious belief. It is an Islamic religious precepts according to the teachings of the Qur'an and the Hadith. The goal of the *Shariah* law is to guide Muslims to live according to their religious conviction. This was systematized throughout the medieval period with many commentaries and provides a wide range of regulations in the relationships with both Allah (rituals) and people (social relations). It also includes ritual practices and ethical standards as a code of behavior according to the Islamic belief system (Coulson, "Shariah: Islamic Law").

114. Parshall, *Muslim Evangelism*, 89.

115. Chedid, *Islam*, 25.

116. Love, *Muslims, Magic, and the Kingdom of God*, 171–75.

and peacemaking is an essential virtue for community, "peacemaking is central to church-planting and church life."[117] In terms of church-planting and its development in the Islamic world, he accentuates the importance of peacemaking as a spiritual discipline in the church community because it "demands active, persistent effort"[118] in the relationship of everyday life with fellow church members and neighbors.

Chapter Summary

In the midst of brokenness and pain, there is a desperate need for people in the Arab world to experience *shalom*. *Shalom* is God's original design for his creation, and he desires human beings to enjoy the fruits of his creation. It is the fallen nature of all creation that, without God's divine intervention, no one will experience *shalom*, and Jesus has fulfilled his task to open the door to *shalom*. Jesus' encounters with marginalized people are marked by a deep heart-response, and his compassion should be reached out to those who are in despair from deadly violence in the region. In his encounters Jesus brought up all the problems, i.e. sins, that had separated people from *shalom*, for true reconciliation. Righteousness through justification by the person of Jesus Christ has brought mankind the way to experience *shalom* through the restored relationship with God. The gospel of peace shows the only way that can transform people and their societies. Therefore, those engaged in Christian mission should provide the message of *shalom* for individual and social transformation. Biblical *shalom* would also transform the social structures that perpetuate spiritual blindness and oppression, especially in the Islamic communities, through the compassionate Christian mission in the region.

As Ireland considers that God's justice and righteousness are expressed in the concern for the poor and needy including orphans and widows,[119] Christian mission must pay special attention to the most vulnerable people in the societies that it serves. In addition, as a more active sense of God's righteousness expressed in Christian mission, cross-cultural Christian workers should demonstrate his righteousness in their ministries so that people to whom they minister may learn how to act and practice justice in their societies.

117. Love, *Muslims, Magic, and the Kingdom of God*, 172.
118. Love, *Muslims, Magic, and the Kingdom of God*, 175.
119. Ireland, *For the Love of God*.

Shalom: God's Ultimate Purpose for the World

What Christian ministry is primarily to be is not merely winning souls to Jesus Christ, but establishing the *shalom* community, the kingdom of God, by the holistic approach of sharing the truth, practicing social justice, building a compassionate community, and planting the church in the cities like "Babylon." The ultimate purpose of the presence of the church and Christian mission is to work for the realization of God's *shalom* community upon wherever it exists. Christian medical mission should try its best not to dichotomize physical and spiritual *shalom* by the holistic approach to people in need.

2

Healing in Islam and the Biblical Approach

SICKNESS AND ACCIDENTS BRING serious fear and instability in the lives of individuals as well as their communities. There are many different ways of approaching healing for the sick in different cultures, which reveal the roots of worldview and theology underneath treatments and remedies.[1] Gaining deeper understanding of the issues related to sickness and healing in Muslim communities is the key to presenting the gospel to Muslims more effectively. God uses the skills of doctors and nurses to treat patients, and sometimes shows his divine power to heal the sick miraculously in a way that science and medicine cannot properly explain. God also uses believers who may have received a gift of the Holy Spirit for divine healing. When the devil makes someone ill, God, who listens to his servants, may heal the person. Both spiritual and scientific approaches for healing attract people's attention. God accomplishes healing in all kinds of ways according to his will.

When I worked at an emergency department as a surgeon in Korea, I took care of a young girl who had been complaining of an unexplained serious stomachache, conducting with normal laboratory tests. Even though her pain seemed unbearable, she was respectful and polite to me. However, she started shouting at her father with a very strange voice as soon as she saw him entering the emergency department. Most medical staff, including her father who was a pastor at a local church, immediately recognized

---

1. Healing: Robert Claxton explains the English word "heal" that originally came from the old Saxon word "hal" meaning "whole," which basically means "to make whole or sound; to cure (of a disease or wound)" (Claxton, *A Christian Doctor Speaks on Healing*, 8).

the fact that there was some kind of spiritual issue with her. Sometimes spiritual forces are undoubtedly involved in both the physical and mental health of human beings.

Miracles occur when confrontation of darkness happens as the evidence of God's power over his creation, and David L. Weddle clarifies: "Miracles in Christian tradition are signs of divine presence in history enacting compassion and defending justice."[2] Human beings are eager to live a healthy life, and try to do their best to get healed when they are sick. The medical ministry that I did for six and a half years in one of the Arab countries gave me a chance to discover the healing approaches in the Muslim community. Taking a careful look at healing issues in the Islamic context helps to evaluate them from a biblical view in order to share the Good News with Muslims. The biblically contextualized message for healing will develop Christian medical missions in the Islamic context, especially in the Muslim community that actively engages in folk practices for healing,[3] by bringing both power and truth encounters.[4]

Islamic View of Health and Disease

The definition of health according to the World Health Organization (WHO), "a state of complete physical, mental and social well-being and not merely the absence of disease or infirmity," was widely accepted in the 1970s and 1980s, with the inclusion of other components such as intellectual, environmental, and spiritual health.[5] In more recent years, this statement has

---

2. Weddle, *Miracles*, 176.

3. Traditional custom reflecting indigenous people's communal lifestyle based on their worldview and belief system and folk medicine is defined as "practiced nonprofessionally especially by people isolated from modern medical services and usually involving the use of plant-derived remedies on an empirical basis" (*Merriam-Webster's Collegiate Dictionary*, "Folk Medicine," 1878).

4. Power encounters are a major confrontation of God's power against the power of false gods or spirits. Through this encounter, a lot of power-oriented people in bondage with fear of the vengeance by their false gods and spirits come to recognize the victorious power of God. Kraft indicates two levels of power encounter: the spirit level and the human level. The Almighty God defeats the false gods at the spirit level, and at the human level, those who have experienced the power encounter may desecrate symbols representing the gods with a challenge of retaliation. The use of power encounter is an eminent means of evangelism by demonstrating the supreme power of God (Kraft, *Power Encounter in Spiritual Warfare*, 1–5).

5. WHO, "Constitution."

been modified to include the ability to lead a "socially and economically projective life."[6] In Islam, Allah is believed to heal all ailments and diseases which include even medically hopeless cases.[7] Muslims also believe that the Qur'an encourages them to maintain their health not only through the maintenance of a health preserving regimen at the individual level, but also through the establishment of a health-protective and promoting system in the community.

Islam emphasizes the importance of health, and promotes activities enhancing the health of individuals. The Qur'an commands its readers to eat from whatever is lawful and wholesome on the earth (Surah 2:168), and from the good things (Surah 2:172). Moreover, it encourages Muslims to have healthy eating habits so that they do not eat and drink excessively (Surah 7:31, 20:81), and advises mothers to breastfeed their children for two complete years (Surah 2:233), which benefits both the mother's and infant's health. Interestingly, certain types of food like the fruits of the palm trees and grapevine are recommended to eat and drink (Surah 16:67). There are also special restrictions for food in Islam as Muslims believe that food affects their body, soul, and spirit according to the Islamic teaching. Halal Certification Services defines *haram* (حرام) as "illicit, forbidden,"—anything that is prohibited by the Islamic faith, which applies to "certain foodstuffs such as alcohol or pork and not certified to be *halal* (حلال, halāl, "permitted")," "certain behaviors such as adultery or abuse," and "ill-gotten wealth obtained through sin."[8] The mark of *halal*, which literally means "permissible," or "allowed," proves that the food is accordingly prepared under Islamic law and tradition.[9] In other expressions, Chedid explains the definitions of *halal* and *haram*:

> Two concepts closely related to the Muslim ethos, constituted as it is by pervasive beliefs, are those of *halal* which is "lawful," and

---

6. WHO, "Constitution."

7. Ateeq, Jehan, et al., "Faith Healing," 299.

8. Sourdel and Sourdel-Thomine, *A Glossary of Islam*, 60; "What is Haram?" *Halal Certification Services*.

9. Sourdel and Sourdel-Thomine, *A Glossary of Islam*, 58. The Halal Food Authority defines "Halal" as the lawful objects or actions according to Islamic law that Muslims are allowed to use or engage in, is commonly used in relation to food products. Animal meats intended for Muslims to consume must be prepared lawfully by following specific instructions: Department of Halal Certification EU. "Islamic Method of Slaughtering."

Shalom: God's Ultimate Purpose for the World

haram which is "forbidden." Both concepts are "an integral part of the religious and ethical system of Islam."[10]

He also indicates that the concepts of *halal* and *haram* are rooted in the Old Testament which gave the Israelites instructions regarding dietary matters with all other laws and regulations. As the blood and meat of dead animals are considered to have germs and other harmful elements, it is believed that *halal* food is necessary to maintain their health as well as spirituality as Muslim. Spiritually unhealthy food such as dead meat, blood, and the flesh of swine is strictly prohibited by Surah 5:3, and all Muslims observe it very carefully.

There are several Islamic practices that Muslims believe promote health and to treat illnesses. One of them is *Wudu'* (الوضوء, ablution), which involves washing parts of the body generally exposed to dirt and dust, including the mouth, before offering prayers in order to be in a pure condition before Allah.[11] This practice is thought to reduce the risks of mouth infections, eye infections, cardiovascular problems, skin infections and cancers. *Wudu'* is believed to give Muslims both physical and spiritual benefits. Another practice is *Istanja* (استنجاء), the act of getting rid of uncleanliness by washing of private parts after urinating. Muslims believe this protects against urogenital infection. For Muslims who do not perform *Istanja* after using the toilet before making *wudu*, neither the *wudu* or *salat* (صلاة, pl. صلوات *salawāt*) are valid.[12] Muslims are also encouraged to clean their teeth with a toothstick (*miswak*, سواك or مسواك), which is considered a practice of purifying their mouths as well as pleasing Allah.[13] This practice is commonly found in Islamic countries and *miswak* should be made by a qualified tree of Salvadora Persica, which is well known for aiding oral hygiene. One of the famous Islamic scholars, Mayank Tripathi, seriously warns that this tree should not be misused.[14] In addition, there is a strong emphasis on drinking clean and

---

10. Chedid, *Islam*, 154.

11. Hussain, *Five Pillars*, 57. The whole process of performing *Wudu'* is described with pictures and the reference from the Qur'an in "Wudu Steps," IqraSense.

12. Said, *Muslim Southern Belle Guide for Teens*, 52. The procedure of *Istanja* is explained: "How to Do Istinja—Part 2," *My Islam*. *Salat* is the ritual prayer for Muslims, which should be performed five times daily in a set form, as one of the five pillars of Islam. *Salat* is supposed to be practiced individually as well as corporately in order to present their submission to Allah (Chedid, *Islam*, 97. The way of observing *Salat* is displayed in "Observance of *Salat*—Daily Prayers," *Understanding Islam*).

13. Adamu, *Medicine in the Qur'an*, 35.

14. Tripathi, "*Salvadora Persica L.* (Miswak)," 24–29. Tripathi warns against

pure water for maintaining health (Surahs 50:9; 67:30). Regarding the manner of drinking water, Muslims are taught not to drink water a "single gulp," but with "pauses," in order to prevent themselves from harmful damages to the respiratory and digestive tracts.[15]

Spirituality in Islam is embedded in every aspect of life, which includes concerns of maintaining health. Adamu defines spiritual health as "a dynamic state of well-being that emphasizes a proper relationship with the spiritual dimensions of living experience," and criticizes the limitation of modern medicine which does not see beyond "its mechanistic view of life."[16] Although this is acceptable in the sense that modern medicine does not exclude the importance of spirituality as closely related to physical illness, Muslims follow various practices based on Islamic belief which are quite irrational according to modern medicine and science. As far as spirituality is concerned, Muslims also believe that their destiny is predetermined, and individual people do not have control over it. What they have control over is a limited free will—that is their actions, their choice to do good or bad—and to believe or reject Allah. According to the Qur'an, those whose hearts are hardened are considered to have the most serious disease: rejection of faith (Surah 2:10). In addition, Muslims emphasize the relationship between spirituality and physical illness because physical illnesses come from the problems of the heart. They believe that Allah only heals illnesses when Muslims change their hearts. Ali Ansari concludes:

> when we, too, have made the *Mi'raj* (holy journey, المعراج) of the prophet to the throne of Allah and back in the twinkling of an eye, then we too have seen the wonders of the heart and can lay claim to perfect understanding and perfect health.[17]

Adam Asar asserts the importance of spirituality for Muslims' healing:

---

exploitation of *Salvadora Persica L.* happening recent decades due to its multipurpose usage, which has threatened the existence of this plant.

15. Adamu, *Medicine in the Qur'an*, 39–41.

16. Adamu, *Medicine in the Qur'an*, 151.

17. Ansari, "Principles and Importance of Spiritual Healing." The *Mi'raj* is believed to be a night journey that the prophet Muhammad took into heaven when he was sleeping in the sacred shrine of Mecca, the *Ka'bah*. The night journey has two parts: The first one is known as *Isra* that Muhammad took from Mecca to the "further place of worship," and the second one as *Mi'raj* to heaven and hell for purification of his heart. The *Mi'raj* is believed to be of great spiritual significance for Muslims ("*Mi'raj*," *Encyclopaedia Britannica*.).

Islamic spiritual healing has been practiced since the dawn of history. This positive energy sophisticated yet miraculous form of healing by Allah is sure cure for all kinds of physiological, psychological and sociological problems, disorders or diseases if manipulated properly. It is a complete natural holistic soul mind body healing.[18]

Hisham M. Kabbani, a Muslim medical doctor, tries to prove spiritual healing in a scientific way, hypothesizing that it happens through a driving energy. His main point is that a healthy heart will be able to heal its sick physical body; so spirituality (for example, asking the meaning of their pain and illness to Allah) is believed to bring both miraculous healing and help medicine work more effectively.[19]

Islamic Views and Practices of Healing Encouraged by the Qur'an

The Qur'an mentions healing (*shifa'a*, شفاء) in several places, and Hanif D. Sherali precisely defines *shifa'a*:

> There is a unique and unparalleled power that Muslims possess, and this is the revealed Word of Allah (SWT) recorded in the Qur'an, which is a guidance, blessings, and, in particular, a *Shifa'a* (healing). This *Shifa'a* is indeed literally a cure against various physical ailments, but more importantly, it is also a cure against spiritual diseases such as pride, ingratitude, jealousy, envy, prejudice and hatred due to personal reasons, dishonesty, lying and cheating, oppression, tyranny, and the exploitation of fellow human beings, among other evils. In addition, the Qur'an provides *Shifa'a* against emotional distress, depression, and disheartening dejection due to the trials and tribulations of life.[20]

---

18. Asar, *Peace of Mind*, 51. Kabbani also states the importance of spirituality for Muslims' healing, sourced from Harvard Medical School's Spirituality and Healing in Medicine, which states that "renewed interest in spiritual healing methods will only help to further the state of modern medicine." (Kabbani, "Spiritual Healing in the Islamic Tradition").

19. Asar, *Peace of Mind*, 51.

20. Sherali, *Spiritual Discourses*, 143. Imam Oyewole explains that healing in Islam—*shifa'a* (healing, شفاء)—is mentioned six times in the Qur'an (9:14, 10:57, 16:69, 17:82, 26:80, and 41:44). These verses generally provide hints to the sources of healing (Oyewole, "Healing in Islam").

Surahs 9:14, 10:57, and 26:80 suggest that Allah should be the one who gives healing, particularly through miracles. Adamu argues that the Qur'an does not support miraculous healing by amulets, charms, or miracles. He does "appeal to reason, knowledge and practice according to the Qur'an and Sunnah," because the miraculous healing through Allah's messengers might possibly be treated as "signs and portents with contempt, mockery or rebellion."[21] Regarding this point of view, he gives an example of Jesus in the Bible who performed the miracles of divine healing, and whose heart was torn with anguish because of the unbelief of people (Matt. 11:18, 17:17, 23:37, and Mark 3:22). This is confirmed by Surah 5:110 in the Qur'an, "when thou [Jesus] did not show them the clear signs and the unbelievers among them said: This is nothing but evident magic."[22] Therefore, Islamic scholars including Adamu encourage Muslims to understand that, although the miraculous healing through Allah's prophets is a manifestation of Allah's power over creation, they are requested to carefully distinguish it from fake miraculous healings performed by evil forces.

However, there are many practices encouraged by the Qur'an which seem to be a part of folk practices. The Qur'an itself is believed to have a divine power for healing, a positive divine energy that may take away a negative energy from patients (Surahs 17:82 and 41:44). So Muslims are encouraged to recite or read certain verses of the Qur'an in front of patients.[23] For most Muslims, there is no need to comprehend the meaning of Qur'anic verses, but they believe it will bring spiritual power and satisfaction.[24] Phil Parshall also observes that the Qur'an is considered a Muslim's comfort in sickness, and that the first Surah of the Qur'an, *Al-Fatiha* (الفَاتِحَة), is frequently recited by patients' visitors.[25] *Al-Fatiha* means "the opening," and is also recited by most Muslim families shortly after the birth of babies. The Imam invited to celebrate a baby's birth usually recites *Al-Fatiha*, which

---

21. Adamu, *Medicine in the Qur'an*, 171–77. The *Qur'an* and the *Hadith* are two main sources of Islam. The former is believed as the direct revelation from Allah through the prophet Muhammad, while the latter is the texts containing the *Sunna*, which is Muhammad's teaching of his words and actions ("What are *Hadith*?" WhyIsalm.org).

22. Adamu, *Medicine in the Qur'an*, 172–73.

23. Asar, *Peace of Mind*, 123–26.

24. Chedid, *Islam*, 161. Love indicates that more than 3/4 of the Muslim world are folk Muslims and emphasizes the importance of power, truth, and cultural encounter for church-planting among these Muslims as a three-dimensional model on the basis of the theology of the kingdom of God (Love, "Church Planting," 87–91).

25. Parshall, *Muslim Evangelism*, 217.

is considered as a parallel to the Lord's prayer in the Bible, in order to open a door for the baby to faith in Islam.[26] Furthermore, some people carry a paper containing Qur'anic verses as an amulet, and sometimes they drink water in which such a paper is completely soaked, believing that it would become holy water.[27] Parshall also shares several typical folk Islamic rituals for healing that do not make sense to those who have a modern scientific education. For example, a verse from the Qur'an written in ink on the inside of a basin will dissolve in water, and the water which dissolves the writing is poured into a glass and given to a patient to drink. An Islamic spiritual leader may recite words of the Qur'an, and then breathe over a container of water, which is believed to have a power of healing for Muslims. Furthermore, he introduces a similar illustration from North Africa:

> At the mosque in Mammam the boys learn the Qur'an from wooden slates which are coated with whiting or chalk. The chapter of the Qur'an which is to be memorized is copied onto the slate with a pen made from a split reed. This is dipped in ink made from charred sheep's wool and gum. The water used to wash the slates clean is called the "Holy Water" and is kept in a large earthen jar outside the mosque. It is reputed to be a certain remedy for many complaints. The patients drink it, and this, of course, is equivalent to drinking the word of God.[28]

However, among Muslim scholars, there is a serious dispute about this practice. Some disagree with its authenticity, and discourage it because it is not proven to have medicinal effect. It may be harmful to personal hygiene because of the chemical toxins associated with the practice.[29]

Based on the belief that Allah is the ultimate source of healing, Muslims believe several substances promote healing. The names of Allah themselves are considered to have healing power, and some Islamic scholars encourage Muslims to use them for miraculous healing. Although it is not mentioned in the Qur'an, *Ash(Al)-Shaafee* (الشافعي) is the name of Allah that means "the healer of all creation." It is found in a narration of the Muslim prophet.[30] This name of Allah is also translated as "the one who cures," and is mentioned

---

26. Chedid, *Islam*, 147.
27. Tursunova, "Cultural Patterns of Health Care Beliefs," 48.
28. Parshall, *Bridges to Islam*, 75.
29. Adamu, *Medicine in the Qur'an*, 172–73.
30. "Ash-Shaafee," *Understand Quran Academy*.

in the Book of Patients by Al-Bukhari.[31] The statement is used whenever Allah's messenger visits the sick: "Take away the disease, O the Lord of the people. Cure him as You are the One Who cures. There is no cure but Yours, a cure that leaves no disease."[32] Muslimah reports the discovery by Ibriam Karim of pronouncing the name of Allah over certain sick parts of the body. As a method of treatment, he instructs patients to put their hands on the place of pain, and praise Allah's names until the pain and sickness goes away.[33] Interestingly, in Surah 16:68–69, the Qur'an describes the healing power of honey, and this is widely believed in Islamic countries. Even in the hospital where I worked in the Middle East, doctors and nurses frequently used honey for the wound care of patients, and patients also insistently asked doctors to use the honey that they had brought. Another source of healing in Islam is water. Many Muslims believe that water has a special power of healing, and it is carefully used for some symptoms like fever. More importantly for Muslims, forgiveness is recommended as one of the moral traits (Surah 7:199; 24:22) necessary to experience divine healing.

Muhammad is reported to have said that there is no sickness for which Allah has not provided a cure.[34] There are some stories of Muhammad healing the sick during his life time, though he did not raise anyone from the dead. Parshall observed that Muhammad's participation in acts of divine healing is rare in the Qur'an and Hadith. He writes: "The norm is the prophet's recommendation of various indigenous remedies for healing."[35] In addition, Muhammad's healing miracles give no indication that Allah provided them through their faith.[36] Asar recommends Muslims to follow the example of the prophet Muhammad:

> Each word of the prayers offered by the holy prophet (peace and blessings of Allah be upon him) in the darkness of the night, in privacy in the midst and outside the company of the people, is characterized by profound sincerity, devotion and eagerness and

---

31. Al-Najdi, *Allah's Names and Attributes*; "Ash-Shaafee," *Understand Quran Academy*.

32. Al-Najdi, *Allah's Names and Attribute*; "Ash-Shaafee," *Understand Quran Academy*.

33. Muslimah, "The Healing Powers."

34. Sahih Bukhari 5678, Book 76 (Medicine), Hadith 1: "The Prophet said, 'There is no disease that Allah has created, except that he also has created its treatment.'"

35. Parshall, *Cross and the Crescent*, 231.

36. Woodward, *The Book of Miracles*.

one feels that the utterer of such prayers is the most exalted person who is perfectly begs from his Lord as a needy person.[37]

Influence of Folk Islam

Seeking well-being is a universal phenomenon; endeavoring to bring healing is as old as human existence. For all human beings, healing is a matter of life and death, a part of the everlasting pursuit of welfare, whether people are sick or well. Frederick J. Gaiser writes:

> Every culture's modes of healing sometimes work and sometimes do not, but as long as cultures stay more or less intact and more or less isolated, people cope with suffering and illness using the available means without a lot of question. Questions abound, however, when different cultures and subcultures, with different methods and definitions of healing, come into contact with one another.[38]

Every religion expresses a significant focus on healing for the sick, and Islam is no exception. Both the "official high" religion based on the Qur'an and the "popular low" religion based on the traditional practices according to Bill Musk's observation,[39] are very frequently found in Islamic countries. He expounds that "popular low" religion "deals with the problems of immediate, everyday life, such as questions of fear, sickness, loneliness, guilt, revenge, shame, powerlessness, longing, meaninglessness, disease, crisis," while "official high" religion tries to "deal with universal issues underlying ideas of origin, destiny and ultimate meaning in life."[40] This distinction is found in every religion, and is also evidently applicable to Islam. It is greatly beneficial for Christian medical mission professionals to understand "popular low Islam" as well as "official high Islam" in order to present the gospel in more proper ways through its missions.

Islam has dominated most of the countries in the Arab world, and many traditional folk practices can be observed. There are various factors that show a degree of cultural and sociological proximity between these

---

37. Asar, *Peace of Mind*, 111. Saadia also states that Muslims are requested to pray for healing by following the example of the prophet Muhammad, because prayer is considered as the source of comfort (Saadia, *The Healing Power of Prayer*).
38. Gaiser, *Healing in the Bible*, 36.
39. Musk, *Unseen Face of Islam*, 184.
40. Musk, *Unseen Face of Islam*, 180.

two religious practices of "popular low Islam" and "official high Islam," while there are other aspects in which the two religious practices seem irreconcilable. Folk practices are something fundamental to traditions in society even if they are completely unrelated to the teaching of Islam. Regarding the relationship of humans to the spiritual realm, the real proximity of Islam to the traditional religious practices lies in the fact that both are more than pure religion. As a matter of fact, even the "official high Islam" offers a framework for assuring many folk practices to address many serious matters of life within the traditional socio-religious world of Islam. In other words, solidarity within the Muslim community creates a religious paradigm of folk practices without changing the unreasonable habits of individual lives.

Practices of fortune telling and remedies for healing are common practices in the Arab world. Charms and amulets are also considered important in protection from diseases and in bringing healing for the sick.[41] Although divination, magic, charms, amulets, or reciting certain incantations for healing are not explicitly encouraged by Islamic teaching, they are easily found in Muslim communities pursuing supernatural help for their illness. Some Muslim scholars assent to the use of amulets and charms with Scriptures as long as this does not lead to *shirk* (شرك),[42] while scholars like Asar are against charms and amulets because they are considered as a means of idol worship:

> The belief associated with good luck charms that they attract good fortune and avert evil is thus committing *shirk*. It was the practice of the Arabs at the time of Allah's messenger to wear lockets, bracelets, beads, shells, etc. as charms. Allah's messenger is reported to have rejected all such practices.[43]

Salih Yucel's summary clarifies the confusion:

> Prophet Muhammad, peace be upon him, had at first forbidden all amulets for fear that they contained certain words that compromised the rigorous monotheism and Islam by invoking spirits and other powers besides God (Rahman 1987, 88). Subsequently,

41. Varner, "The History & Use of Amulets, Charms and Talismans," 6.

42. Adamu, *Medicine in the Qur'an*, 179–81. *Shirk* (شرك): The Arabic word, shirk, means "making a partner [of someone]," and it refers to the association of Allah with other deities, which is the greatest unforgivable sin as idolatry or polytheism in Islam (Surah 4:116) because the fundamental belief of Islam is monotheism (*tawhid*) (Dodge, *Shirk*).

43. Asar, *Peace of Mind*, 132.

he allowed their use but only if their contents were verses or hadiths and the person expected healing from God and not from the amulet itself (Al-Jawziyyah 1999, 29). The verses or hadiths on the amulets can then be read as prayers.[44]

The fundamental motivation of this practice is to be free from disease on the basis of the strong belief that the Qur'an has the miraculous power of healing. Because of the awareness of individual's powerlessness against the evil spirits and sickness, the felt needs in folk Islam towards mysticism must be strong. Many Muslims consciously experience a sense of deprivation when they are in life crisis such as sickness, even if they have a strong belief in Islam and its teaching. Several felt needs of the remedies or practices for healing in folk Islam can be observed.

First, according to Gabriel J. Gomes, Allah in Islam is more remote and less involved in human affairs than God in Christianity is.[45] This belief contributes to Muslims seeking an intercessor who is supposed to help them to be healed. Although the Qur'an is the revelation sent down from Allah, Allah remains unknowable to Muslims. This understanding of Allah is mainly responsible for drawing Muslims into folk practices for their needs of healing. Musk states: "Thus, at times, the orthodox expression of Islam has been consciously ameliorated to include some of the burdens of popular Islam."[46] He continues explaining that folk practices are widely tolerated for maintaining health and healing sicknesses, because "official high Islam" cannot meet the felt needs of Muslims, and Islam is considered to be a way of life which should be absolutely more than a simple religious system. Muslims feel responsible to find a way to maintain their families' and communities' health through folk practices outside of the "official high" Islamic system. Musk's conclusion regarding felt needs is applicable to most Muslims in the Arab world:

> Without a dynamic, divine involvement, contradictory of its own systematic tenets, official Islam cannot hope to compete for the uncompromising patronization of most Muslims, for it cannot meet their most fundamental needs.[47]

---

44. Yucel, *Prayer and Healing*, 39.
45. Gomes, *Discovering World Religions*, 328.
46. Musk, *Unseen Face of Islam*, 214–15.
47. Musk, *Unseen Face of Islam*, 215.

Healing in Islam and the Biblical Approach

Unlike "official high Islam," *Sufis* pursue personal interaction with Allah by repetitive recitation of the Qur'an.[48] Sourdel and Sourdel-Thomine defines-*Sufism* (صُوفِي, *sufiyy*) or *Tasawwuf* (مُتَصَوِّف, *mutasawwuf*) as "mystical movement" in Islam.[49] Parshall explains the importance of *Sufi* spirituality that meets the felt needs of Muslims who seek a solution to the spiritual void in Islam. *Sufism* teaches "a program of spiritual ascent" helping Muslims to be filled with "spiritualism, love, and liberty," by "shifting the emphasis from the external rituals of religions to the mind and heart."[50] Sophia Kim observes the shrine culture in Egypt as a part of folk practices related to *Sufism*, which shows a huge felt need in ordinary Muslims who believe in the personal presence and relationship with Allah in order to resolve their personal problems.[51] It is a popular scene in the Arab world to see many ordinary Muslims as well as *Sufi* Muslims visit shrines of Islamic saints to get help for unsolved current problems.

Second, most Muslims are afraid of the spiritual beings called *jinn* (الجن), "corporeal beings created from a flame without smoke,"[52] because they believe that *jinn* exert all possible efforts to turn Muslims back against Allah. They make their presence known by causing illnesses, especially convulsions, epileptic seizures, fits of madness, and epidemical diseases.[53] Surah 15:26–27 states that *jinn* were created before man, and Surah 55:15 mentions that Allah created the *jinn* from a smokeless flame of fire. They are believed to be a certain spiritual being in a realm between men and angels. They are thought to be invisible as described in the Arabic word *jinn*, coming from the verb, *janna* (جن), of which English translation is to cover, hide, conceal, veil.[54] They are also considered to have free will, unlike angels.[55] They are believed to reside in dirty places like toilets and garbage dumps as

---

48. Parshall, *Muslim Evangelism*, 162.

49. Sourdel and Sourdel-Thomine, *A Glossary of Islam*, 165. The name *sufi* is from the word *suf*, "wool," referring to the garment of woolen patches worn by early disciples. Annemarie Schimmel defines *Sufism* as "mystical Islamic belief and practice in which Muslims seek to find the truth of divine love and knowledge through direct personal experience of God" (Schimmel, *Encyclopaedia Britannica*).

50. Parshall, *Muslim Evangelism*, 162–64.

51. Kim, "*Sufism* in Egypt," 109–11.

52. Sourdel and Sourdel-Thomine, *A Glossary of Islam*, 85.

53. Parshall, *Muslim Evangelism*, 166.

54. Wehr, *Dictionary of Modern Written Arabic*, "*janna* (جن)," 164.

55. Parshall, *Muslim Evangelism*, 33–35.

well as places that humans do not dwell, like mountains, graveyards, and abandoned buildings.[56] Adamu explains how the *jinn* possess man:

> Occasional possession of men by the *jinn* may be due to sensual desires on the part of the *jinn*, capricious whims or even love, just as it may be among humans. However, possession is most often as a result of the *jinn* being angry because some wrong has been done to them. Thus it is to them a punishment for those who wronged them.[57]

Muslims are strongly recommended to recite verses of the Qur'an in order to avoid being possessed by the *jinn*, which will cause various health issues including metal illnesses, because the *jinn* have fiery characteristics. Asar explains the mechanism of possession by *jinn*:

> The *jinn* flow through its newfound host like blood, incrementing its control. The result is the successive infiltration of each organ, limb, and then ultimately the brain, brought under the wing of the *jinn*.[58]

Without proper knowledge about these characteristics and attributions of the *jinn* regarding medical issues plaguing Muslims, a right diagnosis and treatment may not be possible.

Muslims believe that *jinn* are a major cause of occult activities associated with folk Islam, and are responsible for turning Muslims away from Allah to worship other gods.[59] Musk clearly expounds the identity and function of the *jinn*:

> Although theoretically neutral, the *jinn* are conceived of as being bad. They are intensely jealous of human men, women, and children and seek constantly for opportunities to injure them.[60]

Due to the fear of *jinn*, many ordinary Muslims are strongly motivated to appease the *jinn* with various folk practices. It is recommended to recite Surah 23:97–98 to avoid any consequences from manipulation by the *jinn*. This practice for healing might stem from the belief that the holy book of

---

56. Adamu, *Medicine in the Qur'an*, 161.

57. Adamu, *Medicine in the Qur'an*, 161.

58. Asar, *Peace of Mind*, 136. Gholipour reports that many Muslim psychiatric patients attribute symptoms such as hallucinations to *jinn*. This is a common belief among Muslims (Gholipour, "Supernatural 'Jinn' Seen as Cause of Mental Illness Among Muslims").

59. "The World of Jinn."

60. Musk, *Unseen Face of Islam*, 33.

the Qur'an has power over the evil spirits.[61] Exorcism is also recommended to help those who are possessed by *jinn*, but the amulets or talisman for exorcism should not include *shirk* because *shirk* is viewed as idolatry or polytheism which is considered *haram*.[62]

Musk indicates that *qarina* (قرينة), "the spirit double of the human being," is responsible for some sicknesses because it is the companion to *jinn*.[63] He further explains the concept of the *qarina*:

> The concept of *qarina*, or some kind of double of the human individual, is another expression of "being" in the trans-empirical realm. That double is seen as responsible for a variety of occurrences in the life of a human being.[64]

Surah 43:36 mentions *Qareen* which is translated as "companion" (Sahih International Translation). It is considered to be a spiritual being and influences a person to do evil things. The aim of some remedies is to bring bad luck on the *qarina*, and escape from disease.[65] As a person's companion which knows a person's entire life, the *qareen* is believed to be involved in fortune telling in addition to other occult activities.

Third, the fear of the unknown and fear of sickness are strong forces that move people toward animistic folk practices. Because the fear of the unknown future is a universal symptom which affects both individuals and communities profoundly, fetishes, superstition, and divination are the most popular occult activities to relieve this fear. Both the Old Testament and the New Testament criticize these practices.[66] The following definition of "occult" by Leonard G. Goss is helpful:

> For occult practitioners, the occult represents interference with physical nature by using hidden knowledge (gnosis), such as non-conventional practices including reciting formulas, making gestures, mixing incompatible elements, performing healing spells, or performing secret ceremonies attempting to alter physical nature.[67]

---

61. VanRheenen, *Communicating Christ in Animistic Context*, 257.
62. Adamu, *Medicine in the Qur'an and Sunnah*, 166–71.
63. Musk, *Unseen Face of Islam*, 94.
64. Musk, *Unseen Face of Islam*, 163.
65. Musk, *Unseen Face of Islam*, 103.
66. Lev 19:31, Deut 18:9–22, 1 Chr 10:13–14, Isa 8:19, Acts 13:6–12, and Gal 5:13–26.
67. Goss, "What is the Occult?"

Shalom: God's Ultimate Purpose for the World

Divination is frequently utilized when people are trying to find both a cause of disease and certain remedies for healing. It guides Muslims for their healing with occult activities as well as general direction for everyday life. Muslims feel powerless over the future, and nobody can be free from fright and fear, especially when they fall ill. For this purpose, the Qur'an is used to contact the spiritual power that may disclose the cause and the ways to get healed. Musk introduces "cutting the Qur'an" as a common way of divination that Muslims open the Qur'an randomly and interpret any related words with their situation.[68] This kind of divination provides Muslims a way of releasing their fear of the unknown regarding their sickness, as it at least tells them what to do for their situation whether it works or not. Parshall apparently notices that even though mystics have historically sought to shift emphasis from the fear of God to the love of God, there remains pervasive fear on the grassroots level.[69] In the context of animism,[70] extended illness is thought to be caused by sin and be produced by ancestors. Animistic belief is greatly concerned about the causes of illness. Several main causes of illnesses such as soul loss, spirit intrusion, the breaking the taboo, and sorcery can be discovered among Muslims, especially among the *Sufi*. While people who have been influenced by scientific education may naturalize the causes of illness, animists believe that there is some spiritual power behind the naturalist explanation. People who neglect the duty to satisfy their ancestors or spirits might suffer from illness, so they must have a diviner to discern the causes and the ways to escape from it.[71]

There are many examples of "popular low Islam" in the ordinary Muslims' life. For instance, alms, one of the five pillars, can be used for

---

68. Musk, *Unseen Face of Islam*, 62–64.

69. Parshall, *Bridges to Islam*, 119.

70. Animism: A term of animism has a controversy as it is considered to be part of cultural superiority by some scholars who advocate the abandonment of the word. Ingold observes animism as "primitive superstition, systems of belief that allegedly attribute spirits or souls to things, living or non-living, which to any rational, thinking person are 'obviously' mere objects of nature." He compares this concept with the definition of animism by Descola who considers animism with a respectful consideration toward indigenous culture, that "animism is a kind of objectification of nature [that] endows natural beings not only with human dispositions, granting them the status of persons with human emotions and often the ability to talk, but also with social attributes—a hierarchy of positions, behaviours based on kinship, respect for certain norms of conduct" (Clammer, Poirier, and Schwimmer, *Figured Worlds*, 50).

71. Van Rheenen, *Communicating Christ in Animistic Context*, 35–36.

precaution against the "evil eye," and the name of Allah is also commonly applied in the practices of magic. Sam Migliore states:

> The *evil eye* refers to the ability of the human eye to cause, or at least project, harm when it is directed by certain individuals towards others and their possessions.[72]

Zacharias Kotze also argues that "the evil eye is a widespread folk concept that the glance of certain people, gods, animals, and mythological figures can cause injury, illness, or death."[73] Azher Hammeed Qamar explains in the context of rural Punjabi Muslim culture that the fear of the "evil eye" is from "a sense of insecurity of envious human beings and *jinnat* (supernatural beings) that may bring harm to the valued items."[74] Musk also explains the fundamental concept of the "evil eye": "Precious persons or things are constantly vulnerable to hurt or destruction caused by other people's envy. Such envy or jealousy is projected through the eye."[75] Almost all Muslims are influenced by the belief in the "evil eye" to some extent in their everyday lives. As the Qur'an indicates, "Say, I seek refuge in the Lord of daybreak . . . from the evil of the envier when he envies" (Surah 113:1, 5). Envy as a tangible force is considered to be one of the major causes of crises in Muslims' lives, especially many health issues.

Charms or talismans decorated with eye-like symbols, mostly blue- and white-colored, called "evil eyes," are carried in vehicles and placed in houses in order to ward off the "evil eye." Many people also carry it all the time as an amulet, and some truck owners write a slogan or verses of the Qur'an on their vehicles to protect themselves from the "evil eye." An infant is believed to be especially in danger of the "evil eye," so parents and families often give the child an amulet bracelet on its wrist to wear for special protection. The premise of this belief is that a person may cause harm simply by looking at another person or property, and even though protection might come easily by carrying talismans, Muslims cannot be completely free from the fear related to it. Qamar writes that ways of childcare in Muslim families are closely attached to the fear of the "evil eye,"

---

72. Migliore, *Mal'uocchiu*, 13. Evil eye is also defined as "an eye or glance capable of inflicting harm; also, a person believed to have such an eye or glance" (*Merriam-Webster Online Dictionary*).

73. Kotze, "Evil Eye of Sumerian Deities," 102.

74. Qamar, "Belief in the Evil Eye," 398.

75. Musk, *Unseen Face of Islam*, 22–23.

and it pervasively influences their everyday life.[76] There is another popular amulet called *Khamsah*, the hand of Fatima,[77] in the Arab world. Aasia,[78] a local nurse, always carries the hand of Fatima to protect herself and her family from evil spirits.

Muslims are strongly influenced by fatalism which permeates their entire lives. Fatalism is defined by Mark Bernstein:

> Fatalism is the thesis that whatever happens must happen; every event or state of affairs that occurs, must occur, while the nonoccurrence of every event and state of affairs is likewise necessitated. With respect to human affairs, fatalism claims that we lack the power (capability, ability) to perform any actions other than the ones that we do, in fact, perform.[79]

Dalya Cohen-Mor indicates that the frequent mentions in the Qur'an of "being written" or "being in a book" suggest the idea of predestination in Islamic theology.[80] According to the Hadith, Allah casts an angel for a role of dictating the fate of each human being before its birth:

> Narrated Abdullah: Allah's Apostle, the true and truly inspired said, "(as regards your creation), every one of you is collected in the womb of his mother for the first forty days, and then he becomes a clot for another forty days, and then a piece of flesh for another forty days. Then Allah sends an angel to write four words: He writes his deeds, time of his death, means of his livelihood, and whether he will be wretched or blessed (in religion). Then the soul is breathed into his body."[81]

This fatalistic belief is deeply seated in the life of ordinary Muslims, and these deterministic views toward life are closely related to mythological traditions in Islamic society, which promote fear of the future and misfortune. Muslims who feel powerless to change what has been fore-ordained tend to

---

76. Qamar, "Belief in the Evil Eye," 413–15.

77. In Arabic, Khamsah (خمسة) means five, symbolizing five fingers, and Fatima is a daughter of the prophet Muhammad. This amulet is believed to protect from evil spirits (the evil eye) and to bring happiness and good luck (Pelaia, "Learn About the Hamsa Hand").

78. This name has been changed.

79. Bernstein, "Fatalism," 65. The *Stanford Encyclopedia of Philosophy* simply defines fatalism as "the view that we are powerless to do anything other than what we actually do" (*Stanford Encyclopedia of Philosophy*, "Fatalism").

80. Cohen-Mor, *A Matter of Fate*, 4–9.

81. Sahih Bukhari, Book 55: Prophets, Hadith Number 549, Volume 4.

struggle with fearful, fatalistic thoughts. Chedid summarizes their fatalistic theology based on Surahs 3:145, 6:59, 7:188, and 9:51: "Everything is determined by the will of Allah, so that the will of man is rendered futile." While Allah unjustly predestines the fate of every soul, the God of the Bible acts in a way that is consistent with his goodness, grace and justice.[82]

It takes only a short time even for those who are in any Arab countries for the first time to hear the Arabic phrase, *Insha Allah* (إن شاء الله), which means "if Allah wills." When hoping or promising for something good in the future, Muslims are required to say *Insha Allah*. This phrase is used in a multitude of circumstances. Although Christians in the Arab world also use this phrase quite often, the worldview underneath this phrase is quite different from that of Muslims. In practice, it often means that whatever happens is Allah's will. They live in a cloud of fatalism and uncertainty about their future on the basis of Islamic theology. Abdullah,[83] a local nurse who worked with me at the hospital, told me a story of how this Arabic phrase has affected Muslims' lives:

> A man was confident that he would keep his promise of lending some money to his friend the next day. He refused to say, *Insha Allah*, because he was really sure he would lend that amount of money, even though his friend insisted that he should say *Insha Allah*. The same day his son suddenly died, and he was unable to lend the money to his friend.

Ali,[84] a hospital administrator, insisted that his belief should not be related to fatalism, but to a debate over predestination versus free will. He mentioned that the life of this world serves as a test for every soul in both the good and bad things that happen in life, and all of these things cannot occur without the permission of the will of Allah. However, Ali's opinion is more about eschatological insight, while his daily practices seem based on his belief that everything is from Allah and human beings can do nothing about it. Fatalism is the belief that human beings are powerless and cannot change the future and destiny.[85] Many people in the Arab world who I have met express negative opinions about their countries and political leadership while they overemphasize the supremacy of Islamic teaching. Although they are happy with my favorable impression about their country in the beginning of

82. Chedid, *Islam*, 115–16.
83. This name has been changed.
84. This name has been changed.
85. Bernstein, "Fatalism," 65.

Shalom: God's Ultimate Purpose for the World

conversations, they usually end with sighs and complains about their situation and life. They indicate that Allah has helped them, but seem not to have much hope. They confess that Allah's ways are beyond all understanding and his moral character is ultimately unknowable. Muslims do not have assurance of Allah's forgiveness to enter the paradise because they are not certain about Allah's ultimate will and plan for the individual Muslim.

As a matter of fact, popular Islamic thinking and practice are often very fatalistic, especially related to the fear of misfortune. For example, at the hospital, when I would explain the risks of mortality and morbidity related to the surgery due to a patient's critical condition, most of the patient's family said that all consequences would be from Allah and they could do nothing about it. Even though some people knew that patient died from a certain reason, they insisted that this was his destiny from Allah. Fatalism has an impact on all aspects of Muslim society that are governed by the mentality of *Insha Allah*, even in the healthcare system. This usually means Muslims are to submit themselves to whatever happens because it is all from Allah. Muslims do not usually ask probing questions such as *Why does Allah allow diseases, even death?*, since they believe that all Muslims must submit themselves to Allah's will. Allah's justice in the face of suffering is not supposed to be questioned. The fatalistic understanding of Allah's attributes permeates into doctors' and nurses' attitudes toward patients, too. Doctors and nurses at the hospital where I worked had never done resuscitation until I started a basic life support training program. This underdeveloped qualification hindered the doctors and nurses to save lives, which was obviously supported by their fatalistic understanding of patients' destiny.

Bismillah (بسم الله) which means "in the name of Allah"[86]—is one of the most popular phrases in Muslim's life in the Arab world. Foreigners sometimes struggle to understand just what is being conveyed in this little phrase that rings constantly in their ears. Parshall notes: "when a child is able to talk or he reaches the age of four years, four months, and four days, he is taught to say *Bismillah*."[87] This is a very simple illustration of how this Islamic worldview is incorporated into the language. Clearly, Christians and Muslims can agree that the name of God is powerful and mighty, that

---

86. Keene, *This is Islam*, 69. "*Bismillah*" means "in the name of Allah"—"an invocation used by Muslims at the beginning of an undertaking" (*English Living Oxford Dictionary*, "Bismillah").

87. Parshall, *Muslim Evangelism*, 226.

it is a safe shelter, and that everyone should do things in the name of God to express dependence on him.

Hiebert and others expound the challenges of the "magical mentality" in most folk religions that tries to manipulate the powers for their own sake. Christian belief is perceived as another power which is more powerful than their formal gods or powers.[88] Stronger power is always attractive to people in an animistic society. When Barnabas and Paul made a lame man well in Lystra with divine healing power from God, the crowds believed they were gods incarnated and tried to worship them (Acts 14:6–18). The "magical mentality" must be challenged by the biblically-contextualized truth, and be transformed into the biblical worldview rather than the idea that God's divine power is simply exercised over powers in folk religion. In many contexts, folk practices are not easily distinguishable from "official high Islam," or even from Christianity with Muslim-background believers who employ acceptable practices in the Christian belief system. When local churches receive new believers who have been under the serious influence of folk Islam, a distorted message of the gospel becomes a problem in many places. As folk practices attempt to respond to human needs, especially in times of crises, with its own rituals or systems for seeking healing or averting misfortune, they should be dealt with care to present the gospel in biblical ways.

Interview Analysis: Muslims' Understanding of Healing

From these brief interviews, it seems evident that these answers reflect many Muslims' comprehension regarding healing and its religious-cultural value in the Arab world. As noted, failing to understand Muslims' understanding of healing and its related practices within a given culture will certainly hinder Christian medical missions. This interview analysis will empower Christian medical professionals working in the Arab world by enhancing their comprehension of healing in the Islamic context.

One of the most significant answers regarding the procedure for healing in Islamic tradition is *the legitimate Ruqya* (الرقية الشرعية) which was mentioned by nine interviewees. Salih Yucel explains:

> Amulets (Ruqya) and talismans are objects meant to bring protection and good luck. They can be found in many faith traditions

---

88. Hiebert, Shaw, and Tienou, "Responding to Split-Level Christianity," 177.

and cultures. In the Muslim world, people who are uneducated or less educated about religion use amulets that may contain Qur'anic verses, prayers, and symbols. Some people will not seek out modern therapeutic interventions; rather, they will rely on the amulets as a source of healing and protection from the evil powers that cause harm.[89]

It was believed that the prophet Muhammad and his companions performed the *Ruqya*. Khaled Al-Jeraisy indicates that only verses of the Qur'an, *dhikr* (ذِكْر: words in Allah's remembrance) and established prayers are recommended for *Ruqya*.[90] An example of the whole procedure is described on the "Official Ruqyah Website of Abu Ibraheem Hussnayn."[91] The *Ruqya* is observed carefully by most of Muslims in the Arab world. The details of its purpose are described:

> *Ruqya* is the healing and relief of people who suffer and are stuck for years. Secondly, it is a protection of Muslims against shirk and strengthening their faith. Thirdly, it is a door Dawa to non-Muslims because the Quran also cure non-Muslims since sahabas Fatiha healed by a tribal chief healer. Fourthly, it is a fight against witches, Satanists, witch doctors, seers, and their associates and all forms of shirk until it disappears completely.[92]

These interviewees value the *Ruqya* greatly and confidently believe that it works for many sicknesses and diseases, especially those caused by black magic, the evil eye, or *jinn*. Eight interviewees shared their personal experience of divine healing, five of which indicated that it was related to the practice of the *Ruqya*. Al-Jeraisy encourages Muslims to believe in the effectiveness of *Ruqya* to give healing benefits of all physical and

---

89. Yucel, *Prayer and Healing*, 38–39. The *legitimate Ruqya* is considered to be the proper Qur'anic treatment procedure for divine healing in Islam, and is defined as "a treatment using the Qur'an and certain effective supplications or words which have healing effects and are used to cure various illnesses" (Hasanat Ruqya Team, "Hasanat Ruqya: Services of Spiritual Healing").

90. Al-Jeraisy, "Self-Ruqya Treatment," 9–10. *Dhikr* is defined: "*Dhikr*, also spelled *Zikr*, (Arabic: "reminding oneself," or "mention"), ritual prayer or litany practiced by Muslim mystics (*Ṣūfīs*) for the purpose of glorifying God and achieving spiritual perfection." (*Encyclopaedia Britannica*, "*Dhikr*.")

91. Hussnayn, "Ruqya QA."

92. Arrahim, "Ruqya." Dawa (دعوة; Invitation or Call): Dawa literally means "issuing a summons" or "making an invitation" of both Muslims and non-Muslims to know the worship of Allah according to the Qur'an. (Dodge, "The Meaning of Da'wah in Islam").

non-physical illnesses.[93] He also explains: "*Shari'ah* statements confirm the permissibility of seeking healing by Qur'anic citations and the Prophet's established prayers."[94] One interviewee shared a story of his friend who had tried to cure his infant baby with a hole in the heart by feeding him dates and reading Qur'anic verses about dates. Although the infant baby was medically diagnosed to have no hope of survival, it was miraculously cured. The interviewee interpreted this outcome because the father of the baby had a faith in Allah to feed his baby dates although a date is not a kind of food to feed an infant. Another interviewee testified that his relative who had been diagnosed with infertility now had two children because of a treatment with the Qur'an and the legitimate *Ruqya*. Three interviewees specifically mentioned that herbs, dates, honey, and olive oil are an important part of healing.

Ten interviewees clearly indicate that the Qur'an itself has divine healing power in association with the belief that Allah is the only healer. Certainly, faith in Allah is believed to be the fundamental source of divine healing, which greatly strengthened by reciting specific verses in the Qur'an. Interestingly, two interviewees mentioned that all matters of human beings are predestined according to Allah's will. One of these two interviewees shared his story related to *Insha Allah*. He had lost his sensation and movement in his legs after refusing to say it before taking an exam. After asking forgiveness of Allah, his legs were restored. Similar stories bring so much fear to Muslims who might forget saying *Insha Allah* when they talk about any plans for the future. Six interviewees commented that the pursuit of divine healing should be accompanied with the use of modern medicine.

A common phrase in Arabic, *bismillah*, also demonstrates how the language reflects Muslims' thoughts related to their daily practices. "It is the introduction to any work we do," shared Fatima,[95] a local nurse in replying to my query about what she said before the injection of medicine and wound dressing. "It makes the work better. We say it to show that we depend on Allah for everything. If we forget to say it in the beginning of the work—yet, we can never forget to—we say it at the end." Declaring dependence upon God in everything is certainly something we ourselves might champion. However, often this phrase seems not so much intended to glorify Allah as it is invoked like a magic word that conjures up good

93. Al-Jeraisy, "Self-Ruqya Treatment," 9–10.
94. Al-Jeraisy, "Self-Ruqya Treatment," 9–10.
95. This name has been changed.

fortune, luck, success, or wards off evil. "It makes me feel safe," she said. Dr. Muhammad,[96] a local surgeon, also said, "It will make everything very easy for you. Allah will be with you. Allah likes it when we remember his name." The most customary usage of *Bismillah* is before a meal. They told me, "if you do not say *Bismillah* before a meal, you will feel hungry later. When you say it, you feel something inside of you. Even if the food is dangerous, it will not hurt you." Fatima affirmed, "If you say it before you eat, you will not feel hungry afterward even if you only have a little to eat."

This interview analysis provides useful information about the insight of Muslims regarding divine healing and its related practices. On the basis of this analysis and deeper understanding of healing pursued by Muslims, Christian medical mission may be able to approach Muslims with a better process of biblical contextualization in order to present the message of the gospel in this context.

Biblical Contextualization and Healing

In societies where people have diverse worldviews, people use different means or mechanisms for healing because they view the nature and cause of diseases differently. Charles H. Kraft states:

> For example, for most of the traditional peoples of the world, healing was/is a spiritual matter, not a secular one. So is agriculture and human and animal fertility. In the West, however, we have secularized each of these matters.[97]

The crises of sickness bring serious tension and emotional stress to all people, especially Muslims who are strongly influenced by folk practices. They try to find out the causes of the sickness and ways to overcome those crises through various occult practices. Without studying the deeper spiritual reality that extends beyond visible physical causes, Christian mission may face losing a common ground of communication with ordinary Muslims who are in crisis. Musk similarly observes:

> Sickness, then, is one of any number of crises ordinary Muslims have to face. Formal theology might emphasize the sovereignty of God, even in a sense that suggests determinism or fatalism. In practice, however, Muslims spend their days and nights—and

---

96. This name has been changed.
97. Kraft, ed., *Appropriate Christianity*, 365.

hard-earned wages—trying to find ways and means of rewriting what is supposedly maktub ("written").[98]

As Muslim societies in the Arab world integrate folk practices for healing, Muslims' worldview underneath the surface of their traditional daily practices related to folk Islam must be carefully examined in order for Christian mission to strategize more effective ways to present the gospel message. Those who have a modern education, no matter the religious backgrounds, acknowledge that most diseases are caused by substances like germs, bacteria, viruses, or chemicals. They believe that even many of psychiatric symptoms are from interaction among genes, immune and endocrine systems according to the empirical and scientific studies. However, for those who have a folk-Islamic view, causes of diseases are closely related to spiritual matters. Parshall insightfully compared Christianity with folk practices of Islam in terms of felt needs involved in practices for healing:

> All people in the world regard illness as an undesirable reality. The Christian usually responds to sickness with a dash to the medicine cabinet followed by a prayer to God for healing. The folk Muslims' reaction to illness is often of a more mystical nature.[99]

As James 5:14 says that Christians can pray over the sick and anoint them with oil in the name of the Lord for the divine healing power from God. In Christian perspectives, God is supreme above all spiritual forces and subordinate deities, so all human beings must worship and give glory and honor only to God. Gailyn Van Rheenen summarizes:

> Therefore, they must be treated enemies of the cross and encountered both by proclaiming the reality of the sovereignty of God in Christ (truth encounter) and by confronting their power with the awesome power of God (power encounter).[100]

The miraculous gift of healing granted to the Apostles in the early church is still available to the church and the Christian mission nowadays as Apostle James teaches the church (James 5:13–15). Meanwhile, unintended superstition related to the miraculous healing must be well distinguished from healing by the power of the Holy Spirit.

---

98. Musk, *Unseen Face of Islam*, 96.
99. Parshall, *Bridges to Islam*, 122.
100. Van Rheenen, *Communicating Christ in Animistic Context*, 259.

Shalom: God's Ultimate Purpose for the World

Rick Love emphasizes the theology of the kingdom of God to compare the different perspectives of folk Islam to Christianity.[101] The kingdom of God can be defined as "the sovereign reign of God," which means that God is still at work in creation and in history to redeem the world unto himself.[102] God is not remote from human beings, but is close to them and wants to have an intimate relationship with them. The person of Jesus Christ is certainly central to that work, but it extends beyond him to the work of the Holy Spirit in the life of each person, and to the work of God in the affairs of nations and in all his creation. God's sovereign reign deals with the eternal destiny and the spiritual realm of human beings as well as their well-being on earth such as peace, justice, health, provision, and righteousness. God is concerned with the everyday life of individuals who are bearing his image on the earth.[103] Because of this, the promise of healing in Christ's name is given to his people, even if the perfect healing of the whole world still remains as an eternal hope of his second coming. In addition to Love's observation, Musk's comment gives a momentous insight:

> In contrast to the folk-Islamic view, the emphasis of Scripture is also strongly ethical. The Creator, the Lord, is he to whom all creation is accountable, either immediately or ultimately. Whoever or whatever is responsible for disease does not act independently or without prospect of judgement.[104]

He continues to advise Christian medical professionals working with Muslims that the emotional and spiritual issues of sickness or disease should be addressed holistically, even when Muslims accept the diagnosis and treatment such as antibiotics, other medicines, or surgeries, because they may still have a strong fear of the "evil eye," *jinn*, or sorcery that they think might cause sickness.[105]

It is also very important for Christian cross-cultural workers to communicate the message of the gospel to folk Muslims in culturally relevant ways. Scott Moreau develops foundational principles of intercultural communication, and he challenges cross-cultural workers with the insightful comment:

---

101. Love, "Church Planting," 39–46.
102. Love, "Church Planting," 39–46.
103. Love, "Church Planting," 39–46.
104. Musk, *Unseen Face of Islam*, 98.
105. Musk, *Unseen Face of Islam*, 98.

Healing in Islam and the Biblical Approach

> There is no doubt that competence is critical for long-term healthy relationships in a new cultural setting. The ability to live well—in ways that honor your hosts and allow you to live out your Christian convictions in addition to appropriately performing your expected responsibilities—is of critical importance for Christians who choose to live in a cross-cultural context.[106]

For biblical contextualization, every Christian cross-cultural worker has to learn how to communicate properly in different cultures. Moreau presents his research about the different models of contextualization, which assists Christian medical mission to understand the importance of contextualizing the gospel message. He defines contextualization:

> In short, contextualization can be described as the process whereby Christians adapt the forms, content, and praxis of the Christian faith so as to communicate it to the minds and hearts of people with other cultural backgrounds. The goal is to make the Christian faith *as a whole*—not only the message but also the means of living out of our faith in the local setting—understandable.[107]

Without attaining appropriate ways of contextualization, it is almost impossible to share the gospel biblically in situations where medical missionaries deal with folk practices.

Certainly, many Muslims in the Arab world perform practices and rituals for healing on the basis of animistic belief. In the local society, most congenital malformations such as a cleft lip and palate are regarded as curses from evil spirits. One of the most fundamental reasons of fear related to sickness and disease is from the ignorance of the particular medical issues individuals are facing. Proper education about diseases and sickness on the basis of modern medical science may change people's misinformed ideas and thoughts. For people who live in rural areas and do not have modern education, it is necessary to educate them that many of diseases are neither a consequence of curse from the spiritual forces, nor cured by animistic rituals and occult procedures, but by proper medical treatment or surgery. God has created substances on earth that can be made into medicine with healing properties, therefore, medicine should be considered as a part of the whole creation that God has gracefully provided, and should be used to

---

106. Moreau, Campbell, and Greener, *Effective Intercultural Communication*, 226. Four approaches to intercultural competence are suggested: the Cognitive Awareness Model, the Character Traits Model, the Social Skills Model, and the Interactionist Model.

107. Moreau, *Contextualization in World Missions*, 36.

Shalom: God's Ultimate Purpose for the World

treat sickness and disease rather than appealing to mysticism and animistic practices. The biblical truth regarding physical sickness is that it has come as a result of the fall of Adam, and illness is simply a part of the phenomena of the curse after the Fall. Due to this fallen nature of human beings, all will eventually be led toward physical death. However, Christ's redemptive work on the cross has taken the curse away from those who believe in him. Christians would no doubt agree that in atonement, Christ has purchased not only complete freedom from sin, but also from physical weakness and infirmity through his work of redemption.[108] As constant spiritual warfare is acknowledged as a reality in this world, God's divine healing and intervention must not be neglected. In Scripture, people evidently suffered from illness due to possession of demon or spiritual forces, although neither all demon-possessed people were physically ill, nor all of the sick were demon-possessed.[109] Divine healing is a sign to authenticate the gospel message, which shows the reality that the kingdom of God has come and it demonstrates God's attribute of mercy toward those in distress. It is explicitly true that God can heal whatever doctors and medicine cannot heal.[110]

Regretfully, the modern Christian mission movement, taking alongside medical mission, has a tendency of a paternalistic or imperialistic attitude toward local cultures.[111] The underlying beliefs in the folk practices of Islam must be evaluated and understood well without premature judgement or prejudices against the local culture in order to transform animistic worldviews with the biblical worldview and Christ-like humble attitude. Christian cross-cultural mission efforts often have a fallacy of trying to eradicate these folk practices among Muslims through introducing the gospel without properly understanding the underlying beliefs which are not easily identified by outsiders. These folk practices are frequently viewed as unsophisticated activities that can simply be stopped by the introduction of science or modern culture with the Christian belief. However, this transformational change through both power encounter and truth encounter should be thought as a lifelong process, and Christian cross-cultural workers cannot simply ignore or condemn these beliefs, which may encourage people to continue their old ways covertly even after the confession of the Christian faith. Another serious problem is that a number of Christian

---

108. Grudem, *Systematic Theology*, 1063–65.
109. Van Rheenen, *Communicating Christ in Animistic Context*, 116.
110. Grudem, *Systematic Theology*, 1063–65.
111. Mathews, "History of Mission Methods."

cross-cultural workers possess a dualism that divides the world into the supernatural and the natural realities. Hiebert develops a model of the "excluded middle." He highlights that Westerners tend to acknowledge only two worlds, the seen and the trans-empirical world, separating the spiritual and physical realms with no possible interaction between the two. This is a flawed worldview that inherently clashes with eastern or more animistic perspectives.[112] Due to their own educational and cultural background, they intentionally or unintentionally tend to relegate spiritual matters to religion and natural ones to science. Neither modern science, including medicine, should be neglected nor the spiritual realm should be rejected in the places over which folk Islam dominates. The biblical worldview, with proper contextualization, challenges the magical worldview that dominates folk religions and offers *shalom* in the fullest sense of God's righteous and graceful reign.

Contextualization of biblical truth into the situations where Christian missionaries serve is a complex procedure which needs insightful approaches to share the truth of the gospel with Muslims who have a strong background of folk Islam. David J. Hesselgrave emphasizes the importance of the Great Commission contextualization which makes cross-cultural mission efforts more effective in meeting the requirements of Scripture itself as well as in principles of communication, anthropology, psychology, and other social science disciplines.[113] More practically, Hiebert, Shaw, and Tienou indicate the importance of delicate care concerning syncretistic practices related to folk Islam that Christian cross-cultural workers face:

> The danger in responding to folk religions is not so much heresy as it is syncretism—combining elements of Christianity with folk beliefs and practices in such a way that the gospel loses its integrity and message. The problem here is not with old religious beliefs, but with the underlying assumptions on which they are built. The gospel must not only change beliefs, but also transform worldviews,

---

112. Hiebert, "The Flaw of the Excluded Middle," 35–47. Hiebert explains clearly the "Western Two-Tiered View of Reality": (1) "Religion" relating to "faith, miracles, otherworldly problems, and sacred," and (2) "Science" to "sight and experience, natural order, this-worldly problems, and secular." There are questions to the problems of the middle level between these two realities such as "the uncertainty of the future, the crises of present life, and the unknowns of the past."

113. Hesselgrave, "Great Commission Contextualization," 139–44.

otherwise the new beliefs will be reinterpreted in terms of the old worldviews. The result is Christo-paganism.[114]

Martin H. Manser defines syncretism as: "the incorporation into religious faith and practice of elements from other religions, resulting in a loss of integrity and assimilation to the surrounding culture."[115] The danger of being syncretistic is never avoidable because, to some degree, all rituals and practices in Christianity can be syncretistic with ideologies and socio-cultural systems into which it is introduced. God strongly forbade any relationship with the inhabitants in Canaan when he established the Covenant with the Israelites because of the risk that the Israelites could fall into syncretism with pagan religions in Canaan (Exod 34:15–16). One of the examples of syncretistic belief in the Old Testament history is related to the cult of Asherah, and was also precisely exposed on the inscriptions discovered at Khirbet el-Qom which mentions "*Yahweh* and his Asherah."[116] Asherah is known as "the fertility goddess, the mother of Ba'al, whose worship was concentrated in Syria and Canaan and the wooden object that represented her."[117] God resolutely commanded the Israelites to "tear down their altars, and smash their sacred pillars, and hew down their *Asherim*, and burn their graven images with fire" (Deut 7:5, 12:3). God condemned any mixture of the worship to him with the Canaanite religions because syncretism is never compatible with the biblical belief. A good example that the syncretistic belief came into view with God's miraculous power over disease is written in Acts 14:8–18. When Barnabas and Paul healed a lame man in Lystra, people believed them to be gods and the priest of Zeus. People who observed God's powerful intervention offered sacrifices to Barnabas and Paul in their own ways of worship. Whenever the power of the gospel is displayed, there may be a danger of syncretistic belief among people who already have their own ontological belief system. In this particular circumstance, the Apostle Paul approached people in a different way, as Dean Flemming comments:

> In this world of popular pagan piety, the Jewish-oriented arguments used in Antioch would have been both ineffective and incomprehensible. Paul must tailor both the emphasis and the expression of his evangelistic preaching to fit a crowd or rustic

114. Hiebert, Shaw, and Tienou, "Responding to Split-Level Christianity," 17.
115. Manser, "Syncretism."
116. Lemaire, "Who or What Was Yahweh's Ashera?"
117. Newell, "Asherah, Asherim or Ashera."

Gentile polytheists. Stating at the point of their immediate confusion, he directs them the true source of miraculous power. He engages their presuppositions and belief system at the level of foundational *theo*-logy.[118]

The Apostle Paul's contextualized approach to the Lystran stimulates Christian cross-cultural workers to think more strategically about how they should approach Muslims affected by folk practices in their contexts.

Aware of the challenge of defining syncretism in Christian cross-cultural mission, the Congress on the Church's Worldwide Mission adopted the Wheaton Declaration in 1966 which "reiterated the urgency of evangelism throughout the world and condemned both universalism (the doctrine of universal salvation) and syncretism (acceptance of different deities and religious traditions)."[119] Although God's sovereignty over all creation, captured throughout Scripture, should be demonstrated in all Christian missions, practically speaking, the difficulty of properly differentiating between syncretistic and biblically contextualized belief in their cross-cultural contexts can never be facile. Hesselgrave describes the primary principle of contextualization: "Contextualization must balance faithfulness to the biblical text with meaningfulness to the audience."[120] As a matter of fact, Christian cross-cultural mission has been facing enormous challenges of dealing with the issues of syncretism, as Lesslie Newbigin agonizes: "In the attempt to be 'relevant' one may fall into syncretism, and in the effort to avoid syncretism one may become irrelevant."[121] Flemming contributes with his insightful statement about Paul's contextualized message to the Corinthians through 2 Corinthians:

> The life situation in Corinth thus draws out particular theological images and ideas that are a part of Paul's understanding of the gospel, enabling this letter to become a well-aimed message for his audience. At the same time, because Paul's theological reflection has its mooring in the story of Christ crucified, he is able to reframe the gospel in fresh terms without syncretizing or distorting the message.[122]

---

118. Flemming, *Contextualization in the New Testament*, 71.
119. "Wheaton Declaration," 613.
120. Hesselgrave, "Contextualization that is Authentic and Relevant," 115.
121. Newbigin, *Foolishness to the Greeks*, 102.
122. Flemming, *Contextualization in the New Testament*, 113.

Shalom: God's Ultimate Purpose for the World

Careful study about the Apostle Paul's approach certainly assists Christian mission to contextualize the gospel message that becomes more relevant to people in different contexts without serious syncretism.

In the West, for example, Christians commonly believe with cultural superiority that syncretism is the issue in underdeveloped countries. John Stott condemns it by stating "western-style syncretism" which is "the most insidious form of syncretism in the world today because it is the attempt to mix a privatized gospel of personal forgiveness with a worldly (and even demonic) attitude of wealth and power."[123] Newbigin also indicates that the American church is infirm in biblical contextualization, which results in syncretistic worldviews influenced by the fallen secular world.[124] Summarizing Newbigin's contribution, Michael W. Goheen gives three primary elements of biblical contextualization:

1. faithfulness to the primacy of the gospel,

2. avoidance of syncretism and irrelevance, and

3. avoidance of ethnocentrism and relativism.[125]

Ethnocentrism is one of the most perilous hindrances to biblical contextualization, and Hiebert paints cross-cultural missionaries who do not pursue insightful approaches of contextualization as responsible for making the gospel to be "foreign" and "Western."[126] "Critical contextualization," according to his argument, should be developed with the humble attitude of appreciating diverse cultures and understanding their ontological fundamentals in order to contextualize the gospel in biblical ways.[127] Cultural relativism is another possible pitfall of uninhibited contextualization. Modern anthropology acknowledges that all cultures should be treated as equally worthy because no one can possibly judge right or wrong for other cultures. From this perspective, there is no absolute truth in different cultures and therefore the truth of the gospel can also be viewed as relative to the beliefs of individuals and societies when it is newly introduced.[128]

---

123. Stott, ed., *Making Christ Known*, 102.

124. Newbigin, *Foolishness to the Greeks*, 102.

125. Goheen, "Gospel, Culture, and Cultures."

126. Hiebert, *Anthropological Reflections on Missiological Issues*, 81–84.

127. Hiebert, *Anthropological Reflections on Missiological Issues*, 81–84.

128. Relativism is defined: "the denial of any absolute or objective standards, especially in ethic," and "analogously, in epistemology relativism holds that what is true is dependent on the individual or the culture" (Evans, "Relativism").

For various Islamic contexts, there have been remarkable studies helping Christian missionaries share the gospel in more proper ways, but debates about the level of contextualization became more heated. Rick Brown clarifies a danger of syncretism from "insufficient contextualization" that new churches may mix elements of different cultures and worldviews. Brown rightly notes the seriousness of syncretistic worldviews which is a part of darkness as the opposite of the Light.[129] Although his argument for contextualization applied to Muslim communities is persuasive in certain contexts, there is a debate that C5 contextualization called "the Messianic Muslims" has a high risk of syncretism in its practices.[130] "Critical contextualization" is an essential tool for both Christian cross-cultural missionaries and national church leaders to use anthropological principles on the basis of the biblical truth in service to the gospel cross-culturally. Unlike Islam which is inseparably bound to its culture, the gospel should be brought to different cultures without losing its authenticity. Hesselgrave states the effectiveness of contextualization in the conclusion of his article:

> Effectiveness is primarily a matter of contextualizing or shaping the gospel message to make it meaningful and compelling to the respondents in their cultural and existential situation.[131]

---

129. Brown, "Contextualization without Syncretism," 127–33.

130. Travis, "C1–C6 Spectrum." A brief summary of each Christ-centered community described in the spectrum follows: C1: Missionaries establish a church that is basically identical to wherever they are from. C2: The same as C1, except the services are conducted in the language of the region. C3: They have incorporated many non-religious cultural forms of the region into their community, such as dress, art, etc. They still reject any purely Islamic religious elements. C4: They are similar to C3, but they incorporate some Islamic religious elements into their community—like avoiding pork, praying in a more Islamic style, using Islamic dress and employing Islamic terminology. They call themselves "Followers of Isa" or something similar. C5: They retain their legal and social identity within their Muslim community. They reject or reinterpret any part of Islamic practices and doctrine that contradict the Bible. They may or may not attend the mosque regularly, and they actively are involved in sharing their faith in Jesus with other Muslims. They may call themselves Muslims who follow Isa al-Masih, or just Muslims. They may be viewed by their community as Muslims that are a little unorthodox. C6: They keep their faith secret because of an extreme threat of persecution, suffering or legal retaliation. They may worship secretly in small groups. They do not normally share their faith openly and have a 100% Muslim identity.

131. Hesselgrave, "Contextualization that is Authentic and Relevant," 119.

Shalom: God's Ultimate Purpose for the World

Power Encounter and Truth Encounter

Unusual events that do not follow the natural laws are undeniably observable, so many people seek for these extraordinary miracles in their crisis. Furthermore, failure to answer questions related to sickness does not only capitulate to the belief and the worldview of folk Islam, but is unable to respond adequately to people who still desperately ask those questions. David L. Weddle defines a miracle as "an event of transcendent power that arouses wonder and carries religious significance for those who witness it or hear or read about it."[132] From the medical perspective, Claxton confines a miracle to "a rare and wholly inexplicable event, the total, immediate, irreversible cure of an otherwise incurable condition."[133] In the biblical view, miracles are extraordinary acts of God by which God reveals his power and his will for his people. Accordingly, Norman L. Geisler defines a miracle as "a special act of God that interrupts the natural course of events."[134] William O. Carver clearly explains this power in its fullness in the New Testament. The nature of the power is not considered as "a special privilege and extraordinary authority," but "a responsibility entrusted by Jesus Christ as the method of extending his work."[135] He continually defines the scope of the power as "spiritual," and "to be exercised always primarily in the saving of men."[136] God certainly uses his divine power in various ways that validate his message. Believers will sense of awe before God and unbelievers open their hearts toward his message when he manifests himself through miracles according to his own will and reasoning. Miracles are one of the most powerful ways that God reveals his own glory for his own purpose. However, as miracles can possibly be from the enemy, they are not always easily distinguishable from humanity's limited perspectives. Many tend to be deceived by the extraordinary events caused by the evil spirits, and leave their faith in the end.

Millard J. Erickson summarizes that the purpose of miracles is:

---

132. Weddle, *Miracles*. The *Stanford Encyclopedia of Philosophy* defines a miracle as "an event that exceeds the productive power of nature, and a religiously significant miracle is a detectable miracle that has a supernatural cause" (*Stanford Encyclopedia of Philosophy*, "Miracles").

133. Claxton, *A Christian Doctor Speaks on Healing*, 23.

134. Geisler, "Miracle," 449–51.

135. Carver, "Keys, Power of."

136. Carver, "Keys, Power of."

1. "to glorify God,"
2. "to establish the supernatural basis of the revelation especially in biblical times," and
3. "to meet human needs."[137]

His comment on "Providence and Prayer" explains more clearly about prayer for healing:

> It appears from Scripture that in many cases God works in a sort of partnership with humans. God does not act if they do not play their part . . . That is, God wills the healing in part by willing that those in need should bring their entreaties. Thus, prayer does not change what he has purposed to do. It is the means by which he accomplished his end.[138]

In addition, he emphasizes the importance of the relationship between miracles and nature laws, in three conceptions:

1. "miracles are actually the manifestations of little-known or virtually unknown natural laws,"
2. "miracles break the laws of nature," and
3. "when miracles occur, natural forces are countered by supernatural force."[139]

Craig S. Keener provides miracle accounts throughout human history including the Judeo-Christian tradition and various arguments regarding miraculous occurrences in his book, *Miracles: The Credibility of the New Testament Accounts*.[140] With a variety of angles, he gives evidences of supernatural phenomena from ancient to modern history. As a part of his supportive argument for miracles in modern Christianity, he observes a strong emphasis on healing miracles within Pentecostalism, and although there might be exaggeration of occasions with wrong motivation, God certainly has been involved in the healing events for his purpose.[141] His conclusion is greatly helpful:

---

137. Erickson, *Introducing Christian Doctrine*, 144–46.
138. Erickson, *Introducing Christian Doctrine*, 144.
139. Erickson, *Introducing Christian Doctrine*, 145–46.
140. Keener, *Miracles*.
141. Keener, *Miracles*.

Shalom: God's Ultimate Purpose for the World

Not only the Majority World today but also the history of Christianity, including in the West, is replete with supernaturalist claims. The modern Western prejudice against acknowledging or exploring miracle claims rests not on a total lack of evidence for such claims, even in Western history, but on an a priori insistence that they be screened from consideration. Yet such claims belong not only to earlier history or to non-Western cultures; countless examples can be offered today, including in the West.[142]

When God responds to the needs of his people, it is never merely to offer metaphysical falsehood, but to grant actual healing. Jesus healed people who came to him to relieve the suffering caused by such maladies, but never performed miracles for the selfish purpose of putting on a display. Teague advocates miracles as "the third sign-indicator" of "integral mission" that reveals "the true identity of Christ as the Kingdom-in Person," *autobasileia*.[143] It is certain that when Christian mission is truly overwhelmed by the Spirit of God and brings *autobasileia* into the relationship with the lost, miracle is one of the signs that God grants *shalom* through the ministry.

As the view of healing in Islamic belief is closely examined, Muslims see miracles in a very similar way from the biblical view, which sometimes makes it more difficult for Christian cross-cultural workers to convince Muslims with the gospel and the power of God regarding to divine healing. When Christians pray for healing in the name of Jesus, Muslims also pray to Allah for healing. Muslims do not accept that Jesus answers a prayer for healing; instead, their prayer combined with any mystical practices shown in the Qur'an or directed from their tradition is believed to work as a miraculous intervention of Allah. However, God's power certainly overwhelms and makes Muslims think deeply about their unique experience of power encounter, which leads them to seek for the truth. In addition to the fact that power encounter can be relevant in every culture, it appeals to Muslims for behavior changes from their traditional folk practices and emotional fear to the trust in Almighty God who is more powerful than any spirits as a result of the transformed worldview and belief. This personal transformation creates a rippling effect in the families and communities who may experience both power encounter and truth encounter.

---

142. Keener, *Miracles*.

143. Teague, "Integral Mission," 23. *Autobasileia,* coined by Origen of Alexandria, focuses on the reconciled relationship with God through the person of Christ, and it literally means "the Kingdom-in-Person."

Healing in Islam and the Biblical Approach

Although there are arguments that divine healing was limited to the time of Jesus and the apostles, and healing miracles are not a "Christ-commanded assignment for the on-going church,"[144] it is more reasonable to include divine miracles as an important part of Christ's commission to the disciples of making disciples, baptizing them, and teaching them (Matt 28:19–20).[145] The woman with the problem of bleeding (Luke 8:43–48) reveals her superstitious way of seeking for stronger power over her sickness from Jesus. Her hemorrhage made her ritually unclean and anyone who touched her would become unclean, too. Jesus wanted the woman to reveal herself after she was cured completely and openly express the faith which courageously had led her to touch Jesus. The woman's faith in the Messiah came to be accepted and publicly known. Musk interprets this event:

> As Lord, Jesus had seen deeply into her needy life, the life of someone "unclean" in a spiritual as well as a physical sense. He freely granted her wholesome peace. "Daughter" included her in a new family; the persons communicating on a father/daughter, divine/human basis. The woman's closed cosmology is broken open, and now she can truly go in peace, in wholeness.[146]

Gaiser observes a parallel between Jesus' healing (vv. 1–6a) and apostolic healing (vv. 6b–13) in Mark 6:1–13.[147] He explains that "disciples' healing is an extension of Jesus' ministry," and accompanied by Jesus' teaching. Jesus sent his disciples to preach the gospel and conduct a healing ministry, including casting out many demons and anointing with oil many sick people (Mark 6:12–13), so all Christians are sent by him in the same way.[148] God's divine healing is always followed by the invitation to the truth that leads people into his kingdom with the courses of conduct which should be appropriate to his kingdom.

Dean S. Gilliland shares his observation of a prayer service for a Muslim woman who suffered from various diseases, and emphasizes the importance of building up a relationship with people who really need assurance of God's power.[149] Most importantly, because Christian cross-cultural workers who have modern and postmodern educational and cultural backgrounds

---

144. Geisler, "Miracle," 222.
145. United Lutheran Church in America, *Anointing and Healing*, 21.
146. Musk, *Unseen Face of Islam*, 100.
147. Geisler, "Miracle," 224.
148. Geisler, "Miracle," 224.
149. Gilliland, "Ch. 28: The Incarnation as Matrix for Appropriate Theologies," 502–3.

tend to neglect the presence of the spiritual realms and to emphasize only the paradigm of science and knowledge, they should acknowledge the reality of spiritual warfare. Through a sincere effort of connecting with people's felt needs, Christian cross-cultural workers can understand the full scope of the incarnation of Jesus Christ more clearly. He points out their weakness in pursuing God's power over people's physical need:

> Usually the church-trained missionary would have objected to praying publicly about barrenness and would not like the African style of calling on God to meet the woman's need. To truly live with people, as Jesus did, that is, to truly, "pitch one's tent," as it were, in the midst of those we want to love and win to Christ, calls us to meet deep needs in appropriate ways. This is the secret of the Incarnate Word, this Christ, who first emptied himself and then lived as one with us.[150]

His challenge should carefully be applied to Christian medical mission that might sometimes simply regard the spiritual aspect of medical care and the traditional remedies as scientifically unproven practices.

On the contrary, there is also a tendency of overemphasizing miraculous healing as the main part of spiritual ministry with isolation of the truth. It is imperative to remember that healing by power encounter must be followed by truth encounter. Sometimes this tendency neglects proper medical consideration, which results in serious complications of the diseases. This irresponsible implementation of power for healing can surely turn people's away from the truth. The fact that the enemies try to deceive people with miraculous events to break the relationship with God in any way possible should be acknowledged. It is critical to recognize that healing has a different dimension in terms of witness to Muslims from God's direct revelation such as dreams and vision because it involves medicine and health closely related to life and death. Without proper understanding of biblical teaching about healing, imprudent pursuit of healing in Christian mission may cause poignant ethical issues. Additionally, in the strong spiritual communities which commonly practice occult, divination, magic, charms, amulets, and so forth, there is a danger of syncretizing the healing ministry and biblical messages with those in the indigenous contexts. Cross-cultural Christian missionaries must move beyond immediate visible ministries to the long-term task of transforming people's worldviews and beliefs. There remains a danger that the gospel can be confused with

---

150. Gilliland, "Ch. 28: The Incarnation as Matrix for Appropriate Theologies," 502–3.

animistic worldviews when Christian mission simply implements its ministry within the traditional cultural systems. New believers who accept the gospel in folk religious cultures often consider Christian practices as ways of receiving stronger powers for their own benefits. For example, many Muslim background believers who previously lived with folk practices may see Bible verses as amulets and prayers as magic formulas. In this situation, Christianity is perceived as powerful witchcraft and spiritism, but the fear of witchcraft and spirits remains. People's ideas about well-being, misfortune, and evil must be transformed by biblical teaching as much as their understanding of the nature of God.

As a matter of fact, huge felt needs regarding sickness in many Muslims' lives expose the disequilibrium that breaks down inner peace. This is one of the most common reasons why many Muslims get into the occult world, and Christian mission should approach these Muslims with a heart sympathizing their broken relationship with the Sovereign God.[151] As Love says, "miracle is based on relationship, whereas magic is based on ritual,"[152] and cross-cultural missionaries need to consider how they may bring Muslims who experience God's divine intervention of healing into truth encounter, which is an important step toward longing for a true relationship with the living God.[153] In Ephesus during Paul's third missionary journey, God used him to heal people in an extraordinary way. When handkerchiefs or cloths that had touched Paul's skin were placed on sick people, evil spirits were exorcised and illnesses were cured (Acts 19:11–12). Love summarizes that Paul's ministry of signs and wonders was done in the context of a teaching ministry that centered around the kingdom of God, which highlights the distinction between the divine miracle and the magic.[154] Paul demanded true repentance and faith in the truth to experience the true blessing of miracle provided by the Spirit of God. Christian medical mission should pursue both the divine healing promised by the loving God and the presentation of the truth revealed through the person of Christ Jesus in biblical ways with a deeper understanding of people's felt needs in each context.

As far as this matter is concerned, Islam is not regarded as a formal religion, but as a heresy of Christianity that denies and distorts the core belief

---

151. Love, "Church Planting," 91.
152. Love, "Church Planting," 135.
153. Musk, *Unseen Face of Islam*, 224.
154. Love, "Church Planting," 131.

of Christianity. Islam tries to blind people's eyes to the truth by political and sociological oppression. Muslims are spiritually lost and need to place their faith in Jesus Christ, the Son of God and Savior, for their true salvation. The message of the sovereign God who desires his people's trust and allegiance is demonstrated by his power in defeating the spirits and powers of Islam. Sometimes Muslims perceive Jesus as merely a stronger prophet than any other spiritual beings, when Jesus Christ is presented as the powerful Lord over human sickness, even death. Musk concludes:

> Without a full presentation of the truth of who Jesus Christ is, in moments of power encounter, Muslims will probably see Jesus as being like other saints or healers. That Jesus of Nazareth accepted such a view as a *starting-point* in a relationship with himself is demonstrated in the gospel. His intention, however, was consistently to draw the devotee into an encounter with himself as Son of man, as Lord; out of a view of life that allowed no direct relationship with the Creator.[155]

The belief that God hears his people's prayers enables those who previously lived with folk practices to trust in God when confronted with the evils of the immediate life, rather than seeking to manipulate the spiritual powers to do his bidding. The gospel message must be the center on the cosmic conflict between God and gods, as Christ's kingdom confronts the kingdom of Satan, emphasizing the victory that he has won on the cross.

Chapter Summary

Mystical beliefs and practices for healing are very common in every culture and tribe. Not only prolific Muslim Sufi orders, but also charismatic Christians seek supernatural intervention for healing. Understanding the nature of a Muslim's mind and practices for healing helps Christian cross-cultural missionaries present the properly-contextualized biblical message to Muslims. It is believed from Scripture that God always invites humans as co-workers in a kind of partnership for his kingdom's sake. The centurion bringing his request for the healing of a servant (Matt 8:5–13), and the woman with the hemorrhage (Matt 9:18–22) are good examples of faith which resulted in God's working for their requests. God wills healing when believers in need bring their entreaties to him. Thus, prayers are the means

---

155. Musk, *Unseen Face of Islam*, 99–100.

by which he accomplishes his purpose of granting healing to those who believe, rather than changing what he has ordained to happen. The healing power of the Almighty God can only be fully released when Christians and churches truly become the caring, sharing communities as a result of the gospel that is lived out in the world, especially for the lost.

God's ministry of divine healing among Muslims provides a new opportunity for people to join him in the mission that he has already been doing. Christian cross-cultural workers can then enter the thought-world of Muslims with confidence in order to explain the mystery of Christ. Parshall's challenge should be well kept in the hearts of Christian cross-cultural missionaries:

> There is much in Christianity that will appeal to the earnest, God-seeking Muslim mystic. The Christian obligation is to present truth in the most attractive manner possible. This should lead evangelicals to a new consideration of the potentials of a power-encounter ministry that will show Muslims that our God is indeed alive.[156]

God is faithful to bring Muslims into his kingdom through faithful and humble witness of his people. Healing is absolutely God's divine work, and even if healing is never taken for granted because sin and finitude overwhelm the nature of human beings, it always corresponds to God's gracious will. The Lord, *Yahweh*, precisely proclaims his self-definition in Exodus 15:26:

> If you will give earnest heed to the voice of the LORD your God, and do what is right in his sight, and give ear to his commandments, and keep all his statutes, I will put none of the diseases on you which I have put on the Egyptians; for I, the LORD, am your healer (NASB).

Scripture pictures two kingdoms standing in opposition to one another, and the kingdom of God has come with power to defeat the dominion of the enemy. Christian mission has to be aware of the nature of the sovereignty of God in a world where the powers of Satan continue to exist. Christian witnesses should be actively confronting the powers of Satan by showing the promise that God has broken into the world to defeat the powers of Satan through the persons of Jesus Christ and the Holy Spirit.

---

156. Parshall, *Cross and the Crescent*, 236.

3

Christian Medical Mission

FOR MUCH OF CHRISTIAN mission history, Christian medical missionaries have been serving in the context of ongoing war and violence. They have brought the love of God and his peace to people in need. Although there are various advantages of medical mission compared to other types of Christian mission in sharing the love and the truth of God with unreached peoples, recently there have been arguments about the effectiveness and efficiency of medical mission due to the many obstacles and challenges it faces. Some critics observe that the strategies of Christian medical mission still remain underdeveloped in their implementation, and many mission hospitals and clinics have been struggling to survive despite strenuous efforts.[1] For a prudent long-term spiritual influence, Christian medical missions need wisdom and effective strategies. Every Christian medical mission group must humbly learn how to develop its effectiveness, and to evaluate its results and consequences regularly to grow in being a better instrument for God's mission. This book will be a potent tool in providing Christian mission, especially in the Arab world, with specific strengths of the biblical paradigm of Christian medical mission in its pursuit in excellence and professionalism.

Christian medical mission shares the message of Christ Jesus who brings *shalom* to suffering people in a broken world. The basic premise of Christian medical mission is that the fundamental driving force of Christian mission is God who sends his people out to bring the lost into his kingdom. Christopher Wright defines mission:

1. Booth, "Sustainability of Christian Mission Hospitals."

Christian Medical Mission

> Fundamentally, our mission (if it is biblically informed and validated) means our committed participation as God's people, at God's invitation and command, in God's own mission within the history of God's world for the redemption of God's creation.[2]

Ireland summarizes the definitions of "mission" and "missions" referenced by Ott and Strauss, saying, "mission" means "all of God's sending activity in the world," and "missions" refers to "cross-cultural efforts to plant the church and thereby take part in the expansion of God's kingdom."[3] For simplicity in this book, usage of the terms "mission" and "missions" follows the definitions adopted by A. Scott Moreau et al.: "missions has been relegated to the specific work of the church and agencies in the task of reaching people for Christ by crossing cultural boundaries," while "mission is broader, referring to everything the church is doing that points toward the kingdom of God."[4]

The Arab world has experienced turmoil, disagreement, confusion, and violence for millennia, making this geographic area a bubbling cauldron of unrest. It seems to be filled with contention and terrorism, and any attempt for peace seems impossible. Drastic events have continued in this area of the world. Beginning with Tunisia and Egypt in 2010, nation after nation in the region went through protests, demonstrations, and riots against dictatorial regimes. Although some countries seem to be settled, many countries in the region are still engaged in a self-destructive process of sectarian polarization and violence. The wars and unrest have devastated people's lives and the region's heritage. In addition to political unrest, the Arab world has been maintaining a greater resistance to the gospel than most other religions, and has the most unreached people groups according to demographic information about religions in the Arab world.[5] For a long time, Christian faith among Arabs has been restricted to traditional church communities such as the Coptic churches in Egypt, the Maronites in Lebanon, and some other Catholic and Orthodox churches. Christian medical mission groups must be committed to the best practices because, whatever it does, it reflects who God is and what the gospel of Jesus says for the peoples in need. Just as the resources that God has given are useful and precious, but limited, Christian medical missionaries also have to acknowledge their calling to be

---

2. Wright, *Mission of God*, 22–23.
3. Ireland, *For the Love of God*.
4. Moreau, Corwin, and McGee, *Introducing World Missions*, 17.
5. Joshua Project, "Affinity Bloc: Arab World."

good stewards in order to respect people's dignity and to sustain itself with the resources it has in the contexts that it serves.

Many countries in the Arab world are considered to be restricted countries to the gospel because they neither allow any Christian missions to come in and do evangelism, nor to proselytize Muslims. Some mission agencies prefer a term of "creative access nations" (CANs).[6] However, Christian medical missions are still regarded as one of the choice platforms for entry into these restricted countries because professional medical skills are welcomed and able to earn credibility in places closed to traditional missionaries. The CANs carefully monitor, restrict, or even keep out any Christian who tries to do traditional mission work. Jeff Palmer and Lynda Hausfeld define a "platform" as "anything that is done to give a person/team something to stand on in order for them to gain access to their target population."[7] They find this term inappropriate when it is used for describing a way of only gaining access to the CANs, arguing that it may be disingenuous or simply relegate compassion as a means to an end.[8] There are Christian cross-cultural workers in the CANs who simply try to get their residency and work permit by using business or profession as a front, yet do not intend to create a legitimate business nor work professionally. Rather, they want to use most of their time to establish relationships for sharing the gospel and focus on spiritual ministry. This approach certainly does not portray a good testimony of what it really means to follow Jesus Christ in everyday life and work to those to whom they minister. Furthermore, this distorts the whole message of the gospel, which possibly establishes unhealthy theology within emerging local churches. Christian medical missions must understand the problematic issues of the "platform" approach and faithfully serve local individuals and communities through professional medical skills that enable them to enter local communities and develop deeper relationships with the belief that authenticity and legitimacy are vital to interpersonal relationships. Understanding the problematic usage of "platforms," this book continues to use this term for describing various ways or forms of approaching the CANs. Christian medical mission groups should diversify their approaches to the CANs in order to overcome current challenges and share the gospel through biblical principles and strategies in various contexts. The platforms of Christian medical mission should

6. "Creative Access Nations," *IBMGlobal.org*.
7. Palmer and Hausfeld, "Compassion and Unreached People Groups."
8. Palmer and Hausfeld, "Compassion and Unreached People Groups."

reflect the holistic nature of God's kingdom, and never be a mere means to an end. The healthy platforms of Christian medical mission groups will provide many opportunities that unreached people can experience the values of God's kingdom and the message of *shalom* through the encounter of Jesus Christ.

Christian Medical Mission History and Current Challenges

Christians have engaged with healthcare for the sick since the days of the early church. Although miraculous healing was one of the main ministries of Jesus and the early church as an important manifestation of God's kingdom inaugurated through Christ Jesus, there is little medical work mentioned in Acts and other parts of the New Testament. Nevertheless, fathers and missionaries of the early church actively took part in both medical and healing ministries. Summarizing these ministries of the early church, Robert H. Munson states: "It appears that a wide range of activities to prevent or cure illness or reduce suffering can be seen as ministerially valid."[9] From Medieval Roman Catholicism to the Protestant Reformation, compassionate medical care for underprivileged people was a fundamental part of church ministries, as Palmer and Lynda describe: "Pioneer evangelical mission work often went hand in hand with medical and healthcare ministries as well as others addressing the needs of target populations."[10] Contrary to the positive reflection of medical and healthcare as a part of Christian mission, care for the physical body was sometimes discouraged by unbiblical theology and syncretistic folk practices influenced by heresies of Christianity and other religions.[11] However, it is obvious that Christian medical missions have played a central role for Christin mission throughout its history. In many resource-poor areas and countries today, Christian mission clinics and hospitals are still the only local infrastructure to get any reliable medical care. Nevertheless, alongside of the fact that modern science and medicine have seen remarkable development since the nineteenth century, it is inevitable that Christian medical mission also has shifted its priorities to different emphases.

John Wilkinson asserts three reasons that theology of medical mission and the church's mission are identical:

9. Munson, "Changing Priorities and Practices."
10. Palmer and Hausfeld, "Compassion and Unreached People Groups."
11. "The Theology of Medical Mission," *Rendle Short Lecture*.

1. "the phases of the medical mission development are identical with the church development,"
2. "as inter-church aid[12] is an expression of the mission of the church found in the medical mission, there is no need to find a separate theology for the medical mission," and
3. "the modern rediscovery of the ministry of healing of the church supports the idea that the theology of church mission clearly explains the theology of the medical mission."[13]

Although his assertion that medical mission does not require a separate and specific theology makes sense, as it is aligned with the theology of the Church's mission, there are many theological issues to deeply consider related to medical mission itself.[14] He also observes the four stages of the modern Christian medical mission, which follows a particular pattern.[15] To begin, in "the Pioneer Stage," most of medical missions focuses on curative medical care at a very simple facility, mostly run by individual medical missionaries. During "the Mission Stage," medical services become more diversified, with preventive healthcare at the mission hospitals or clinics established with resources from outside mission organizations or churches. The local indigenous church comes to exist through the medical mission and takes responsibility for offering medical care to its own local people independent of foreign resources and control at "the Church Stage." Finally, in "the State Stage," the national government takes responsibility of providing the healthcare system to its citizens, initiated by local churches. Although the secular health system under the national government may possibly have fundamental Christian values and provide proper healthcare to all citizens with Christian principles of love and justice, this still does not fulfil the end goal of reconciliation with God through medical practices.

Gaining a deeper understanding of these stages enables Christian medical mission to evaluate the issues related to initiatives, controls, and resources. All these patterns of the medical missions are neither always

---

12. Inter-church aid: Wilkinson mentions inter-church aid as the relationship found in Acts 24:17, Romans 15:25–28, 1 Corinthians 16:1–2, 2 Corinthians 8:1 to 9:15, of the collection which Paul made from the Churches of Asia Minor and Greece for the relief of the Church in Jerusalem (Wilkinson, "Making Men Whole," 12).
13. Wilkinson, "Making Men Whole," 11–12.
14. Wilkinson, "Making Men Whole," 12.
15. Wilkinson, "Making Men Whole," 11.

observable in the mission fields, nor appear sequentially. In some contexts, as Wilkinson observes in Nepal, the medical mission develops stage by stage, and at the final stage, national health services may take over Christian medical missions. This is desirable in terms of sustainability, but there is a high risk that the ministry platform becomes completely secular and no longer gives any Christian influence to the communities that it has served for a long time. In addition, he considers the medical mission as part of the healing ministry of the church and as the counterpart of evangelism, which is a simple dichotomy between preaching the gospel and serving one's neighbors.[16] Wilkinson's four phases have a similarity to the Rendle Short Lecture that presents four different phases in the modern Christian medical mission history: "the era of preachers and pioneers," "the curative era" by "the hospital builders," "the community era" focusing on "the primary healthcare bandwagon," and "the training era."[17] These phases can be observed in many countries since the nineteenth century, and in some places these four phases still exist symbiotically. This four-phase schema summarizes modern Christian medical mission to help Christian medical mission communities strategize their ministries in their own context with proper evaluation of strengths and weaknesses related to different phases.

Medicine itself has advanced more in the last fifty years than ever before in history, and will do more in coming years. Further, as medicine becomes more and more complicated with the advancement of knowledge and technology, there are enormously complex ethical issues that the Christian faith has to address. Under these circumstances, Christian medical mission groups have been facing tremendous challenges, and these are not only found in medically-developed countries, but also reach to the resource poor areas which receive short-term and long-term medical missions. Focus on the materialistic view of modern medicine prevails in medical practice, and this leads medical professionals to perceive patients as cases who carry abnormalities rather than whole persons. The phenomenon that scientific data and measurement predominate in diagnosis and treatment of patients reinforces inhumanity in medicine. This common tendency takes away the fundamental interpersonal relationship from medical practices, and the medical missionaries who have medical training in this kind of environment become more incongruent in the cultures that value these relationships. Furthermore, because modern medical practices

16. Wilkinson, "Making Men Whole," 14.
17. "The Theology of Medical Mission," *Rendle Short Lecture*.

excessively rely on laboratory data, radiologic tests, and highly-developed instruments and equipment, medical professionals become more incompetent in the resource-poor areas due to the huge gulf between where they were trained and where they serve in mission. Besides, all advanced medical technologies get more expensive and demand a considerable amount of cost to sustain the medical mission clinics and hospitals.

Moreover, as pure scientific evidence rules the field of modern medical education, many indigenous ways of healthcare which have not been examined yet by the western medicine are simply neglected. Medical missionaries trained in the Western medicine education system tend to look down on traditional views of local health and medicine without any proper investigation, which causes indigenous reluctance to have foreign medical professionals in their communities. Min Chul Kim, who is a former medical missionary to Nigeria, challenges medical missionaries who are strongly influenced by modern Western medicine:

> Distorted concepts of healthcare have been transplanted to the underdeveloped countries of Africa. Many Africans have abandoned a traditional, holistic understanding of healthcare that incorporates the well-being of the physical, social and spiritual aspects of human beings. As a result, community-initiated primary healthcare—which is cheaper and more cost effective—has been discouraged. Broadening the concept of health may give more ministry opportunities to the medical missionary.[18]

In addition, as almost all governments and their indigenous medical professionals have been building up barriers against continued foreign medical practice in their countries without proper licensure, long-term and short-term medical missions are strictly controlled by the local government and are no longer welcomed in many countries unless they bring visible benefits to the local medical communities.

Concept of Integral Mission and Holistic Ministry

The false dichotomy between "the sacred" and "the secular" is deeply rooted in Christian belief throughout history,[19] and this dichotomized

---

18. Kim, "Missionary Medicine."

19. The Sacred and the Secular: Buenting indicates that Augustine (354–430 AD) is a foundational theologian who brought a dichotomized idea that life can be divided into the sacred (spiritual) and the secular (physical) as he states, "Jesus' earthly purpose was

thought leads people away from the biblical approach to the mission of God. Debra Buenting summarizes the split of "the sacred" and "the secular" which became sharply divisive in evangelical Christian society in the early twentieth century.[20] According to her observation, those who were engaged more in social transformation through spiritual repentance by the gospel emphasized the active participation in the change of the unjust structure of their societies while the other side focused on the personal relationship with God and soul-saving activities, which mainly resulted from individualistic cultures.[21] The former became involved in relief and development ministry among marginalized people and communities, and the latter pursued evangelism for individual soul-saving.[22] Modern western culture based on scientific evidence operates according to compartmentalization rather than integration. Integrating biblical faith into personal life and professional work is a task of great difficulty, particularly in compartmentalized cultures. Furthermore, there is a dichotomy between truly biblical ways of stewardship for the creation and possible unbiblical ways that lead to the fallen worldliness. Resolving this division is a great challenge because of the limit of human understandings. The dichotomy influences the purpose and everyday practices of Christian mission as well. DeYoung and Gilbert mention the "bait-and-switch argument" regarding compassionate ministry and evangelism.[23] Their emphasis on evangelism to meet people's spiritual needs as "a deep and profound act of love for another person"[24] is understandable, but the argument for evangelism related to compassionate

---

to 'release souls of light from the prison of their bodies." She explains that this dualistic belief system results in a split Christian mind that anything related to the spiritual activities is considered as sacred while others as secular. She gives an example of vocation: "The offices of the pastor or priest, missionary, monk, nun, or deacon were considered spiritual vocations and given much more value and authority than the secular vocations of bricklayer, farmer, teacher, lawyer, storyteller, artist or businessperson" (Buenting, "Evangelicals and Social Action," 16).

20. Buenting, "Evangelicals and Social Action," 15–19.
21. Buenting, "Evangelicals and Social Action," 15–19.
22. Buenting, "Evangelicals and Social Action," 15–19.
23. DeYoung and Gilbert, *What Is the Mission of the Church?* 227–29. "Bait and Switch" can be defined as (1) "a sales tactic in which a customer is attracted by the advertisement of a low-priced item but is then encouraged to buy a higher-priced one" and (2) "the ploy of offering a person something desirable to gain favor (such as political support) then thwarting expectations with something less desirable" (*Merriam-Webster Online Dictionary*, "Bait and Switch").
24. DeYoung and Gilbert, *What Is the Mission of the Church?* 229.

ministry of the church should be developed more deeply from the dichotomized thought of what Christians and the church are supposed to do. God's ultimate plan for humankind is *shalom* as harmony of intimate relationship restored through Christ, which shapes every aspect of life and perceptions of the world. Melanie McNeal lays a strong emphasis on discipleship as one of the most important mission paradigms, which brings the holistic and transformational changes in people and their communities:

> Discipleship as a process of journeying into growing, maturing relationship with Jesus Christ embraces the whole of life; spiritual awakening, social interactions and responsibilities, identity and security, lived daily life in community. Mission therefore would have a concern for the whole of people's lives and seek the welfare of the individual and their community.[25]

Paul Bendor-Samuel, an enthusiastic proponent of "integral mission," also indicates a serious concern of the trend to reductionism in the mission paradigm as a result of "the dichotomization of the spiritual and material." He writes: "This spiritual schizophrenia legitimizes talk of the primary of evangelism and church-planting over other expression of the Lordship of Christ."[26] In recent decades, magnificent scholarly endeavors among the evangelical mission community have brought up the issues related to the dichotomy in Christian mission and observed remarkable advancement in the theology of Christian mission.

Background: Evangelistic Mandate and Social/Cultural Mandate

God the Creator is sovereign over all physical, spiritual, social, and political systems, and all authorities on earth are ultimately responsible to him. The root definition and nature of holistic ministry emanates from the debate between the evangelistic mandate and the social/cultural mandate of the Church. Unfortunately, although the integral mission or holistic mission can be defined with words, it is an extremely complex concept in practice,

---

25. McNeal, "Mission Paradigms," 74.

26. Bendor-Samuel, "Discipleship," 98–99. Reductionism is defined as "the act of oversimplifying an issue, breaking it down into small parts that don't reflect how complex it actually is" according to Vocabulary.com ("Reductionism," *Vocabulary.com*) There have been serious debates that some evangelical Christian groups may accuse others of reductionism that the gospel is too much simplified to the message of individual soul saving without understanding the whole concept of the gospel and the biblical truth.

especially in the cross-cultural context. Nobody can successfully execute missions with these two aspects perfectly integrated because certain context requires or allows stronger emphasis on one aspect than the other—although sometimes these two aspects cannot be clearly divided into two. The perspective of evangelicals has been broadened from an exclusive Christianity to an inclusive Christianity that embraces the world, and recent theological understanding has taken beyond the evangelistic mandate.[27] This recent endeavor of deepening the understanding of the gospel in the socio-cultural complex has awakened the evangelical churches to the necessity of integrating the social mandate in evangelical Christianity. God's people are called to proclaim the excellences of him (1 Pet 2:9), which surely includes the whole loving and righteous attributes of him through word and deed so that people may experience transformation from darkness to his marvelous light. Philip M. Steyne defines both mandates: "The evangelistic mandate speaks of God's concern for man's salvation and the cultural mandate speaks of man's responsibility for creation and for his fellow man."[28]

Perspectives from the creation account should be examined to grasp God's fundamental purpose since the beginning. God directly announced his purpose for the creation of human beings in Genesis 1:26–31. God created human beings in his own image and in his likeness and set them to rule over the created order. Undoubtedly, he conferred the most glorious honor on all human beings. D. James Kennedy explains the identity of human beings as "God's junior partners" for the world that he created, and describes the cultural mandate for his people:

> That mandate is still in force today. As the vice-regents of God, we are to bring his truth and his will to bear on every sphere of our world and our society. We are to exercise godly dominion and influence over our neighborhoods, our schools, our government, our literature and arts, our sports arenas, our entertainment media, our news media, our scientific endeavors—in short, over every aspect and intrusion of human society.[29]

The cultural mandate is based on the purpose of God's creation experiencing the ultimate message of *shalom*. After the Fall, the original mandate in Genesis 3:20 needed to include spiritual reconciliation with God as well as with

27. Reimer and Banda, "Doing Mission Inclusively."
28. Steyne. *In Step with the God of the Nations.*
29. Kennedy, *Led by the Carpenter*, 7.

Shalom: God's Ultimate Purpose for the World

the whole creation. DeYoung and Gilbert explain the essential characteristics of the cultural mandate by studying two Hebrew words, *abad* ("work") and *shamar* ("keep") as the precise job description given to mankind through Adam (Gen 2:15) and the priests of the Israelites (Num 3:8; 18:1–7).[30] The connection between God's original mandates to Adam and the priesthood was not coincidental; the cultural mandate clearly illustrated that Adam, as a representative of humanity, is not only the one who rules over creation as God's vice-regent, but also the priest who intercedes with God for the whole world.[31] Because all mankind is sinful after the Fall, humanity's great honor has been damaged and wrenched concurrently. Jesus Christ's redemptive ministry on the cross is the only way to experience fulfilment of God's *shalom* in all aspects of life. In addition, Jesus' high priestly prayer (John 17), clarifies Christians' roles and attitudes toward the world as God's royal priesthood (1 Pet 2:9); they are called to be in the world to bring *shalom* with the ultimate reconciliation through Christ Jesus to the fallen world. Until the end of the age, God's people still live in a world governed by the enemy, where the consequences of sin remain, yet they are called to be his vice-regents to rule over creation and intercessors for his redemptive reconciliation.

The Old Testament prophets persuaded the people of God to become righteous and to act justly in order to be exempted from his wrath. Israel's priests violently broke God's law and profaned his holy characteristics; her officials shed blood and killed people to make unjust gain; her prophets proclaimed false visions and lying divinations; the people of the land practiced extortion and committed robbery; they oppressed the poor and needy and mistreated the foreigner, denying them justice. When people were separated from the Lord, they were totally evil. As the prophet Amos proclaimed that doing justice and living righteously is more important than religious feasts and assemblies (Amos 5:21–24), God's people must live righteously by his law. God's people who have experienced his redemptive love should live as the vice-regents of God. The Apostle Paul admonished Christians to offer their bodies as living sacrifices, as their spiritual act of worship and not to conform any longer to the pattern of this world, but to be transformed by the renewing of their mind (Rom 12:1–2). The Lord said persistently from the Old Testament to the New Testament that his people should keep the law, not in order to become God's people, but because they

---

30. DeYoung and Gilbert, *What Is the Mission of the Church?* 208–13.
31. DeYoung and Gilbert, *What Is the Mission of the Church?* 208–13.

are God's people. Therefore, the Lord demands total loyalty to himself and his mandate should penetrate every aspect of corporate and individual life.

Although God's social/cultural mandate was given in the beginning, his redemptive mandate became fundamental and indispensable after the Fall. God's constant mercy towards his people was demonstrated to his people and the Gentiles through the Exodus (Exod 3:9–10) and his consideration of the great wicked city of Nineveh (Jonah 4:9–11). The fundamental truth is that God's people should see the world through God's eyes and with his agenda. Kennedy describes Jesus' commandment as the Great mandate:

> The second mandate, the Great Commission, was given at the dawn of the new creation, at the very beginning of the Christian era, soon after the death and resurrection of Jesus Christ. We find the Great Commission in Matthew 28:19–20: Here again, we see one of the reasons for the mess the world is in today—and once again we have to confess that it is our failure as the Church of Jesus Christ to carry out God's second mandate, the Great Commission.[32]

In Acts chapters 10 and 11, the Lord's vast purpose for salvation of all nations is evident. The Lord presented his purpose through Peter's vision and the salvation of Cornelius's household. The Apostle Peter confirmed the church's commission: that God called his people for the purpose of declaring the gospel as his chosen people (1 Pet 2:9). Even if the evangelistic mandate is fundamental, the social/cultural mandate should never be neglected in Christian mission. These two mandates are inseparable, and the tendency to emphasize one or the other leads to a faulty conception of God's mandate. Every Christian ministry must lay emphasis on the integration of both the evangelistic and the social/cultural mandate, because one without the other does not represent the whole message of the gospel.[33] *Shalom* will

---

32. Kennedy, *Led by the Carpenter*, 8.

33. The Lausanne Committee for World Evangelization and the World Evangelical Fellowship sponsors international consultation on the Relationship between Evangelism and Social Responsibility. An Evangelical Commitment (LOP 21) shares three kinds of relationship: (1) social activity is a *consequence* of evangelism, (2) social activity can be a *bridge* to evangelism, and (3) social activity not only follows evangelism as its consequence and aim, and precedes it as its bridge, but also accompanies it as its *partner*. "It has been said, therefore, that evangelism, even when it does not have a primarily social intention, nevertheless has a social dimension, while social responsibility, even when it does not have a primarily evangelistic intention, nevertheless has an evangelistic dimension." [Lausanne Movement, Evangelism and Social Responsibility: An Evangelical Commitment (Lausanne Occasional Paper 21).] The equal integration of the two mandates is essential for Christian mission to demonstrate the whole message of the gospel

ultimately be experienced through the integration of both the evangelistic and the social/cultural mandate in the Christian mission.

Definition of Integral Mission and Holistic Ministry

The ultimate goal of Christian missions is to bring *shalom* to the lost by making Jesus Christ known through demonstrating his love and compassion. Christian missionaries have developed a variety of approaches to overcome the barriers which prevent people from hearing the gospel message, especially in the Islamic countries which resolutely resist the Christian mission. Not only to pull down this stronghold against the gospel or to overcome the barriers, but also to demonstrate the truth through holistic ministry amongst the neediest peoples, Christian mission must develop more effective methodologies in order to contribute to God's mission. DeYoung and Gilbert identify "a difference between a church and a bunch of Christians," by the difference in their role in mission:

> The mission of the church seems to be something narrower than the set of all commands given to individual Christians—it's proclamation, witness, and disciple making (which includes teaching everything that Jesus commanded).[34]

This assertion does not seem consistent with the emphasis on the fact that the message of the gospel should not be reduced. The church is supposed to carry out God's mission by understanding the holistic nature of the gospel proclamation, but historically there was a tendency of slipping away from God's fundamental calling to proclaim the gospel holistically.[35] Christian missionaries make Christ known by living and working together with people in need, and through these relationships, individual lives and communities transformed through encounter with Jesus Christ would be seen.

---

to experience *shalom*.

34. DeYoung and Gilbert, *What Is the Mission of the Church?* 208–13.

35. The church is the fundamental instrument of God's mission from the New Testament times. Winter introduces "the two structures of God's mission" which are the church and the missionary band: the former is the structure of fellowship that consists of believers carrying our God's mission and the latter is all "missionary endeavors organized out of committed, experience workers who affiliated themselves as a second decision beyond membership in the first structure." Winter clarifies the importance of both structures in God's mission and urges collaboration with mutual respects for the fulfillment of the God's mission.(Winter, "The Two Structures," 121–39).

"Integral Mission" and "holistic mission (ministry)" are interchangeably used, although there is a different emphasis from various evangelical circles. The Micah Declaration clarifies its definition:

> Integral mission or holistic transformation is the proclamation and demonstration of the gospel. It is not simply that evangelism and social involvement are to be done alongside each other. Rather in integral mission our proclamation has social consequences as we call people to love and repentance in all areas of life. And our social involvement has evangelistic consequences as we bear witness to the transforming grace of Jesus Christ.[36]

Bendor-Samuel defines holistic ministry as "the ministry from the fullness of God, through the whole person and Christian community bearing witness to the whole gospel for the transformation of individuals, communities and nations."[37] This definition emphasizes transformation that may explain Jesus' use of the term for salvation in the Gospels more clearly. Salvation might have been used for a sense of reduction to "soul-saving," while transformation includes a meaning that the individual "minister," and Christian community must see their lives as a whole.[38] In other words, as traditional mission efforts within some mission groups tends to narrow down salvation to soul-saving, the concept of holistic ministry emphasizes transformation in people's whole lives through teaching the whole gospel that Jesus presented. Furthermore, Parshall clearly indicates in a similar need for missionaries in the Islamic context:

> Missionaries have traditionally dealt with Islam as a "high religion" based on the Qur'an and tradition. This approach is inadequate. Research must be aimed toward uncovering the real (as opposed to the ideal) system of beliefs that touches every segment of the Muslim's life.[39]

The mission of God is basically for reconciling all creation through Christ, therefore, the Christian mission purposefully intends to make disciples in all aspects of life, by worship, proclamation, and fellowship, which bear witness to the whole character of the Lord Jesus Christ.

---

36. Micah Network Global, "Declaration on Integral Mission."w
37. Bendor-Samuel, "Holistic Ministry in an Islamic Context," 2–3.
38. Bendor-Samuel, "Holistic Ministry in an Islamic Context," 2–3.
39. Parshall, *Muslim Evangelism*, 102.

Ireland highlights the importance of compassionate care for God's chosen people and communities to reflect who God is and his righteous that reigns over all creation.[40] The fundamental definition of compassionate missions can never be separated from the whole message of *shalom*. Compassionate care of Christian mission requires active involvement in an action or a work of helping the people in need to experience God's righteousness, and Ireland clearly indicates: "We might also recall that Jesus spoke of righteousness not primarily as a state of being but as an action."[41]

The debate of how proclamation of the truth and compassionate care could be brought to people and their communities through Christian mission is fundamentally important but needs to advance to a deeper theological understanding. Teague uses the term "Integral Mission," based on the *autobasileian* theology of reconciliation.[42] "Integral Mission" finds the concept of Christ as "the Kingdom-in-Person"—*autobasileia*—rather than the holistic balance between word and deed. *Autobasileia*, a term coined by Origen of Alexandria, focuses on the reconciled relationship with God through the person of Christ,[43] and the *autobasileian* theology has a strong emphasis on the message of re-creation in that reconciliation with God brings humans back to Eden where they were under God's complete reign. Through an encounter with the person of Christ, new fellowship with Christ restores God's image in fallen human beings. His application of the *autobasileia* to "integral mission" is well stated:

> Plainly speaking, integral mission is more than a simple holistic integration of word with deed. It is a return to the Garden with all the theological wealth that is implied by Eden. If we settle on just trying to balance word and deed, we are missing the real point of integral mission.[44]

While many missionaries and scholars have grasped the theological concept of "integral mission" over the last fifty years, the debate about the priority between words and deeds expanded to the concept of how Christian missions can deliberate the ultimate purpose of God's mission as the reign of God in the person of Christ being proclaimed and fulfilled through integration of both words and deeds.

40. Ireland, *For the Love of God*.
41. Ireland, *For the Love of God*.
42. Teague, "Integral Mission," 13–22.
43. Sanders, "The Kingdom in Person."
44. Teague, "Integral Mission," 19.

Christian Medical Mission

The primary identity of the church is the community of faith as the body of Christ, and the instrument of God's mission. God has chosen the church as his primary instrument in his mission to the world; therefore, it is not the mission of God if there is no visible or invisible church conducting Christian missions. The churches in the Arab world carry the primary responsibility for mission among their peoples. All Christian missions, including Christian medical missions, intentionally plant churches or empower the church where it exists. In church mission practice, there is often a tendency to dichotomize the professional ministry from spiritual ministry. Ireland rightly states:

> Concern for the lost always occupies the central place in the mission of the church. Evangelical compassion must consistently exhibit a robust concern for the lost, with the understanding that only Jesus can redeem sinful humanity from its fallen state.[45]

Although the role of missionaries may vary in different contexts, he also adds that making disciples should include an active "indigenous compassionate response of the local church."[46] In many countries, indigenous churches have grown and self-confident local leaders have taken over the leadership for their own missions. The foreign cross-cultural mission force and the local indigenous church have become more inseparable in pursuit of God's mission, and the intimate partnership exemplifies the kingdom of God that demonstrates the realization of *shalom* to the lost.

The holistic approach to mankind's health issues is not only emphasized among Christianity, but also widely stressed in many societies. The broad usage of holistic care has brought confusion to Christians and churches developing their incomplete doctrine regarding medical holism. Common usage of spiritual words for unbiblical holism often confuses Christians who do not have understanding of their message and leads them to the pitfalls created by the New Age movement. Jane D. Gumprecht insightfully describes the concept of "holistic health or wellness" as an unbiblical understanding, influenced by the postmodern New Age movement on the basis of teaching by Edgar Cayce (1877–1945), a psychic master, who has been called the "sleeping prophet" and "father of holistic medicine."[47] Gumprecht observes:

---

45. Ireland, *For the Love of God*.
46. Ireland, *For the Love of God*.
47. "Who was Edgar Cayce?" *Edgar Cayce's ARE*.

Shalom: God's Ultimate Purpose for the World

> Satan has made this God-given concern for our physical and mental well-being a vehicle to bring the occult into the church, in a seemingly innocent way. Christians are asleep. They are not aware of the bond between the holistic health movement and the secular, humanistic New Age movement, which is energized by the spirit of the antichrist.[48]

She seriously warns Christians not to fall into the deception of "the holistic health" largely influenced by the unbiblical New Age movement, and yet there seems to be confusion, especially regarding oriental medicine which approaches health and medicine with a completely different concept. Chuanxin Wang defines "the holistic medicine" as an ancient system of healthcare that takes the whole person into consideration for approaching health and healing.[49] This approach emphasizes the connection of mind, body, and spirit for maximizing well-being by bringing people in harmony with nature.[50] Gumprecht clarifies that this approach is certainly part of "spiritism," rather than the work of the Holy Spirit, and the wholeness from this approach means "becoming one with collective consciousness or divine mind."[51] However, oriental medicine using acupuncture and herbal medicine has scientifically developed, and some are already approved for applying to patients without any influence of the New Age movement. Although there is a danger of falling into unbiblical holistic care, this warning should not be generally applied with ignorance of local traditional ways of healthcare. More extensive studies could bolster this subject with recognition of the cultural, religious, and spiritual dimensions.

Historical Considerations of Integral Mission

The issues regarding the relationship between verbal proclamation of the gospel and social action have been a debate of long standing in the history of Christianity. There became a sharp conflict of opinion between fundamentalism and liberalism in modern Christian history, but both came to face the theological challenges by postmodernism and fragmentation within traditionally liberal and conservative circles.[52] In the late nineteenth

---

48. Gumprecht, *Holistic Health*, 1–5.
49. Wang, "Holistic Health Definition."
50. Walter, "Holistic Health."
51. Gumprecht, *Holistic Health*, 223.
52. Grenz and Franke, *Beyond Fundamentalism*, 6–7.

and early twentieth century, theological liberalism critically influenced the Christian community and Christian mission.[53] Johnson summarizes this period of history:

> The practical issues that necessitate such a discussion grow out of the legacy of the fundamentalist-liberal divide of the late 19th and early 20th centuries. With the rise of theological liberalism that challenged the authority of the Bible, all that was left was the Fatherhood of God and the brotherhood of man. In cross-cultural missions this meant no need for conversionary evangelism, rather social action and bringing civilization was required. Evangelicals who held to the authority of the Bible rejected this view and reacted against it. Mission came to be seen as only evangelism and the planting of the church.[54]

Liberation theology developed in Latin America in the 1960s, which emphasized the social responsibility of church for those oppressed by the unjust economic, political, social structures rather than soul-saving through the person and work of Jesus Christ.[55] In the North American context, evangelical Christian groups were actively involved in various ministries to meet the spiritual and physical needs of the underprivileged before the twentieth century, but the rise of liberal groups in the early twentieth century made Evangelicals withdraw from these ministries in order to distance themselves from the social gospel movement.[56] Among evangelical circles, there has been serious tension between those who traditionally emphasize church-planting in terms of soul-saving and those who are more interested in compassion ministry oriented toward social responsibilities as Christians.[57] Over the last fifty years, Evangelical church leaders have deepened

---

53. Evans, "Liberation Theology."

54. Johnson, "Missions and Compassion."

55. Evans, "Liberation Theology."

56. Corbett and Fikkert, *When Helping Hurts*, 43–44. Social Gospel Movement: Evans identifies three characteristics from the definition of Social Gospel in American Protestant history that tried to integrate evangelical and liberal theological circles: (1) "Social idealism from its distinctive liberal synthesis," (2) "a belief that a primary objective of religion was to advocate for systemic social changes," and (3) "a motivation to promote a vision of America as a religiously and culturally pluralistic society" (Evans, *The Social Gospel*, 2–3).

57. Johnson compares these polarized positions: "On one side are those who see cross-cultural mission as only properly involving proclamation of the gospel and planting the church, while on the other people can only conceive of mission in compassion and humanitarian terms" (Johnson, "Missions and Compassion").

their comprehension about how Christian mission should function to share the gospel message more effectively. Although they agree with the basic notion of social responsibility regarding justice, human rights, and responsibility to the poor and the oppressed, as well as evangelism to teach and proclaim the word of God, opinions vary on the details of what extent the church should be involved in various social concerns. Furthermore, when these issues are raised in cross-cultural contexts, methods and degrees of Christian mission involvement are extremely complicated. During the last several decades, discussion about the concept of integral mission has developed among the international evangelical conferences.

The Congress on the World Mission of the Church (held at Wheaton in 1966) admitted that the evangelical community was responsible for not actively pursuing the application of scriptural principles to the problems that the world faces such as racism, war, population explosion, poverty, family disintegration, social revolution, and communism.[58] The World Congress on Evangelism (Berlin, 1966) consisted of conservative Protestant leaders from around the world and was an important start of discussion about ways of increasing cooperation in evangelistic work among worldwide churches.[59] It greatly influenced the inauguration of the International Congress on World Evangelization (1974) and the International Conferences of Itinerant Evangelists (1983 and 1986). The Lausanne Movement began in the early 1970s as an evangelical attempt to "reframe Christian mission in a world of social, political, economic, and religious upheaval."[60] Its founders believed that the church must know how to apply the gospel to these rapidly changing contemporary issues more biblically across the globe. The Lausanne Movement confirmed that evangelism and social responsibility are equally important and Christian mission efforts must integrate both.[61] At this congress, the common belief regarding the mission of the church in the mid-twentieth century was well revealed by Billy Graham's statement:

> If the church went back to its main task of proclaiming the gospel and people converted to Christ, it would have a far greater impact on the social, moral, and psychological needs of men than it could achieve through any other thing it could possibly do.[62]

58. "Wheaton Declaration," 458–76.
59. "One Race, One Gospel, One Task," *The World Congress on Evangelism*.
60. Lausanne Movement, "The Legacy of the Lausanne Movement."
61. Lausanne Movement, "The Lausanne Covenant."
62. Teague, "Integral Mission," 19–22.

The Chicago Declaration of Evangelical Social Concern (1973) took a further step for the concerns of evangelical Christians' social responsibility by confessing failure to demonstrate the love of God toward the oppressed and those suffering social abuses.[63]

The Prioritism-Holism debate surfaced more intensively at the First International Congress on World Evangelization (Lausanne, Switzerland, July 1974), and witnessed a major diversion in evangelical thought concerning evangelism and social responsibility.[64] The fifth covenant of the Lausanne Covenant declared the social responsibility of church with passion:

> The message of salvation implies also a message of judgment upon every form of alienation, oppression and discrimination, and we should not be afraid to denounce evil and injustice wherever they exist. When people receive Christ they are born again into his kingdom and must seek not only to exhibit but also to spread its righteousness in the midst of an unrighteous world. The salvation we claim should be transforming us in the totality of our personal and social responsibilities. Faith without works is dead.[65]

Teague notes the objection after the Lausanne Covenant, raised by the conservative circle that felt that this would weaken "the primacy of proclamation in evangelism," and that evangelical leaders have strived to clarify the relationship between proclamation of God's words and social response.[66] According to Ireland, the Consultation on World Evangelization (COWE) in Pattaya, Thailand (1980) restored the priority of evangelism, although social responsibility of the church remains necessary.[67] The International Consultation on the Relationship of Evangelism and Social Responsibility (CRESR) held in Grand Rapids (1982) followed to address the issues more clearly, but evangelism and social response still remained separate like "two blades in a pair of scissors or the two wings of a bird."[68]

As the concept of "integral mission" became a major issue among international evangelical leaders, the statement of integral mission was declared by the Consultation of the Church in Response to Human Need (Wheaton,

---

63. Christians for Social Action, "Chicago Declaration of Evangelical Social Concern (1973)."
64. Ireland, *For the Love of God*.
65. Lausanne Movement, "The Lausanne Covenant," 5.
66. Teague, "Integral Mission," 20.
67. Ireland, *For the Love of God*.
68. Stott, ed., *Making Christ Known*, 102.

Shalom: God's Ultimate Purpose for the World

1983) so as not to limit the church to traditional evangelism, but also to address the social issues in the local society that do not reflect the whole message of the gospel.[69] In addition, the affirmation of the church's mission to the world has transformed eschatology of the coming of the God's kingdom to the idea that God reigns over the whole creation beyond the idea of escaping into the distant future. The concept of "integral mission" enabled evangelical mission groups to obtain deeper understanding and make practical plans of bringing the whole life under the lordship of Jesus Christ.[70] The definition of "integral mission" was further developed with the Micah Declaration (Oxford, 2001) stating that evangelism and social involvement are not tasks to be done alongside, but should include both social consequences of the gospel proclamation and evangelical consequences by the social involvement through the witness of Jesus Christ.[71] Currently "integral mission" is more clearly defined by Lausanne Movement:

> The mission of God is "to reconcile to himself all things, whether things on earth or things in heaven" (Col 1:20), and our part is crossing geographic, cultural, politic, economic, and social barriers "with the intention of transforming human life in all its dimensions, according to God's purpose, and of enabling human beings to enjoy the abundant life that God wants to give to them and that Jesus Christ came to share with them."[72]

Integral Mission with Christian Medical Mission

Christian medical mission can be described as cross-cultural mission through medical work and pursues the holistic approach. Based on his experience, J. Dudley Woodberry writes: "The history of medical ministry gives credibility to Christian work. But it must be seen as only part of a holistic ministry."[73] Christian medical mission should not only aim to improve the medical and healthcare system, but also take care of the whole person. Modern medicine tends to focus on diseases and curative attempts more than on people who need holistic restoration from their health problems. Jean Johnson refers to

---

69. Padilla, "Integral Mission and Its Historical Development."
70. Lausanne Movement, "Integral Mission."
71. Micah Network Global, "Declaration on Integral Mission."
72. Lausanne Movement, "Integral Mission."
73. Woodberry, *Muslims & Christians on the Emmaus Road*, 301–2.

Christian Medical Mission

the concept of "McDonaldization" of society from sociologist George Ritzer (characterized by efficiency, calculability, predictability, and control) regarding modern Christian mission.[74] Christian mission groups have a tendency of focusing more on productivity related to the numbers of churches planted or new believers through its missions, rather than seeing the quality of restored relationships which is often not measurable.[75] The impact of modern fast-food culture can also be observed in many Christian medical missions including short-term medical missions, and tends to lead them to focus on materialistic outcomes. Rather, holistic medical mission should be able to deal with diseases and health issues, and, furthermore, demonstrate how to eradicate their pathogens which come from both physical conditions and the spiritually-fallen nature of human beings. Not only miraculous healing by God's divine power, but also the holistic care of Christian faith itself provides health benefits, especially to those who have mental health problems and terminal illnesses. Alex Bunn and David Randall indicate:

> While it is striking that faith appears to be associated with improved health outcomes, the Christian faith is not to be judged by its material benefits, but by whether it is true. Christianity's holistic emphasis on human beings whose physical, mental, relational, and spiritual dimensions are all vitally important is an important corrective to the reductionism of modern medicine. Patients do not simply present biological problems to be solved. Rather, effective medical interventions should address all the dimensions of our humanity. It is clear that most patients value and seek this form of holistic care.[76]

Tetsunao Yamamori describes four characteristics of biblical holism:

1. Holism is w-holistic,
2. Holism is synergistic,
3. Holism is restorative, and
4. Holism is Christocentric, or Christ-centered.[77]

---

74. McDonaldization: Ritzer, well-known sociologist, introduced the concept of McDonaldization in 1993. He observes a sociological phenomenon in modern society that people are very much influenced by in-and-out fast-food culture. He refers to McDonaldization as a "process of rationalization" which results in "an efficient, logical sequence of methods that can be completed the same way every time to produce the desired outcome" (Ritzer, *The McDonaldization of Society*, 13–15).
75. Yamamori, "Christian Health Care," 98–103.
76. Bunn and Randall, "Health Benefits."
77. Johnson, "Counterintuitive Missions in a McDonald's Age."

Shalom: God's Ultimate Purpose for the World

The modern Christian medical mission force has enormously contributed to the establishment and development of medical services in many medically underdeveloped countries all over the world. It is obvious that medical missions have been an effective instrument of sharing the gospel and love of Christ in many countries.[78] Mark A. Strand reports that over a half-million Christians in Nepal have been influenced by medical mission work in various ways. Furthermore, eighty percent of the Christians in India claim that a Christian mission hospital is related to their becoming a Christian.[79] The important role played by medical missions in the preaching of the gospel is undeniable. Peter Parker, the first medical missionary to China (1804–1888) and his team in the 1830s were convinced during their missionary medical service that the spread of the gospel message was "inextricably bound with the spread of all forms of knowledge."[80] Despite their successful medical mission effort, they received complaints from the directors of the American Board about "neglecting their primary duty to preach the gospel" and agonized over being caught in the middle between medical profession for mission and spiritual ministry.[81] Frequently, medical mission work has simply been viewed as a mere affiliation for spiritual ministries.

Caring for the sick with the compassionate heart of Jesus has been the primary purpose of Christian medical mission groups over the centuries, which has also enabled it to proclaim the gospel to the lost. John Greenall observes that most cross-cultural medical missionaries were implementing their ministries either in a hospital or in a clinic in 1969, and very few were involved in other types of ministry.[82] It is undeniable that there was a certain level of opposition toward the Christian medical mission, and some evangelical mission leaders viewed it as a mere tool to share the gospel or a kind of inducements to attract people to Christianity. However, this has been changing since early 1970 when many Christian medical mission leaders began deeply thinking about the medical care as an important part of integral mission. Green insightfully explains how Christian medical mission is an essential part of the integral mission:

> Medical missionaries must be clear in their theology of medical mission; it is not "bait" to catch fish, nor is it just treating people

---

78. Hardiman, ed., *Healing Bodies, Saving Souls*, 5–9.
79. Strand, "Medical Missions in Transition."
80. Lazich, *Seeking Souls through the Eyes of the Blind*, 75.
81. Lazich, *Seeking Souls through the Eyes of the Blind*, 75.
82. Greenall, "What is the Future of Medical Mission?"

without pointing them to Christ. Instead medical missionaries must couple evangelistic zeal with genuine compassion for humans, whether people respond to Christ or not. Indeed, holistic care through church-linked community health is seen by many as the best and perhaps the only way for true integral mission to take place.[83]

How Christian medical mission groups should function in relationship to the overall Christian mission efforts is still complicated, as modes of medical mission have diversified according to their contexts since 1970. The greatest transition has been from medical platforms of curative care to preventive care for underprivileged communities. The importance of preventive medicine over curative medicine has been emphasized because some medical missionaries came to realize that the same people kept returning to the hospitals and clinics with the same preventable illness. This focus on preventive medicine is not only due to the realization of preventive medicine's importance, but also because curative medicine at either a mission hospital or clinic became more expensive and difficult to sustain with funds from outside in many countries. The heavy burden of raising funds caused the hospital or clinic based mission strategy to lose sustainability sooner than later. The effort for preventive medicine within Christian medical missions is more effective in medically underdeveloped countries and more cost-efficient in its implementation. This trend seems to be one of results of taking desperate measures under the pressure of necessity in Christian medical mission to sustain with less foreign resources. In this circumstance of facing various challenges Christian medical mission leadership has been forced to diversify the modalities of its missions.

As a part of preventive medicine in the context of Christian medical mission, Community Health Evangelism (CHE) was highlighted as an effective way of integral mission. This program integrates evangelism and discipleship with a Christ-centered development program focusing on health education as a part of preventive medicine.[84] Medical Ambassadors International defines CHE as a "strategy for individual and community development through training that brings physical and spiritual change."[85] Suzanne Hurst introduces CHE as an excellent example of "Best Practice Program Models":

83. Greenall, "What is the Future of Medical Mission?"
84. CHE Global Network, "Community Health Evangelism (CHE)."
85. Medical Ambassadors International, "Community Health Evangelism (CHE)."

Shalom: God's Ultimate Purpose for the World

> CHE takes the basic elements of best practice and combines them with appropriate Bible lessons to create a Christian-based community development and disease prevention program that can be launched by a local church group or by a larger community interest group. CHE's emphasis is on empowering local groups and individuals through training trainers. Community participation, ownership, and sustainability are key elements of the CHE DNA.[86]

CHE has been implemented in various contexts to meet the physical and spiritual needs of local communities through holistic ways that include both ministries of compassion and spiritual discipleship with the principles of community development. Because it approaches many different contexts of culture and religion, the principles are applied with flexibility to empower local people in partnership with the local church when it exists.

In addition, medical missionaries came to realize the importance of training local medical and healthcare workers in addition to caring for the sick. When the local healthcare system is primarily dependent on foreign resources of medical professionals, it tends to remain underdeveloped due to the huge gulf between the local and the foreign. The local people trust foreign mission clinics and hospitals more than their own indigenous medical care facilities because the quality of medical care at the Christian mission clinics and hospitals is not comparable to the local medical care in many places. The Christian mission clinics and hospitals are influential because they provide a better quality of medical services to their patients, but create undesirable effects on the local medical care system because they usually have their own strategies focusing on the delivery of high-quality medical services to patients rather than interacting with the local medical care system for its development. In addition, in many contexts, the local medical care system does not have enough resources to provide quality medical services with low medical fees compared to the Christian mission medical services which bring resources from outside. This brings critical issues in the relationship between the Christian medical mission and the local medical care system. Realizing the importance of training local medical and healthcare workers alongside caring for the sick, which empowers the local medical care system, may possibly be one of the greatest tactics of integral mission.

---

86. Hurst, "Best Practices in Compassionate Mission."

Integral Mission in the Islamic Context

Generally speaking, many Muslims in the Arab world have preconceptions against Christianity because of various socio-political, cultural, and historical reasons, which blind Muslims to the gospel message. Commonly, Christian missionaries, without proper effort to comprehend people's thought and worldviews, hastily get into arguments with the intention of presenting the gospel to save the lost. Greg Livingstone defines "church-planting" as

> the whole process of evangelizing, discipling, training, and organizing a group of believers to a level of development permitting it to function as a viable church independent of the agent(s) who brought it into being.[87]

He insightfully states a tendency of apologetics that missionaries usually try to do for Muslims:

> All too often, well-intentioned missionaries to Muslims find themselves seeking to defeat the Muslim with western logic, unaware that their memorized arguments from formal education may be addressing questions that few Muslims are asking.[88]

It is critical to remember as a missionary in Islamic countries that people's hearts are hardly touched without first building close relationships, even though the presentation of the gospel is essential for evangelism and church-planting, especially in Islamic countries which are hostile to the Christian mission. Jesus' earthly ministry demonstrates the principles of what Christian mission should look like in the Arab world, too. Christian missionaries should be willing to embrace Muslims with the same heart that Jesus poured his love and compassion upon the lost who sought healing not only physically, but also emotionally and spiritually. When Christian mission professionals embrace Muslims whose hearts have been hurt by fear and anger, God will bring reconciliation to them through the witness of Jesus. Teague emphasizes this issue:

> The purpose of mission work is to bring people to encounter the Kingdom-in-Person . . . It is the King reigning, doing, conquering and healing . . . In the New Testament, the gospel is a

---

87. Livingstone, *Planting Churches in Muslim Cities*, 73.
88. Livingstone, *Planting Churches in Muslim Cities*, 139.

pneumatic encounter with the person of Christ. If we forget this, we forget everything.[89]

In addition, Parshall's insightful comment should be kept in mind:

> Missionaries must present the word of reconciliation in such a way that it fits well into the value system of the society in which it is being proclaimed. The transforming of the worldviews and allegiances of Muslims should be carried out as a process that involves minimal social dislocation.[90]

There is a group of church planters in the Islamic context who think it is best to win souls by defeating Islamic theology through logical arguments, but Livingstone encourages them to try building intimate relationships with Muslims first, as they hardly earn people's hearts without these relationships.[91] It is essential to build intimate relationships in order to make the gospel message more persuasive, but there is the risk of creating a dichotomy between reaching Muslims relationally and reaching them apologetically. Nabeel Qureshi's fine work from his former identity as a Muslim, *No God But One, Allah or Jesus?*,[92] demonstrates the importance of apologetics in conveying biblical truth to Muslims. These two approaches must be included together, and all Christian workers need to convince Muslims with the biblical truth. Melanie McNeal summarizes the importance of discipleship which should bring changes in mission paradigms and strategies. As the circumstances in Christian mission change, the task of mission should be changed. Various mission agencies have their own focus according to their professions and visions. While evangelism and church-planting are essential to every Christian mission, equipping, empowering, and serving local church should not be neglected in Christian mission as well. The importance of discipleship is clearly demonstrated, and transformational holistic ministries become more crucial, especially in the Arab world.[93] As discipleship involves every aspect of Christian' lives and ministries, which grows complex in the cross-cultural context, the importance of holistic ministry and biblical ways of building up partnership should be considered

---

89. Teague, "Integral Mission," 23.
90. Parshall, *Muslim Evangelism*, 111.
91. Livingstone, *Planting Churches in Muslim Cities*, 139.
92. Nabeel Qureshi, *No God But One*.
93. McNeal, "Mission Paradigms," 48–97.

carefully during the whole journey of ministries in order to effectively present the message of the gospel.

Although many missionaries agree about the importance of integral mission in the cross-cultural context, serious debates surround the question of how much Christian mission has to be involved in various socio-political issues. As integral mission desires to see every aspect of life transformed by the gospel, deliberation on various socio-political issues is inescapable. Johnson states that the dimension between proclamation of the good news and Christian social response in real life can be considered as primary to the other even though these do not have any conflict at the theological level.[94] He distinguishes issue-based ministry, which is more concerned about social issues in the context such as water problems, human trafficking, abortion, or poverty, than about spiritual ministry, such as primary evangelism and church-planting. There are serious concerns about this approach especially in cross-cultural mission, and Johnson explains well:

> Social issues are on the radar of local churches that embrace God's mission in their society, but when Christians from on social setting take issues from their setting and address it in a new setting, it is likely not to be a successful intervention from an indigenous church perspective. It may be satisfying to the individuals who do the intervention but not effective on the ground.[95]

When cross-cultural Christian missionaries try to fix any social concerns from their own cultural perspectives, without proper knowledge about cultural structure of the host community, there may be undesirable involvement in politics which results in negative consequences to the spiritual ministry of gospel proclamation and church-planting. To facilitate social activism, it would be better to be patient until the local people cast vision and take initiative for change instead of trying to fix the issues with proposed intervention and funding. Local governments may perceive this kind of expatriate involvement as a political threat rather than of appreciating the endeavor. Even if it takes longer than expected, it is important for the locals to see the issues from the biblical perspective and take it with ownership for sustainable changes. It is agreeable to Johnson's statement that "the fully-integrated approach" with active indigenous local church involvement for its own social issues is more desirable as its response to the

---

94. Johnson, "Counterintuitive Missions in a McDonald's Age."
95. Johnson, "Counterintuitive Missions in a McDonald's Age."

Shalom: God's Ultimate Purpose for the World

message of the gospel which transforms its perspective toward the social concerns and issues.[96]

Debate about which has a priority between spiritual ministry and social responsibility in Christian cross-cultural ministry misses the important point. Christian missions should never dichotomize these two dimensions of Christian life and ministry, but this phenomenon is found everywhere not only because of different theological understandings, but also because of the implication these principles have on different levels of ministry in a wide range of contexts. Evangelism and discipleship be intentionally brought together in ministry from the beginning at both the individual level and the church community level so that participants acknowledge these two dimensions should not be done serially, but be integrated as a whole. Johnson concludes regarding compassion ministry in practice:

> Practicing compassion with a deeper commitment to the founding and maturing of an indigenous church movement carries with it the hope of lasting fruit and people with increased capacity to care for their own needs and that of their community and who see God providing for them.[97]

Christian mission must have the perspective of wholeness that brings *shalom* to the community as Jesus demonstrated how he could integrate many different aspects of the whole gospel to people in very different circumstances and situations. Christian mission should be able to call people to Jesus through presenting his life and truth that they may eventually realize the biblical message of *shalom* in their personal lives and their communities by becoming more like him through growing in the intimate relationship with him.

According to Livingstone, Christian medical mission work is one of the essential parts of the holistic process in church-planting in the Muslim societies.[98] Christian medical missions are a platform for entry into restricted countries, and in many ways they are able to open the doors for Christian professionals to work in those countries with proper social status like professional positions and residential permits. Although some scholars find the term of "platform" irrelevant and offensive, arguing that it is disingenuous and simply relegates compassion as a means to an end, this definitely provides places for Christian professionals to interact with local

---

96. Johnson, "Counterintuitive Missions in a McDonald's Age."
97. Johnson, "Counterintuitive Missions in a McDonald's Age."
98. Livingstone, *Planting Churches in Muslim Cities*, 90–91.

professionals and people, which enables them to build intimate relationships and share the Christian faith. Intelligible and non-threatening roles of professional missions through various platforms would be viewed by host communities as a positive contribution even though they are laid to suspicion at certain levels. The quality of professional work and daily living will break down negative stereotypes toward outsiders and Christians, which are mostly perceived through Western media associated with its immoral secular culture and political preconceived ideas. Livingstone recommends entering Muslim communities by finding employment in Muslim companies so that Christian mission professionals may have more opportunities to build up meaningful relationships with the local people.[99] Staying in the Muslim milieu sometimes presents challenges of security and safety and temptation to compromise Christian values in certain situations. Livingstone points out that the western companies or governments could be a greater hindrance to the gospel because they do not want to lose their benefits of collaboration with the local companies and government by getting accused of religious activities.[100] In the same line of assertion, Christian medical mission needs to mingle with the local Islamic medical institutions such as health projects, clinics, hospitals, and medical education systems like medical colleges, rather than separating itself by establishing and running its own mission platforms.

Relief, Rehabilitation, Development and Transformation

There have been many scholarly articles about mistakes that many Non-Governmental Organizations (NGOs) have made with donor-driven development projects within underdeveloped countries and societies. Even many Christian organizations and mission agencies have tried these sorts of projects with good intention, but their results have not always turned out positively. Small differences in the fundamental principles of these missions can have dramatic consequences for all endeavors. The stories tell how foreign resources provided by both government organizations and NGOs have broken down the local communities and even the image of the local churches. Sadly, this is also true for many Christian missions providing compassionate care in underdeveloped areas, as Ireland indicates from his experience:

99. Livingstone, *Planting Churches in Muslim Cities*, 94.
100. Livingstone, *Planting Churches in Muslim Cities*, 95.

Shalom: God's Ultimate Purpose for the World

> As a missionary living in West Africa, I have heard countless tales told by African pastors describing how donor-driven projects connected to NGOs have ruined the image and effectiveness of the local church.[101]

Hurst also mentions that Christian mission must consider the consequences of good intentions to help in the cross-cultural settings:

> While our motives need to be pure, good motives and kind hearts do not necessarily guarantee that we understand the context where we are working or that we cognizant of possible unintended consequences.[102]

Corbett and Fikkert insightfully draw a picture of the dynamics related to shortsighted missions: "Material Definition of Poverty + God-complexes of Materially Non-Poor + Feelings of Inferiority of Materially Poor = Harm to Both Materially Poor and Non-Poor."[103] Many local churches which work with those NGOs become too dependent and tend to pursue materialistic possessions, which leads both church leaders and ordinary members to lose their willingness to serve each other with joy. This phenomenon seems to be universal and can be commonly found in the Arab world as well. Ireland diagnoses this as "the results from the loss of compassionate virtues and ethics as part of the disciple-making process."[104]

Relief is defined by Corbett and Fikkert as "the urgent and temporary provision of emergency aid to reduce immediate suffering from a natural or man-made crisis"; rehabilitation as activities to "seek to restore people and their communities to the positive elements of their pre-crisis conditions"; and development as "a process of ongoing change that moves all the people involved—both the 'helpers' and the 'helped'—closer to being in right relationship with God, self, others, and the rest of creation."[105] These definitions can be applied to many occasions that the Christian mission faces. In a similar way, Medical Ambassadors International (MAI) explains three categories of "the ways to help communities":

---

101. Ireland, *For the Love of God*.
102. Hurst, "Best Practices in Compassionate Mission."
103. Corbett and Fikkert, *When Helping Hurts*, 155. Although this equation is about the effects of short-term missions on poor communities, this is also found to be relative to the issue raised in this chapter.
104. Ireland, *For the Love of God*.
105. Corbett and Fikkert, *When Helping Hurts*, 99–100.

1. Relief Ministries—Provides temporary short-term assistance without addressing long term needs nor using community assets. It is doing things for people because of an observed need.
2. Betterment Ministries—Tend to create short-term positive, caring beneficial environments and relationships that offer participants respite or positive experiences.
3. Development Ministries—Focus on measured changes in knowledge, skills abilities or conditions of the participants.[106]

Corbett and Fikkert strongly emphasize the importance of this determination:

> It is absolutely crucial that we determine whether relief, rehabilitation, or development is the appropriate intervention: One of the biggest mistakes that North American churches make—by far—is in applying relief in situations in which rehabilitation or development is the appropriate intervention.[107]

Although it is often difficult to identify whether "relief," "rehabilitation," or "development" is the proper terminology for each situation, determining the situations and applying principles accordingly is the key for Christian missions to prevent unnecessary adverse effects of mission works and bring the best ways to help out the communities.

When Christian mission groups strive to transform local communities with missions and projects, it must reach into the root of socio-economic phenomena rather than simply deal with what can be seen on the such as poverty, injustice, ethical issues, or socio-political corruption. Darrow Miller proposes that Christian missions should influence people and their communities with the biblical worldview through various missions and projects. In his observation that "ideas have consequences," he suggests paying special attention to the worldview of people in order to bring transformation to their community.[108] His assertion is that the fallen world suffering from poverty, violence, disease, and countless consequences of human depravity is enslaved by the power of darkness which has permeated entire cultures as well as human beings. The comparison of the three major worldviews—animism, theism, and secularism—and the explanation

---

106. "Urban CHE Overview: Community Health Evangelism," *Medical Ambassadors International*.

107. "Urban CHE Overview: Community Health Evangelism," *Medical Ambassadors International*, 4.

108. Miller, *Discipling Nations*, 34.

about how these worldviews can impact people's lives are persuasive. Both secular and religious organizations conduct development projects to eradicate poverty, but it is sadly true that there have been undesirable sequelae because of the insufficiency of proper knowledge and experience. It is crucial to establish better principles and strategies to transform the story of relief and development with stewardship. Miller defines development as "a process of discipling both people and cultures, founded on the creative and redemptive work of God and based his story."[109] The key concept of biblical development he suggests is "stewardship," which is closely related to the cultural mandate as the vice-regents of God mentioned previously. Miller clarifies development on the basis of the biblical concept of stewardship in comparison with secularism and animism:

> Development, understood as stewardship, maintains a dynamic tension between conserving and progressing. The biblical development worker, then, is best described as a progressive conservative (or a conservative progressive). What a contrast with secularism, which progresses without conserving, or animism, which conserves without progressing.[110]

Understanding the worldview reflecting people's theological belief is an essential process for the Christian mission to bring transformational changes to the communities.

The root of many undesirable consequences from Christian cross-cultural missions lies in insufficient comprehension of the prevailing local culture and worldview as well as self-centered perspectives toward local socio-economic circumstances. Cross-cultural missionaries who serve underprivileged people and communities tend to see their needs from their own perspectives and simply try to meet those needs with resources from outside, without properly considering the long-term effects to the communities. Their desire for compassionate care is admirable, but never good enough for bringing transformational changes. Many missions and projects tend to pursue measurable materialistic products or outcomes more than immeasurable inner transformational process of people and communities. Although Christian cross-cultural workers are very well aware of the importance of people who may experience life transformation through these development projects, it is always immensely challenging to implement principles for measuring the unmeasurable outcomes and products in

109. Miller, *Discipling Nations*, 177.
110. Miller, *Discipling Nations*, 232.

people and their communities. Nevertheless, the Christian mission group must commit itself to constantly return to the root of the worldview and theological belief system related to the social concerns observed in the local culture. They should patiently try to transform people's distorted worldviews due to the fallen humanity to the biblical worldview that brings the complete restoration in the broken relationships. This comment by Corbett and Fikkert regarding poverty alleviation brings an important insight that all Christian missions should not neglect:

> Material poverty alleviation is working to reconcile the four foundational relationships[111] so that people can fulfill their callings of glorifying God by working and supporting themselves and their families with the fruit of that work.[112]

They place great emphasis on people rather than projects, since the goal of Christian mission is "to see people restored to being what God created them to be."[113] One of the most serious undesirable consequences of these types of development efforts is dependency created by foreign-funded projects. JoAnn Butrin and A. Chadwick Thornhill indicate the definition of poverty as neither economic nor materialistic, but as relational.[114] This unique definition of poverty leads Christian mission to a different approach of alleviating poverty. They assert: "Though we may have good intentions in trying to provide for the lacks, we may create an unhealthy dependence."[115] Ireland also highlights: "Compassionate efforts that are most fruitful are those that avoid the creation of dependency, which often robs those we would serve of their God-driven dignity as divine image bearers."[116] In the same line, Corbett and Fikkert highlights the necessity of avoiding "the poison of paternalism" as the primary rule of thumb.[117]

After determining whether situations are suitable for relief, rehabilitation, or development, the Christian mission has to follow the essential

---

111. Four foundational relationships: Relationships with God, Self, Others, and the Rest of Creation (Corbett and Fikkert, *When Helping Hurts*, 54–59). Corbett and Fikkert adapt four foundational relationships for each person from Myers, *Walking with the Poor*, 27.

112. Corbett and Fikkert, *When Helping Hurts*, 74.

113. Corbett and Fikkert, *When Helping Hurts*, 77.

114. Butrin and Thornhill, "Defining Poverty and Need."

115. Butrin and Thornhill, "Defining Poverty and Need."

116. Ireland, *For the Love of God*.

117. Corbett and Fikkert, *When Helping Hurts*, 109.

Shalom: God's Ultimate Purpose for the World

principles for practice. Johnson introduces the indigenous principles of compassion missions.[118] He emphasizes "the indigenous principle of self-support," which respects the dignity of individuals and establish self-sustaining indigenous ministries. Historically, one of the most remarkable indigenous principles is the "Three Selfs" of self-support, self-governance, and self-propagation which were introduced by Venn and Anderson in the 1850s and applied in the ministries of John Nevius and Roland Allen.[119] The "Three Selfs" principles of Christian mission reject "foreigners' influence on the church leadership, foreign financing and foreign missionaries,"[120] and has impacted the early church in Korea and China. Hark Yoo Kim reflects the self-support principle in Christian mission history in Korea:

> In case of Korean mission history, the self-support principle has played a very important role in the rapid growth of the church. Most mission scholars point out that one of the most influential and effective mission principles in the Korean peninsula was the self-support principle.[121]

Johnson gets to the point using the Apostle Paul's church-planting principle, stating that all churches should be "responsible for themselves in all dimensions" and "participate in God's mission and take the gospel to their social worlds and beyond."[122] Corbett and Fikkert highlight the momentous principle of "asset-based community development (ABCD)," which is "consistent with the perspective that God has blessed every individual and community with a host of gifts."[123] Here, there is a comparison between asset-based community development and needs-based development that

---

118. Johnson, "Counterintuitive Missions in a McDonald's Age."

119. Jones, "The Christian Church in Communist China," 186. Three-Self Principles: These principles were developed by three protestant missionaries, Henry Venn, Rufus Anderson, and John L. Nevius. The fundamental idea of these principles is that all national churches and ministries should become quickly independent from the mother churches mainly in Europe or North America. These principles asserts that all foreign mission forces have to establish local churches and ministries with "self-governing, self-supporting, and self-extending" structure, and then turn over the control to local leadership. These principles were an important driving force for local churches to grow. Nevius, a Presbyterian missionary in China and Korea, observed a meaningful success of these principles in China and Korea (Three-Self Principles in *Encyclopedia of Protestantism*).

120. "Three Self Church."

121. Kim, "What Sort of Relationship Does the Sending Church Want with the Receiving Church?" 83–84.

122. Johnson, "Counterintuitive Missions in a McDonald's Age."

123. Corbett and Fikkert, *When Helping Hurts*, 119–20.

sees the needs in the life of a person or a community and tries to meet their needs by bringing resources from outside.[124] Ireland also asserts that development as a way of compassionate care should focus on people's assets more than their needs, and serve them with dignity.[125] He explains:

> A driving idea behind development principles is that of sustainability. This means simply that compassionate efforts should be able not only to persist, but thrive, even without missionary presence and involvement. Such an approach requires tremendous humility and long-term commitment. The missionary who engages in development work cannot be in the spotlight or play the dominant role. Development requires empowering and training local people. This idea finds its ultimate basis in Jesus' own mission, as he came not to be served, but to serve (Matt 20:28).[126]

Distinguishing these two different principles is not a matter of either good or bad, but they should wisely be applied according to the context. This process helps make the perspectives of Christian cross-cultural development workers more biblical and continually reminds them of the root of the problems that they face on fields. Corbett and Fikkert highlight:

> The point of ABCD is not to deny those needs or the deep-seated brokenness that undergirds them. On the contrary, the point of ABCD is to recognize—from the very start—that poverty is rooted in the brokenness of the foundational relationships and to start the process of restoring both low-income people and ourselves to living in right relationship with God, self, others, and the rest of creation.[127]

ABCD values the local people and their assets as the foundational cornerstone of sustainable community development with the acknowledgment of their potential and worth. Christian mission should play a role in enabling the local people and communities to open their eyes to discover what they already have, and in utilizing it for maximum effect. This way will increase local people's dignity and motivate them to continue finding their own ways to use their assets to develop themselves and their communities no matter how disadvantaged or impoverished they are. Awareness of a certain situation and application of right principles accordingly are the keys

---

124. Corbett and Fikkert, *When Helping Hurts*, 120.
125. Ireland, *For the Love of God*.
126. Ireland, *For the Love of God*.
127. Corbett and Fikkert, *When Helping Hurts*, 120–21.

for the Christian cross-cultural mission to avoid potential negative effects and bring the most effective long-term solution. This will bring biblical transformation to the individuals and their communities by the full restoration of broken relationships, *shalom*, through the truth presented by Jesus Christ. DeYoung and Gilbert advise,

> In today's cultural climate, where the accolades come quickly to those with humanitarian strategies and the opprobrium falls fast on those with evangelistic concerns, it is even more imperative that we keep the main thing the main thing.[128]

One must not neglect the fundamental truth that, throughout all the efforts of relief, rehabilitation, and development, the key is ultimately placed on the transformation of people's worldview closely related to their theological belief system.

Chapter Summary

Every human being is remarkably unique as they demonstrate the image of God. Even without God's divine involvement of miraculous healing, life itself is a miracle; because billions of miracles that modern science still may not properly explain are simultaneously at work to sustain the life of every individual. Medicine is a visible way of bringing reconciliation for the broken physical body and of demonstrating God's love to the lost. The Scriptures display the story of how God calls his people to bring the message of reconciliation to those who have rejected him. His unconditional love and compassion may spare nothing to them, and medicine is certainly an important part of his mission.

Millions of people all over the world are excluded from adequate medical care, and many are dying due to shortages of resources and trained healthcare workers. Some conservatives simply blame the nature of the fallen world and the choices that individuals make for themselves. However, Christ turned this upside down through his sacrificial love on the cross and has brought the hope that members of his kingdom will realize complete reconciliation with God, the Creator. Christian medical mission has been one of the best practical instruments of demonstrating God's compassionate love and the truth of the gospel in integral ways, which enables Christian mission to reach out to the most unreached areas as a bridge of

---

128. DeYoung and Gilbert, *What Is the Mission of the Church?* 238.

bringing the message of how relevant and powerful God is. As an essential part of God's mission, Christian medical mission also pursues integral mission and tries to strategize with the principles of community development. Still, there are many opportunities for Christian medical professionals to become involved all over the world despite so many barriers that hinder the gospel message from being shared. Deeper consideration of how Christian medical mission can influence the individuals and the communities more biblically and effectively is very important for God's mission. Christian medical missions should foster Christ-centered compassionate care, which will eventually make Jesus known to the lost who will experience *shalom* through reconciled relationships with him by his redemptive work.

4

Principles and Strategies of Christian Medical Mission in the Arab World

CHRISTIAN MISSION WORK FACES enormous challenges as the world constantly changes at a remarkably rapid pace. At the same time, a variety of new opportunities are presented for Christian mission to meet people who used to live in countries very closed to the gospel as God opens doors in unexpected ways. This recent situation requires Christian missionaries to rethink their work. The revolutionary development of science and technology has impacted Christian mission with the dramatic changes in the strategies of reaching out to unreached peoples. As various types of Christian medical missions have been serving people in different contexts, research about how they have been developing their strategies to meet the needs and what their struggles are will be greatly beneficial to understand current challenges and to suggest ways of overcoming those challenges. Timothy C. Tennent describes seven megatrends that are shaping twenty-first century missions:

1. The Collapse of Christendom;
2. The Rise of Postmodernism: Theological, Cultural, and Ecclesiastical Crisis;
3. The Collapse of the "West-Reaches-the Rest" Paradigm;
4. The Changing Face of Global Christianity;
5. The Emergence of a Fourth Branch of Christianity;
6. Globalization: Immigration, Urbanization, and New Technologies; and

Principles and Strategies of Christian Medical Mission in the Arab World

7. A Deeper Ecumenism.[1]

Understanding these megatrends helps Christian mission shape its current structure, and requires mission leadership members to respond to these changes in biblically appropriate ways. These complex global changes make some traditional ideas about Christian mission invalid in particular circumstances.

The Arab world lies in constant turmoil with disagreement, confusion, and violence. The needs increase as the region is dotted by continual wars, unrest, religious fanaticism, and persecution, and the situation has been getting more aggravated in recent decades. The resulting humanitarian disasters are only topped by the corresponding spiritual catastrophe and hopelessness. The land where the love of God birthed hope for all human kind is now filled with hatred and despair. Local churches in this region, which are God's instrument to witness his *shalom* and love, have seemed powerless for a long time and have continually been recipients of resources from the West to survive. These local churches have been suffering from being a minority secluded from the majority Muslim population. In addition, some countries in this area do not allow any form of churches, while others do under very restricted rules with invisible and visible social persecution.

Nevertheless, during the last decade, some local evangelical churches have been experiencing spiritual revival, which enables them to grasp the mission of God and bring them into the pursuit of missions in the Arab world. It is stronger in some sections than in others, but a number of churches have begun sending missionaries to other Arab countries. In addition, Christian medical mission work has also come into blossom in many places, although it has been limited in its scope. It finds itself in a time of transition as there have been remarkable changes and developments in healthcare systems all around the world. Even in medically underdeveloped countries, especially in the urban sector, many local clinics and hospitals have arisen with advanced medical faculties and facilities. The local governments have been developing their own healthcare systems independently, and local doctor's associations have been pressuring their governments to protect their own profits against any foreign medical activities. These current changes have both pros and cons toward Christian medical mission, but certainly require mission leadership to reshape traditional principles and strategies.

1. Tennent, *Invitation to World Missions*, 18–52.

In this current situation, Christian medical mission work has to find the right niche for God's mission and search for the unique role to play in Christian mission endeavors. It is important to find a way to encourage the growth of something that is indigenous and will be able to bear long-term spiritual fruits. Many of these endeavors have traced and retraced the same steps for decades. There is something that Christian medical mission work should acknowledge and learn about to no longer foster division and disunity in Arab churches. It is critical to find ways of growing the church in the understanding of its task and ability to perform it together. This is particularly momentous for Christian medical mission because it tends to separate itself from the local church due to its professional nature of independence, which cannot be simply criticized.

This research proposes the missiological role of Christian medical mission in the Arab world, predominantly influenced by the Islamic culture and worldview.[2] Based on the previous discussion about the integral mission, Christian medical mission primarily exists to be salt and light to the world through professional medical practices. The missiological foundation of Christian medical missions is to be a faithful Christian presence in non-Christian societies as trustworthy medical practitioners who intentionally seek to position themselves as gospel witnesses, directly when possible but also indirectly, according to the context. This chapter unfolds practical suggestions that may help Christian medical mission professionals strategize to overcome its current challenges and develop healthier structures to continue to serve the lost in the Arab world.

Challenges that Christian Medical Mission Faces, and Suggestions to Overcome Them

Although the Christian mission force, mostly from the Global North, has been playing a key role in advancing the gospel to unreached peoples with a pioneering spirit and sacrifice over the last several decades, sadly it also has planted undesirable influences like unbiblical individualism and

---

2. Pew Research Center reports that the twenty-two countries in the Arab World have the highest percentage of Muslim-majority countries. Indeed, more than half of the twenty countries and territories in that region have populations that are approximately 95 percent Muslim or greater (Pew Research Center, "Mapping the Global Muslim Population").

materialistic prosperity in the mission fields.³ In addition, mission agencies have to humbly reflect on the reality of having built kingdoms of individual mission agencies which disempowered local indigenous churches and their leadership. Inadequate understanding of the local cultures and languages have produced unbiblical contextualization and misunderstandings against the gospel massage as well. Furthermore, for different reasons, protestant churches and missions have become increasingly fragmented and divided, which is never a good example to the global church. Christian medical mission is not able to escape from these condemnations and sometimes seems to exist in the right middle of these problems. Christian medical mission must face matters squarely and confront these challenges boldly in order to be a better instrument of God's mission in the Arab world.

Sustainability

It is undeniable that remarkable Christian medical professionals have provided outstanding care in medically underdeveloped countries for centuries as a fundamental instrument of God's mission. A PRISM survey reports that there were "786 mission hospitals globally, with 883 missionary doctors," which have served "approximately one million and five hundred thousand in-patients and eight million out-patients," as of the year of 1958.⁴ Christian medical mission clinics and hospitals that started with large outside funding raised by missionaries and intended to provide compassionate medical services with free or very cheap medical fees created expense system that are almost entirely dependent on the foreign funds from outside the country. This type of compassionate medical service at many mission hospitals and clinics has been facing unavoidable financial challenges, which create a bottleneck in management. This financial struggle of the Christian medical mission clinics and hospitals is an actual challenge, and Kim shares his experience in Nigeria:

3. Global North and Global South are more favorable terms for referring developed vs. underdeveloped countries. These terms were used by Carl Oglesby in the late 1960s and are being used widely these days. Lemuel Ekedegwa Odeh analyzes these two economic worlds and summarizes the concept of these two terms. He explains four broad indicators distinguishing these two groups of countries: the Global North is typically politically stable, technologically advanced, economically wealthy, and has demographics that trend towards zero population growth, while the Global South is the opposite of these characteristics (Odeh, "A Comparative Analysis," 338–40).

4. Strand, "Medical Missions in Transition," 4.

Added to this is the fact that Nigerian mission hospital buildings are old. With little support from the government, they are struggling to pay employee salaries that have gone up while foreign assistance has dropped. Labor unions or local communities also prevent the reduction of mission hospital payrolls. The government neither provides free land for mission hospitals nor gives them any tax benefit.[5]

It is a common occurrence that many famous Christian mission clinics and hospitals all over the world struggle to continue providing their services. The major challenge that they are facing is the lack of both financial resources and human resources, as they are mostly dependent on foreign supporters. Ruth Maclean reports that even the famous Lambarene hospital, founded by Albert Schweitzer, cannot find enough resources to sustain its services, and is caught in a struggle for control between local authorities and foreign supporters. The local staff was accused of corruption and stealing, while they accused the Europeans of racism and colonial views.[6] The criticism raised in her article should be carefully examined:

> The staff has also changed since Schweitzer's day. One of the criticisms levelled at him was that he did not train enough local doctors and nurses. The hospital keeps its tradition of accepting volunteers from Europe for long or short stints but most of the staff are Gabonese—except the new French director.[7]

Many Christian mission hospitals may face similar fates, unless Christian medical mission groups set reasonable goals and strategies. Many Christian mission clinics and hospitals are located in rural areas to provide medical care for those in greatest need. Because most developing countries experience intensive urbanization, and indigenous medical professionals are accustomed to the advantages of living in a big city, it is becoming more laborious to recruit well-trained indigenous medical professionals for service in rural areas where most Christian mission hospitals and clinics are located. It is natural for families to provide their children with better educational opportunities, and to desire better salaries than mission hospitals can offer. As many Christian medical missions, both short-term and long-term, seek to provide medical care to those in need in rural areas, there

---

5. Kim, "Missionary Medicine in a Changing World."
6. Maclean, "Crisis Engulfs Gabon Hospital."
7. Maclean, "Crisis Engulfs Gabon Hospital."

Principles and Strategies of Christian Medical Mission in the Arab World

is consistent difficulty in establishing a long-term collaboration between Christian medical missions and indigenous healthcare professionals.

The United Nations announced the seventeen Sustainable Development Goals (SDGs)[8] in 2015 as a following step of the eight Millennium Development Goals (MDGs)[9] in 2000 because it recognized the importance of setting up long-term, achievable goals. The SDGs place a strong emphasis on partnership for real and sustainable changes in the world.[10] Though secular in focus, these goals urge Christian mission groups to deeply reflect on what has been done in the last centuries and to evaluate how it can serve individuals and communities as a better instrument for God's kingdom. One of the most important principles for sustainability within Christian medical mission is to build up a partnership with the local healthcare system from the beginning of its establishment and hand over the missions to the local leadership sooner rather than later. This is never an easy task, because there are many obstacles to establishing this partnership. One of these obstacles is that foreign medical missions may be perceived as competitors or intruders to the local medical professionals rather than supporters or assistants. Especially in the areas of honor-shame cultures, local medical professionals may strongly feel insecure and ashamed before the advanced medical skills and technologies that are not familiar to medically underdeveloped countries.[11] Strong resistance against the foreign medical mission force trying to interfere with the local leadership of the underdeveloped healthcare system is frequently observed. In addition, without proper local language and cultural understanding, Christian medical mission will not

---

8. United Nations, "Sustainable Development Goals."

9. United Nations, "Millennium Development Goals."

10. United Nations, "Sustainable Development Knowledge Platform."

11. Guilt oriented- versus Honor-Shame oriented cultures: Christopher L. Flanders compares two distinctive cultural orientations. Although there are certainly personal variations and no "guilt cultures" or "honor-shame cultures" per se, Western culture is more guilt-oriented while Eastern culture is more honor-shame-oriented, as a culture may stress one more than the other. Flanders explains guilt as "feelings of self-condemnation, regret, or remorse about what people have done," which is more related to "their own internal moral compass, the individual conscience," while shame is "a purely private affair, experienced when the self fails to achieve a goal or desired state, which is related more to what others think." (Flanders, *About Face*, 58–64). Hiebert defines guilt as "a feeling arising when people violate the absolute standards of morality and their conscience within themselves," and shame as "a reaction to other people's criticism, an acute personal chagrin at people's failure to live up to their obligations and the expectations others have of them" (Hiebert, *Anthropological Insights for Missionaries*, 212–13).

be able to construct a meaningful partnership in a short period of time, especially when operating from a needs-based approach.

In another aspect, there is a visible possibility that Christian medical missions which have been successfully established may lose their purpose and core values when the ownership of such Christian medical missions is handed over to the local leadership that does not share the missions' biblical values. This is obviously problematic in many Christian medical mission clinics and hospitals. Nevertheless, when the original intention of Christian medical missions is to assist and empower the local health system and is well accepted through intimate relationships built by proper language and cultural understanding, sustainability for the missions is certainly more likely. It may take a longer time to found a sustainable structure for the local healthcare system, but such a structure would be invaluable and strongly influential once established. Throughout the process of implementing medical missions, local medical professionals should not only be trained in their medical practices, but also be challenged with the holistic approach of medicine so that they may be influenced by the kingdom values and the truth of the gospel. This will make Christian medical missions continue to be influential in their communities in partnership with the local healthcare professionals even after the foreign mission force is withdrawn gradually or completely.

Although the rapid growth of medical skills and technologies benefits all human beings, the cost of medical care is obviously getting more and more expensive, and sadly a large number of people cannot afford it. As a matter of fact, Christian medical mission should grasp this reality and accept the limitation that, unlike a couple of decades ago, it will not continually have a positive influence in its local community with resources from outside because the running cost and expenses of its own institutions are growing ever costlier. The global Christian medical mission community carries the burden to continually support these mission clinics and hospitals, so rather than establishing large general clinics or hospitals, building smaller specialized clinics—if it is really needed in the context—may be more effective and manageable in terms of long-term sustainability. This approach would also be safer, as it can avoid double-minded local leadership that may try to take advantage of the properties the mission has created.

Conflicts with the Local Medical and Healthcare System

Christian medical mission groups have to deal with their relationship and function with the local medical system. Although medically underdeveloped and developing countries previously welcomed medical professionals to assist their medical and healthcare systems, now barriers against this influx of foreign medical mission are growing higher because it is perceived as a strong competitor or intruder to the indigenous medical healthcare system. To protect their own medical and healthcare system, many countries' local governments restrict medical practices by foreign-licensed medical professionals. In addition, most of the countries have their own equivalent authorities to the American Food and Drug Administration (FDA) in their government system, which provide a close inspection of medicine brought into the country. All medicines and medical equipment have to be inspected by this government authority, although it is intended to be used to meet the needs of for the marginalized. In this sense, bringing medicine and medical supplies without registration to the local authority of the country can be considered smuggling, which is certainly an illegal activity and is not consistent with the biblical values that all Christian medical missions want to share. Sharing the love of God and the truth of Christ Jesus with the lost cannot justify all possible unethical activities of Christian medical missions. In addition, Christian medical mission groups must reflect on their biblical characteristics toward the local medical and healthcare society which is mostly underdeveloped compared to the nations sending most Christian medical mission professionals. These sending countries or agencies of Christian medical missions are enculturated by "top-down McDonaldization methods of global mission," which "ignore the local worldview, localization and traditional values," according to Johnson, who views this tendency as "modern colonialist tendencies."[12] Good intentions to serve people should not be used to justify all the consequences of illegal activities, which is never a good testimony to the individuals and the communities which Christian medical mission serves.

Sadly, many Christian medical missions have failed to establish faithful local leadership and medical professionals. Because medicine is a complex science that requires extensive education and training, not many Christian medical missions have invested time and energy in this complicated process for the next generation. Rather, foreign medical professionals

---

12. Johnson, "Counterintuitive Missions in a McDonald's Age."

have focused more on treating patients as a means to share the gospel for spiritual fruits. More fundamentally, it has to humbly admit that as a part of the paternalistic attitude characterizing modern Christian mission, foreign medical professionals are responsible for giving no desirable endeavor to raise up indigenous leaders to take over the leadership of the missions. This is also an issue of the attitude that Christian medical missionaries do not trust local partners who should potentially become the leaders of their missions. Some Christian medical missionaries are certainly skeptical about handing over leadership of the clinics and hospitals to the locals, and do not make a practical plan to raise up the next generation. As a result, many of those mission clinics and hospitals have faced serious challenges of transferring leadership to the indigenous leaders in the end, especially when it faces the lack of resources from outside. However, in certain contexts like South Korea, numerous medical missionaries set a good example preparing indigenous leaders, as Kim indicates from the history of Christian medical mission in Korea:

> Indigenous people should assume the leadership of mission hospitals as they gain the ability to do so. When Dr. Stanley Topple left Korea for Kenya in the early 1980s, he left the rehabilitation center in Korean hands. The three-self principle (self-government, self-support and self-propagation), which became a driving force for church growth in Korea, was also successfully applied to Christian medical facilities.[13]

Partnership with mutual respect and trust is the key for indigenous development of Christian medical missions by minimizing any possible conflicts with the local healthcare system. Rather than separating Christian medical mission itself from the local healthcare system, it must pursue practical strategies and plans to build up partnership with the local healthcare system from the beginning of its mission.

As strategies of utilizing medical practices for the benefit of the community are pursued, Christian medical mission must modestly acknowledge that the ultimate responsibility of medical care should lay on the local churches as well as the local medical society and government. Valerie Inchley shares her insight about the role of national professionals and churches related to Christian medical missions provided by professional expatriates:

---

13. Kim, "Missionary Medicine in a Changing World."

The first is the progressive hand-over to national medical professional colleagues, and the other, the increasing responsibility that national churches are assuming for various aspects of medical work. The former is an exciting sequel to the years of training invested, and the latter, an equally exciting outworking of the holistic theology of the younger churches.[14]

Indigenous people in many medically underdeveloped countries tend to make light of their own medical and healthcare system, and do not give much trust to their medical professionals. Instead, they admire Christian mission clinics and hospitals when they experience high-quality medical services and encounter the attitude of Christian servanthood. This is invaluable for Christian witness, and yet this obviously brings a serious dissociation between the local people and their local healthcare system, which is ultimately a poor testimony in the long-term perspective of Christian mission. Local medical professionals certainly feel the dignity of their profession become impaired, and lose healthy self-esteem toward their own people, which can result in animosity toward Christian medical missions and medical professionals. Christian medical mission should try to be assistants or facilitators for the local healthcare system, rather than to be competitors or intruders that may bring distrust into the relationship between the local people and their local healthcare system. It must function more interactively with the local healthcare system so that the gospel message and the kingdom values may influence the local healthcare system for positive long-term transformational changes.

Security and Safety Related to Christian Medical Mission in the Arab World

As political instability, religious intolerance, insecurity generated by globalization, and the recent refugee crisis in the Arab world unfold, ethnocentrism and extremism grow accordingly. Injustice to certain people groups has angered many others in the Arab world. Militant forces in the Arab world have sprung up in recent decades, performing acts of terrorism which are justified as freedom fighting. Suicide bombings as well as other acts of violence have terrorized people not only in the Arab world, but also in the whole world, making peace harder and harder to imagine. Many fundamental Islamic groups influence and recruit the young, impressionable,

14. Inchley, "Medical Mission."

and angry into extremist causes. In this long-standing chaotic situation, there are significant security concerns that the Christian community and churches in the Arab world wrestle with as political and religious forces have come to restrict any Christian missions that engage in proclamation of the gospel message. In certain areas, it is almost impossible to talk about what Christian medical mission does because Christian workers and organizations can be targeted for terrorism or kidnapping. All this means that it becomes harder to do Christian missions in many places in the region where the needs are greatest. This raises a variety of issues such as prayer support, generating financial support, and mobilizing Christian professional workers more widely as churches and Christians are afraid of being involved in the critical incidences. Most evangelical churches in the Arab world have been struggling as minority groups against Muslims, and many Christian missions engaged in the area have relied almost entirely on outside funding.

During the last few decades, security and safety issues became more critical because the direct threat toward Christian mission and local churches has sharply increased in the countries dominated by Islam. Christian mission continually asks itself how to reduce or avoid exposure to risks and prepare for the consequences of faithfulness to God. Christian mission and many indigenous churches in the Islamic context cannot escape from conflict and offense toward the message of Christ. Although the conflict may not necessarily stem from irrelevant behaviors or attitudes of Christian mission, sometimes it obviously comes due to the nature of Christian mission that cannot compromise the gospel and kingdom values. Christian medical mission is in the same situation, although it may be not seen as obvious as direct spiritual ministries, like church-planting and evangelism. All Christian medical missions must follow a well-prepared protocol with close monitoring of the security incidents related to their daily activities in order to prevent any unnecessary exposure to security incidents.

Summary

The challenges that Christian medical mission currently faces are not easy to overcome, yet, simultaneously, they open many new paths that welcome Christian medical professionals to get involved in cross-cultural contexts as medical professors, trainers, advocates, health educators, and health professionals for secular or government organizations. Christian medical mission groups need to make these various opportunities effective platforms of God's mission rather than consistently adhering to the Christian mission clinics and hospitals which serve as a comfort zone for Christian medical professionals. In order to make Christian medical mission approaches more successful and fruitful, they should pursue the competencies that Hurst lists: "Community-based, People-centered, People-owned, Participative, Focuses on targeting the root cause of the problem, Measurable, and Sustainable."[15]

In addition to the purposes of Christian medical mission that provides both physical and spiritual care to the sick, more importantly it should not neglect that it can share the fundamental Christian values within any healthcare system, even those strongly influenced by the essentially secular system or other religious values. This is a more complex issue that challenges Christian medical mission to deeply reflect and wrestle. In spite of humanity's rejection of him, God has instituted his divine plan to reconcile with his creation through Christ Jesus for eternal fellowship with himself. To bring this message into the health system that Christian medical mission serves, there should be a long-standing and holistic plan that facilitates the kingdom values to permeate into the local health system. The debate of the priority over either physical or spiritual care through Christian medical missions is outdated and does not necessarily contribute to Christian mission in many contexts. God's people, like Joseph, Esther, Nehemiah, and Daniel, as well as the early church, lived in the pagan empires of Egypt, Babylon, Media, Persia, and the Roman Empire, and the Bible teaches how these people of God lived a godly life and influenced people in the pagan culture and religions with the kingdom values. Furthermore, God wanted his people to seek the prosperity of these cities (Jer 29:5–6), so the pagans would eventually understand the love of God through the presence and the godly life of God's people among them. Christian medical mission is responsible for developing its strategies and plans in order to provide sustainable changes among the people for whom it provides care more effectively and biblically.

---

15. Hurst, "Best Practices in Compassionate Mission."

Example 1: Christian Medical Ministry at a Local Government Hospital

Background

One of the most important strategies for Christian medical missionaries is to closely work with the local healthcare system to empower local medical professionals. Previously, many countries in the global south welcomed Christian medical missions to come and help their people, but as their medical and healthcare systems develop, foreign medical services are no longer favorably accepted because they become competitors to the local medical and healthcare system. PRISM reports:

> 64.8 percent consider the local government to be highly favorable or favorable to their presence as a foreigner, but 32.3 percent agree that compared to when they first arrived, getting permission to initiate effective long-term medical work for expatriate medical workers is getting harder.[16]

In this sense, approaching a local government clinic or hospital should be considered as a primary way of finding collaboration with the local medical and healthcare system in spite of various obstacles. It may take a longer time to establish a desirable medical and healthcare system under local leadership due to likely resistance to any changes. This is in comparison to the model of Christian medical mission clinics and hospitals, which allow the expatriates to exercise strong leadership from the beginning for well-developed medical and healthcare system, thanks to their experience and resources. Unless there is an intimate relationship built on mutual trust, which may require considerable amounts of time and a humble attitude, local leadership will not respond to the call for change from the expatriates. In addition, in Islamic countries, many expatriates working with non-governmental organizations are considered as a possible threat or intruder to their socio-religious system, so local people view them suspiciously. Furthermore, it is a big challenge for medical missionaries to build up relationships with local leadership that might be involved in corruptive and unbiblical practices. Although these practices are sometimes widely accepted in the local society, many of them cannot live together with Christian values and identity. Christian medical missionaries should deeply think about how to

---

16. Strand, "Medical Missions in Transition," 8.

build an intimate relationship with local leaders without compromising the gospel message.

A medical project started in 2006 at a government hospital in one of the Arab countries that opened a door for several Christian professionals to work with the local medical staff. The hospital provided a hospital wing as a platform of medical and nursing training programs for local doctors and nurses. Local doctors and nurses allocated in the wing as local partners actively took part in managing both the wing and the surgical and nursing training programs. All the training programs were designed to develop their surgical knowledge and nursing skills, which practically benefited them, and to challenge the local staff to transform their worldviews and values of their lives that had been distorted and corrupted by their culture and religion. Their core values of life, in addition to their underdeveloped medical knowledge, were obviously modified through this medical ministry. The training programs intentionally focused on raising the local leadership and were completely given over to the local staff in 2011 after five years of service.

The ministry strategy was to strengthen the skills of the medical professionals and the healthcare system by enabling well-equipped Christian medical professionals to train the local doctors and nurses at the government hospital. Through this medical ministry platform, Christian doctors and nurses were able to minister holistically to the physical, emotional, and spiritual needs of local people, both the local hospital staff and patients. The ministry has certainly impacted local people with the message of the gospel in words and deeds. Many encountered powerful healing experiences both by divine intervention and by medical treatment, which opened Muslims' hearts to the gospel throughout this medical ministry. Intimate relationships between Christian expatriates and the local hospital staff were the key to bringing the truth into their hearts, and to cause a Muslim to make positive inquiries toward the gospel message being communicated throughout the ministry.

Strategic Elements

This ministry at the government hospital followed the model of integrated holistic ministry that would bring sustainable transformation among the hospital staff. The purpose of the ministry was to see transformational changes in the lives of individuals and the hospital community that could sustain themselves and last for a long time. It tried to move the local community from dependency to dignity by challenging people to utilize their full potential through discovering their own capacity and resources on hand. It has been the foundation for scores of initiatives in the Arab world that succeeded where other approaches had failed. The local colleagues, doctors, nurses, and many hospital workers were influenced from increased understandings of medicine, surgery, and nursing to the new level of spirituality through the training programs. This project strived to establish a model of compassionate, counter-cultural Christian presence and witness in addition to a high standard of ethics and medical professionalism. The expatriate staff tried to integrate Christian values into the training programs, and the project brought about results which would have a multiplying effect. Because medical and surgical needs were immense in this area, the local hospital staff and patients recognized that this project definitely had met their needs. After the local surgical and nursing staff was exposed to training programs provided by qualified foreign teaching staff and overseas training hospitals, they showed a strong desire to take part in the training program and develop themselves.

During the last two years of the project (from the middle of 2009 to early 2011), the focus shifted towards leadership development to make the project self-sustainable by the local staff. More local surgical and nursing staff who were willing to learn and participate in the project were recruited. Through the work demonstrating Jesus' love and compassion as well as Christians' integrity, some of the local staff and patients started asking various questions about Christianity, and some embraced the gospel. After 2011, the nursing training committee consisted of the local nurses who had successfully finished the seventh Fundamental Nursing Training Program and the third Critical Care Nursing Training Program by themselves, and continued without expatriates' support even in light of a very unstable political situation in both the country and the hospital in 2012. They were also asked to help other hospitals in the city start these programs in those hospitals. In addition, all the local nurses in the nursing training committee trained were appointed as head nurses in other wings at the hospital even though many of them were still young in age. The hospital recognized them as integrated, faithful, and better equipped nurses to take the higher positions and to bring transformational changes to other departments in the hospital.

Principles and Strategies of Christian Medical Mission in the Arab World

There were many opportunities for sharing the Christian faith while living and working among local people as a part of sowing seeds. When the local staff became seriously interested in the gospel, they were introduced to another team which shared the gospel more deeply with the local believers. When local people came to learn more about the Scriptures, the seed sowers connected these local seekers to the underground churches with a process of evaluation for their genuineness. Because the country is one of the most conservative Islamic countries and does not allow any activities proselyting to the Christian faith, most Christian workers got resident permits through either humanitarian aid or business platforms. Church-planting teams in the country consisted of individuals who were directly but secretly involved in Bible studies and local underground worship services, and a couple of medical staff were also part of these church-planting teams. This was done cautiously so as not to bring unnecessary persecution to the underground churches and the teams. Most Christian workers in the country are considered seed sowers as more than 90 percent of local people belong to unreached people groups and have not heard the gospel before. A team-based approach is more effective in terms of both medical training and sharing the gospel in conservative Islamic countries. Through the team ministry, the local staff learned the kingdom values of love, fellowship, honesty, compassion, and integrity. The mission strategy of making Jesus Christ known through integrated ministry, in partnership with the global church, among local people, was shared with the expatriate medical professionals and other church-planting missionaries. By placing Christians with skills in these areas to serve individuals, churches, and communities holistically, they played an essential role of being the real salt and light of the communities extensively ruled by the enemy. This project enabled the local workers and the expatriates to work together to address the physical, emotional, and spiritual needs of the local people. The vision throughout this project was to positively influence all the individuals who were involved, from the local staff and trainees to patients with compassion and integrity. Furthermore, this project strengthened local underground churches in many ways, such as providing better healthcare for their families and relatives and better ideas about how to live as a committed Christian for his kingdom. This project certainly increased the potential for the spread of the gospel and the growth of the church in the region.

Shalom: God's Ultimate Purpose for the World

Various Training Opportunities for the Local Medical Staff

Every year, local doctors and nurses chosen through training programs were invited to affiliated hospitals in Korea for their overseas exposure to a more developed healthcare system at clinics and hospitals. The doctors and nurses who visited Korea came to be strongly motivated to develop their work at the hospital after returning. They said they were greatly impressed by how well-organized and developed the medical care system in the affiliated hospitals in Korea was, as well as by the devotion of the Korean medical professionals who cared for patients just like their family members. Most of the local staff used to complain of poor supplies and resources in their hospital because of the underdeveloped condition, but their attitude shifted to a strong vision to develop their hospital services for the poor of their own country. They found their real identity as medical professionals called to help the sick. They presented many practical ideas and a strong desire to help the situation of the hospital, and their attitude changed a lot in a very positive way. In addition, the local staff set a rule to stop any unethical behaviors such as bribery, which was one of the most common endemic practices related to the medical and nursing work at government hospitals. It was common for nurses to give injections and surgeons to do operations only when they received a certain amount of money.

From another perspective, churches and Christian medical professionals in Korea actively participated in these overseas training opportunities for the local staff with the thought of being part of God's mission in their own medical practice and ministry. Even without deeper cultural understanding and communication in the local language, hospitality, practical medical training, and helping the local staff put it to practice shaped their understanding about the cross-cultural mission which might be happening far away. This brought great joy to those who helped the local trainees as they were able to be part of God's mission in their own workplace.

More importantly, the project provided opportunities for global churches to participate in holistic medical ministry. By bringing the committed Christians with professional skills to serve individuals and communities holistically in this area, God demonstrated his love and truth to both the local people and the expatriates participating in the project. Various short-term medical teams offered seminars and workshops related to the ongoing surgical and nursing training programs every year. As the short-term teams utilized their specialties more effectively for the local medical professionals, the level of the short-term team satisfaction was very high, compared to the random one-time primary care that most of short-term medical missions do. Rather than a lot of patients being treated by foreign medical professionals, patients were carefully selected in advance for the local doctors to have more chances to practice and learn from short-term teams. The local doctors and nurses greatly appreciated the contribution from short-term teams and showed their willingness to learn from them, which demonstrated the importance of partnership between the local healthcare professionals and the Christian medical mission force for transformational and sustainable changes. The patients who were not treated by short-term teams received good care from the local professionals with continual assistance by long-term medical expatriates on the scene after the short-term teams left. The short-term teams effectively empowered the local healthcare system and strengthened the relationship between the long-term medical missionaries and the local medical professionals. The effective collaboration between the long-term missionaries and the short-term mission force has brought kingdom values to medical practices as well as medical excellence to the local healthcare system with appreciation from both sides.

Summary

Many local hospital staff working with the project used to say that there was no hope in their hospital and country because of the underdeveloped administration system, corruption, and poor resources. Since they had little resources in their hands, all that they were interested in seemed to be material resources for better medical practices. They blamed their government for lack of support and thought that their medical service would instantaneously improve when they had resources like advanced medical equipment and facilities. Through the project at the hospital, many of the hospital staff and leadership were transformed by the kingdom values and principles and challenged themselves to be more equipped through training programs. They came to realize that medical instruments and equipment may be useless if human resources are not well-developed and trained for utilization of those material resources. The training programs at the hospital enabled the local leadership to continue to develop their own system and to extend to the healthcare network in their city. The hospital leadership received honor and praise from the medical communities as well as many patients who were taken care of at the hospital, which encouraged them to grow continually and independently.

Example 2: Medical Ministry for Refugees Residing in Lebanon

Background

The recent refugee crisis in the Arab world has brought serious hostility between different ethnic and religious groups. This crisis is not only in the Arab world, but also in European countries and North America, due to the fact that the ethnic background of refugees has changed tremendously over the past several decades, thus growing hostility and fear against refugees from the Arab world. Ongoing conflict that has been tearing apart Syria and Iraq requires urgent care. The church must show the love of Christ since this conflict has created millions of refugees and displaced people. Crises have been ravaging the Arab world since 2010, and the catastrophe of the refugee crisis from these ongoing wars and civil unrest is observed in Yemen, Syria, Iraq, and many other neighboring countries. Other countries around the world have also seriously been affected directly or indirectly by the wars in the Arab world and the refugee crisis. Nasser Yassin reports:

> The Syrian crisis, in its magnitude, intensity, and protracted nature, has amplified a new wave of anti-immigrant and anti-refugee reactions and sentiments in Syria's neighboring countries and in the Global North. It is the largest humanitarian tragedy and the biggest displacement crisis since World War II.[17]

Although forced migration and displacement are not new in the region, no one could have imagined such extensiveness of scale before, and the sheer magnitude of the refugee crisis is overwhelming. Furthermore, the spread of terrorism shakes the globe as disquietude prevails on every individual. Therefore, the fragility of the society as well as the gigantic scale of basic human needs to survive in the region have strongly influenced both Christian mission efforts and the humanitarian sector.

The United Nations High Commissioner for Refugees (UNHCR) reports that 65.6 million people are currently forcibly displaced worldwide,

---

17. Yassin, *101 Facts & Figures on the Syrian Refugee Crisis*, 9.

and the number of refugees is calculated as 22.5 million.[18] According to the "Syria Regional Refugee Response" of UNHCR, the number of persons fleeing Syria totals more than 5.6 million, and all of these people are residing either within official refugee camps or among people in host countries as semi-permanent migrants.[19] In addition, there are 6.5 million internally displaced Syrian refugees within Syria, including 2.8 million children. This is figured as "the biggest internally displaced population in the world."[20] Most refugees in the region, including Syrian refugees, are experiencing exhaustion of resources after a life of long-term displacement, which results in serious problems from basic foodstuff for nutrition, clothing, and housing to education and healthcare. Above all, refugee children as well as elderly people are the most vulnerable. Yassin mentions in his report:

> Syrian refugee children's health is particularly affected by the interaction of numerous influences. Many are living in informal settlements and substandard shelters with minimum hygienic practices and unsanitary living conditions which have augmented their risk of infectious diseases.[21]

In addition to the refugees themselves, the local governments of host countries as well as international organizations have been struggling from this challenging situation. This extensive refugee flux has changed the whole nature of states and communities in the region; therefore, Christian medical mission organizations must develop constructive strategies to respond to the situation of refugee crisis in order to share the message of *shalom* through integral missions.

Strategic Elements

As the massive exodus of Syrian and Iraqi refugees continues to escalate, Christian medical missions are stepping up efforts to alleviate suffering and to bring hope in the midst of desperate circumstances. The refugee crisis demands large-scale humanitarian assistance, especially in the areas of relief, healthcare, and basic education for children, which create many

18. United Nations High Commissioner for Refugees, "UNHCR: Figures at a Glance."
19. United Nations High Commissioner for Refugees, "UNHCR: Syria Regional Refugee Response, Operational Portal: Refugee Situations."
20. United Nations High Commissioner for Refugees, "UNHCR: Syria: Internally Displaced People."
21. Yassin, *101 Facts & Figures on the Syrian Refugee Crisis*, 68.

Shalom: God's Ultimate Purpose for the World

opportunities for Christian medical mission to serve. The end vision for this ministry is to see a movement of refugees from Syria and Iraq praising God and telling the nations of his glory. This medical mission seeks to empower a church-planting ministry among the refugees by providing excellent, professional medical services to meet their physical, emotional, and spiritual needs. It also tries to equip refugees with skills to improve their healthcare for their own physical needs. High standard professionalism in the works and relationships are always pursued through empowerment among local communities. To bring about transformation both in personal life and in communities, Christian missionaries aspire to positively influence individuals through the compassion and integrity of Christian mission. In addition, they have initiated strong partnerships with local Lebanese evangelical churches and Christian organizations, and developed Lebanese teams that facilitate holistic care within refugee communities. As many evangelical churches have long existed in Lebanon, Christian mission organizations have a different role in this context as compared to the country where I served previously, where there is no visible church and the invisible church faces exorbitant persecution. The World Council of Churches reports: "Lebanon was Christianized as of the first century AD. With the Arab conquest and Islamization in the seventh century, it became the area with the highest proportion of Christians in the Middle East."[22] It is essential for Christian medical missions to perform their work with local churches in any ways possible. More ministries should be partnering with the local churches and Christian organizations involved in the relief and development work in the areas of health, education, economic, vocational training, environmental, community development, and so on, as advocates for the rights of the oppressed, vulnerable and marginalized. With the intention to transform people and society by building and supporting sustainable projects, Christian medical missions play very important roles in the partnership with local churches.

Programs of the Medical Ministry

Elpis HOME Clinic[23] was inaugurated in 2014 as a medical mission platform for refugees as well as the marginalized in Lebanon, and it has

---

22. World Council of Churches, "Lebanon."

23. Elpis is a Greek word, ἐλπίς, meaning hope, and HOME stands for Health Outreach to the Middle East, and is "a Christian, non-denominational organization that

become an effective medical ministry. It has been trying to provide excellent primary medical care for those in need. In addition to the stationary Elpis HOME Clinic, serving the highly populated area of refugees in Beqaa and the eastern part of Lebanon, mobile clinic activity takes the healing message of Christ as well as primary medical care to the neediest of the population in isolated areas. This mobile clinic travels to extremely poor areas packed with Syrian refugees which lack medical institutions, offering quality healthcare to people in need. Most of the poverty-prone refugees are deprived of education and therefore have little knowledge about how to maintain good health and its benefits in life. To live as a refugee, a disease-free and healthy lifestyle is essential. Therefore, to address the needs, Elpis HOME clinic feels the urge to educate the underprivileged and uninformed about health rights and services through health education experts. The primary objective of this health awareness program is to keep people disease-free through prevention and education about adopting a healthy lifestyle and preventing unwelcome diseases.

Another important program of this ministry is to visit patients' homes, which provides several advantages. Patients who do not come to the clinic due to various reasons are taught how to take care of themselves at home and are encouraged to come to the clinic for their advanced healthcare. A visiting nurse and her staff take care of family members by providing a teaching session of preventive medicine in their own setting where they are more at ease. Furthermore, gaining a greater understanding of the family's current living circumstances helps those families build up intimate relationships with caregivers. Considerable physical and emotional support has also been found in the visiting staff-patient alliance. As the bond of trust between patient and physician is vital to the medical care process, this medical ministry offers opportunities to significantly improve the quality of life and health status of refugee families.

From its beginning, Elpis HOME clinic has been offering a counselling program by a local Christian psychologist to support families that are struggling from serious emotional and spiritual issues. The UNHCR statistics shows that more than forty percent of refugees from Syria are children up to eleven years old,[24] many of whom have experienced pro-

---

exists to offer physical and spiritual healing to people in need in the Middle East by providing medical care and education." "Health Outreach to the Middle East (HOME)."

24. United Nations High Commissioner for Refugees. "UNHCR: Syria Regional Refugee Response: Inter-Agency Information Sharing Portal."

found loss and survived devastating events that can seriously impact their emotional development and long-term functionality. Their journeys from their home countries to Lebanon are often rife with violence and instability, and are characterized by long periods without the most basic childhood needs met, such as proper nutrition, housing, and education. Despite the extreme adversity that they face, some children and their families demonstrate profound strength and resilience in their survival strategies, coping mechanisms, and abilities to adapt within what are often completely unfamiliar environments. Nevertheless, the intense psychological and spiritual pressure deep within their hearts must not neglected. The counseling program for these vulnerable families is only beginning to understand the full impact of armed conflict, displacement, and resettlement on children's development and overall well-being. The counselling program tries to help refugee families learn to cope with their emotional and spiritual issues. This ministry provides important resources in the lives of these refugee children and their families and tries to enhance society's understanding of their experiences and needs.

Summary

The medical mission for refugees residing in Lebanon has been responding to urgent needs in the region. Through the compassionate care for refugees facing desperate needs, it provides relationship-based holistic medical care, and various programs of the medical mission create many opportunities for refugees to experience the love of God and to encounter the gospel. In addition, one of the most important roles of the medical mission in Lebanon is to support local churches that are actively involved in the ministry for refugees and the marginalized. Collaboration with local churches should be put as top priority of the medical mission as medical professionals help local churches to build up trust and intimate relationships with people. The medical mission cultivates the kingdom culture of love, compassion, integrity, and righteousness. Furthermore, this will continue to encourage Arab Christian medical professionals to cast a vision of God's mission in the region and provide a place of collaboration with the global church in reaching out to the unreached people groups in the Arab world.

Interview Analysis: Medical Missions
(Christian Mission Clinics and Hospitals)

This analysis is based on interviews with five Christian medical professionals working in the Christian mission clinics or hospitals in the Arab world. The interviews were conducted by either email or face-to-face interview. These brief interviews reveal the challenges and the opportunities of medical missions in the Arab world in order to shape new principles and strategies for Christian medical mission on the basis of understanding the current situation.

All five interviewees have more than eight years of experience working at a Christian mission clinic or hospital. Only one physician has been involved in training local Egyptian doctors, although most beneficiaries of medical services are Muslims. The main purpose and goal of the other four physicians are to serve the poor and Muslims with professional, compassionate medical care. The main source of running expenses for the ministry can roughly be divided into an external foreign fund of donations and internal income, mainly from patients and local churches. As Christian mission clinics and hospitals try to help the marginalized in the community, their income from patients cannot cover all expenses in most cases. One physician indicates that his mission hospital sustains itself on a day-to-day basis with medical fees paid by patients, and, in his opinion, this may be applied to most Christian mission clinics and hospitals in the region. They seem to have a trifling profit themselves because they used to be highly dependent on external funding sources to maintain and develop, which have mostly been decreased or discontinued. One of the hospitals tries to extend their medical services by constructing new buildings with external funds graciously given by donors, but they must have a constructive strategy to maintain and continually develop as the ministry is grows larger and more difficult to manage.

At the Christian mission hospitals where the interviewees work, one of the main challenges is to recruit younger medical professionals because a hefty patient load demanding a heavy labor of physicians and lack of advanced medical equipment hinder quality of training for them to become better specialized. This is a vicious cycle prohibiting competitive medical services, and although these trainees become better physicians after the training period, local Christian doctors struggle to find positions at more well-known hospitals dominated by Muslims. Christian mission clinics and hospitals hardly obtain well-trained specialists because they cannot provide adequate salaries, which is the most serious long-term challenge. Some can commit themselves to be part of the missions in theory or vision, but reality reveals that poor salaries might not keep them for a long time, especially in medical missions. One interviewee states that Christian medical mission organizations have to make a practical plan to recruit highly-qualified specialists with satisfactory financial support, which will eventually bring more patients and trainees to the missions. Another interviewee emphasizes the importance of the hospital leadership and administration system, which will manage the missions more cost effectively and efficiently.

Training programs at the Christian mission clinics and hospitals should be well established and maintained so that experienced medical faculty may continue to have opportunities of influencing the medical staff and the next generation. This also gives a sense of Christian community which enables the committed Christian medical staff to hold fast to the same vision in spite of many challenges. Unfortunately, two of the interviewees cannot give the principles and strategies of the medical missions in which they are involved. Many Christian medical missions in the Arab world seem to struggle with a paucity of principles and practical goals for their medical missions, evident as all of the interviewees have only given very broad ideas. This suggests that each medical mission should set more specified principles and strategies in their context for all the staff to follow. Throughout its development, these principles and strategies should be examined regularly and be reformed as needed according to changes of the situation. Without holding comprehensive visions, principles, and strategies in common, Christian medical mission will not be able to successfully serve those in need for a long time.

Survey Analysis: Short-Term Medical Mission

An online survey about short-term medical mission was conducted over a three-week period in March 2018, and twenty-three people replied. The responders included seventeen physicians, one oriental medicine doctor, three nurses, one nursing student, and one Bible teacher. Only one of them participated in short-term missions within their own country, Korea, while the rest have taken part in short-term medical missions in cross-cultural contexts. Nine of them have participated in more than ten trips, which reflects the fact that they have a lot of experience and

Principles and Strategies of Christian Medical Mission in the Arab World

thoughtful ideas about short-term medical missions. Forty-seven percent of the respondents(eleven of them) mentioned that their motivation to be part of the short-term medical missions was from the request of their faith communities, including churches and Bible study groups, which means that faith communities play a very important role in recruiting medical professionals to short-term medical missions. The other half answered that their motivation was to be part of God's mission by serving people.

Respondents' opinions of how short-term medical missions impact health issues of the local community varied, and the majority said that it had helped the ministries of missionaries and local churches in terms of sharing God's love and the gospel message. Four people firmly mentioned that there had not been much help to the local healthcare system, while three people thought that their missions had contributed by health promotion through health awareness programs and medical screening. One responder interestingly clarified: "Positive impact on direct beneficiaries of medical care, but negative effect to the local healthcare system." The main reasons why their short-term team has not made an important impact were:

1. Lack of medical equipment and facilities in host areas as well as lack of understanding of the local culture and health-related circumstances,
2. The tendency toward a one-time event because the team visited different locations without consistency, and
3. Time limitations that did not allow the team to build relationship with local people and to follow up patients who need consistent care for their chronic illnesses.

Two respondents mentioned that a lack of collaboration with local healthcare systems was the reason for limited influence of the short-term medical team. The encouraging fact is that seventeen responders indicated their short-term medical teams did interact with the local care providers in their services, which include both Christian medical mission clinics or hospitals and the local healthcare system, while eight answered that there was not any interaction with the local healthcare system.

The main reasons that their short-term medical missions failed to meet the needs were:

1. Lack of preparation to grasp the local circumstances,
2. Lack of consistency, and

3. Lack of time and capacity to take care of complicated and chronic illnesses.

To overcome these problems, many suggested that the short-term medical missions should develop ways to collaborate with local public healthcare centers or hospitals, which will then be able to provide important information about local circumstances before the team goes as well as better medical equipment and facilities that the short-term teams can utilize. Better ways of organizing short-term medical missions should include training opportunities for local healthcare professionals to sustain better ways of healthcare that the short-term teams bring for their own people. Another important suggestion gleaned from the answers is to make a very practical plan of consistent visits to a certain area that helps everyone build up intimate relationships between short-term teams and the local health communities. Through these relationships, the short-term teams will be able to impact individuals and communities more positively and effectively with better preparation on the basis of close ties and proper communication. An interesting tactic suggested by one respondent is to develop a remote care system that may enable the short-term team and its medical professionals' network in their home country to continue providing medical care needed for chronically ill patients or complicated cases for whom the short-term team could not provide a care on the spot.

The expectation of the short-term medical teams toward local churches seems simple and plain:

1. Providing medical and spiritual care for those who have come to see the short-term medical teams even after the team leaves,
2. Providing venues for medical practice and connecting local people to the team, and
3. Translation, logistics, and administration.

These three answers indicate that local churches are encouraged to approach their healthcare system to connect it with the short-term medical teams. Nineteen responders (82.6 percent) answered that they were planning to get involved in short-term medical missions again in the near future, which is a great encouragement. At the same time, the leadership of Christian medical missions should feel responsible for developing better strategies to facilitate these short-term medical mission desires. Most of these responders believe that the short-term medical mission plays an essential role in God's mission, and they are eager to utilize their medical professions to share his love and message. There are negative impressions about the short-term medical missions to consider:

1. Lack of consideration of the local culture with inappropriate attitudes such as paternalism and a needs-based approach,
2. Abusive usage or misuse of medicine without proper diagnosis, and
3. Dependency created by the mission force.

When medicine is used as a part of Christian mission efforts in a different cultural and medical context, it should be carefully planned to avoid any adverse effect to the local community. This survey is greatly beneficial to understand various experiences and opinions from the participants in order to suggest better ways to develop short-term medical missions.

Short-Term Medical Missions and Their Functions

Short-term Christian missions have been an important part of Christian cross-cultural mission to both mission fields as well as the global church.[25] Remarkable development of transportation and telecommunication has enabled this new generation of the Christian mission force to travel around the world with a passion to share the love and the truth of God. Corbett and Fikkert summarize:

> The phenomenal growth of short-term missions (STMs) over the past decade is accompanied, or fueled, by much positive press. Reports claim that STMs accomplish much in the host community and have a positive impact on those who go, especially in terms of their becoming further engaged in missions through giving and becoming long-term missionaries.[26]

Through short-term Christian mission, a new generation of the global church is more actively involved in and exposed to the spiritual and physical needs of the unreached people groups in cross-cultural contexts. In addition, those who have professional skills and experiences desire to utilize them in effective ways for people in need overseas while they are mainly living in their home countries. God certainly uses this new generation of the Christian mission force to boost significant changes in people's lives.

25. Livermore, *Serving with Eyes Wide Open*, 21–22.
26. Corbett and Fikkert, *When Helping Hurts*, 151.

Modern Christian medical missions can simply be divided according to the time period of service to the categories of long-term and short-term medical missions, both of which contribute largely to medically underdeveloped countries. Short-term medical missions can be utilized effectively to meet the needs in places where local medical services are not available and contribute to Christian mission in a variety of ways.

However, short-term medical missions should humbly acknowledge that it has also created multi-faceted adverse effects within the local communities that it serves. Corbett and Fikkert indicates:

> The core problem with STMs to poor communities is that STMs tend to reflect the perspective of poverty as deficit, the idea that poverty is due to the poor lacking something.[27]

In addition, most short-term medical missions occur in contexts that require development projects, rather than relief or rehabilitation, and follow the strategies of relief or rehabilitation in those contexts irrelevantly. Many problems that short-term medical missions have caused for local communities are serious. Without proper laboratory tests and radiologic equipment, it is a great challenge for physicians to make a correct diagnosis. Misdiagnosis with little understanding of language and culture is evidently common, which may cause harmful complications or side effects from the prescribed medicine or treatment. If a short-term team provides medicine brought from their home context for the chronic illnesses like hypertension and diabetes, the patients may not be able to find the same medicine after consuming what is given by the team. In most countries, medical practices by foreign physicians as well as medicine brought in by the team are against local government law and regulations, which is not consistent with biblical values that a Christian short-term team is supposed to bring to the local communities. Without realization, a short-term medical team may break rapport between the local healthcare system and the local patients. In many medically underdeveloped countries, foreign physicians and medical teams are highly respected in comparison to local healthcare workers, which creates a negative effect in the local communities once the foreigners have departed. The impacts and consequences of short-term medical missions are seldom evaluated by healthcare professionals; rather, evaluation simply reflects with numbers of patients for whom the team offered medical care. Accordingly, Arnold Gorske lists thirty-three reasons that "patients are at

---

27. Corbett and Fikkert, *When Helping Hurts*, 155.

much greater risk of serious harm from drugs in the short-term mission setting."[28] Christians who are willing to participate in short-term missions certainly do not want to harm people and communities in the mission field, but sometimes they face unintended harmful consequences in their ministries. Especially in the cross-cultural context, there are many possibilities of seeing these unforeseen undesirable consequences regarding medical missions. Corbett and Fikkert rightly assert:

> Unfortunately, STM teams are generally in needs-based mode, bringing their knowledge, skills, and material resources to poor communities in order to accomplish a task as fast as possible. Indeed, there is not even time for the STM teams to identify existing resources in the recipient communities. As a result, paternalism rear its ugly head, and we undermine local assets and increase poverties of being, community, and stewardship.[29]

Kind, well-intentioned people with a desire to help those in need are not enough to bring biblical transformation in the local community, and, moreover, they might be misused or abused in various contexts. It certainly requires quite a long time to come to know and understand the context in which Christian missions are working, but the fact that this long-term endeavor can possibly reduce harmful and undesirable consequences should be kept in mind.

Jennifer Bido reports on the result of interviews about how a short-term medical mission trip called "Operation Walk Boston" in the USA visited a Dominican hospital and brought meaningful changes to both the short-term medical mission team and the host hospital in Dominica. Bido finds that "cultural norm and organizational structure are important determinants of program sustainability."[30] One of the sustainable changes at the host hospital in Dominica is "an evolution in nursing culture" with "greater independence in decision-making," and the observable obstacles of changes are "language" and "organizational hierarchy."[31] In addition, this short-term mission trip positively impacts the American participant's

---

28. Gorske, "Harm from Drugs in Short-Term Mission," 7–16. The thirty-three reasons include: lack of knowledge of patients, inadequate medical records, not enough time for obtaining patients' medical history, unreliable medical laboratory test, poor equipment and facilities, proper communication due to poor understanding of local language and culture, noncompliance, and so on.

29. Corbett and Fikkert, *When Helping Hurts*, 158.

30. Bido, et al., "Sustainability Assessment," 944–49.

31. Bido, et al., "Sustainability Assessment," 944–49.

medical practice with "better appreciation for different providers' roles and for managing cost in a resource-constrained environment."[32] As this research indicates, short-term medical missions always have to consider the bidirectional influence to both participants of the short-term team and the local host medical organizations with better preparation and plans, which will bring meaningful changes to the local communities.

Medical mission tends to build its professional force of mission without close relationships with local churches and other mission agencies because medicine is a relatively complex profession compared to other types of missions. These characteristics make medical mission isolated, and it has its own types of secondary spiritual activities. In addition, medical missions tend to take the needs-based mode rather than the asset-based mode because discovery of local assets and strategic development plans without building up a close relationship with the local healthcare system and local churches are almost impossible. It is a fundamental truth that Christian medical mission should work together with local churches as well as global churches and established mission foundations that will be able to sustain partnership. Glenn Schwartz's study suggests best-practice principles should be developed for the long-term healthy impact on the communities.[33] Melissa K. Melby and others evaluated short-term experiences that medical students take part in with overseas educational programs, and suggested ethical principles for these short-term experiences, which gives insightful guidelines for short-term medical missions:

1. skills building in cross-cultural effectiveness and cultural humility,
2. bidirectional participatory relationships,
3. longitudinal engagement that promotes sustainable local capacity-building and health systems strengthening, and
4. embedding within established community-led effort focused on sustainable development and measurable community health gains.[34]

These principles cannot be easily obtained immediately, but require much effort and time. As these principles can minimize harmful consequences and maximize desirable bidirectional benefits, all the short-term medical

---

32. Bido, et al., "Sustainability Assessment," 944–49.
33. Schwartz, "Short-Term Medical Missions," 27–34.
34. Melby et al., "Beyond Medical 'Missions,'" 1–6.

missions ought to commit themselves to follow these principles. In the same vein, Robert H. Munson also asserts four goals in medical missions from his research regarding the short-term medical missions in Philippines: "R.E.A.L. for Right motives, Effective partnering, Active community participation, and Long-term strategy and planning."[35] His comment challenges short-term missions' participants to think more deeply about how they should utilize their professional gift for the mission of God:

> Medical Missions and the broader long-term ministry in a community is a spiritual work. The ministry is God's ministry, not our own. This dimension of the work must never be forgotten in all of the research, evaluation, goal-setting, strategizing, and training involved in the activity. However, the spiritual dimension must never be used as an excuse to ignore the more mundane (or mechanistic) components of preparation and implementation of the ministry. In fact, proper planning and strategizing should freely and fully incorporate prayer, meditation, seeking God's will, and other activities that are often considered, rightly or wrongly, as more spiritual. These different activities should be considered not only complementary, but synergistic.[36]

From this perspective, below are suggested some more practical principles for short-term medical missions based on my own experience. Primary care for the local people without any partnership with the local healthcare system should not be prioritized unless the situation truly requires urgent care for relief in a situation like natural disasters or war. Short-term medical missions always need to find a way to empower and strengthen local healthcare systems rather than to do their own medical practices separated from the local healthcare system. The fact that a onetime primary medical service, maybe once or twice a year, hardly contributes to the improvement of the local healthcare system should seriously be considered. Furthermore, when medical services are provided free of charge by short-term medical missions, they are sometimes thought to be poor-quality medical services, although nobody expresses it to their faces, and people do not take medicine in the way instructed by short-term team doctors. This may damage trust and rapport between doctors and patients

---

35. Munson, "Healthy Medical Missions." This article is based on some of the findings in his dissertation, "Strategic Use of Medical Mission Events in Long-Term Medical Mission Events in Long-Term Local Church Outreach: A Consultant-style Framework for Medical Mission Practitioners in the Ilocos Region, Philippines."

36. Munson, "Healthy Medical Missions."

because patients tend to blame recurrence or consistency of their symptoms on the treatment or medicine that they have received, not on their failure of taking medicine, nor on not following the physician's prescription of treatment. This frequently happens for tuberculosis patients, as medicine for tuberculosis is free of charge in most countries, and although they are carefully instructed to take the medicine until complete remission for at least nine months, patients do not consistently take the medicine when they no longer have symptoms. This is one of the reasons that tuberculosis patients often experience a recurrence of the disease and resistance to medicine.[37] Even if the medicine that the short-term medical team provides works well, this positive result might also cause negative consequences in the local healthcare community, as local healthcare professionals can be blamed for their failure of treatment. Short-term medical missions have a great potential for Christian medical missions when they are well-planned and -strategized by the right principles. Many harmful results that short-term medical missions have caused should be humbly reflected on and allowed to become a lesson to current short-term medical missions.

Suggestion of a Healthy Paradigm for Christian Medical Mission

As the socio-political situation in the Arab world has been experiencing enormous changes since 2010, this might be a critical opportunity for Christian medial mission groups to demonstrate the message of *shalom*. Corbett and Fikkert explain three common triggers fostering changes for individuals or groups:

1. a recent crisis;
2. the burden of the status quo becoming so overwhelming that they want to pursue change; or
3. the introduction of a new way of doing or seeing things that could improve their lives.[38]

All of these triggers are observable in the current situation of the Arab world, especially in Muslim communities, and Christian medical missions has to find its role to bring transformational changes with biblical principles

---

37. "TB Treatment—TB cure, how is TB cured, TB drugs, treatment duration," *TB-FACTS.org*

38. Corbett and Fikkert, *When Helping Hurts*, 208.

and strategies. The way of medical missions is focused on providing medical care to the marginalized by founding of Christian mission clinics and hospitals may no longer be a superb strategy in many contexts of modern Christian medical mission. There is a great need to shift the paradigm of Christian medical mission to overcome new challenges that it has been facing. Diversifying platforms of Christian medical missions, which moves from the traditional mission clinic and hospital-based models to partnerships with various local organizations, is absolutely necessary to be more effective and sustainable. The key paradigm shift is partnership that brings all possible relationships into the values of God's kingdom, and through which Christian medical mission may experience *shalom* by sharing the message of the restoration of the whole relationships.

For facilitating indigenous medical missions in the Arab world, important methodologies are suggested in order to experience a vision of indigenous medical mission among Arab Christian medical professionals who leave their own countries to serve Arabs in different countries or ethnic groups in the Arab world. When the first-century church started its missionary ministry, many physical and spiritual events and circumstances lined up to allow this to happen. A parallel set of events and circumstances being prepared by the Lord has lately been observed among Arab Christian medical professionals. These Arab Christian medical professionals, compared to expatriates, better understand the cultural background and language in the region. The Christian medical mission force from the Global North, which has much experience and resources, may still be helpful for the Arab medical missionaries who still need spiritual, academic, social, and financial resources. To bring a healthy network of Christian healthcare organizations and resources into the Arab world, all have to humbly commit themselves to equipping and sending with mutual respect and accountability.

At a medical mission leadership meeting in 2009, an Egyptian pastor who used to be a medical doctor shared his struggle that Egyptian evangelical churches had no theological foundation of the mission of God. Most Christian churches in the Arab world did not have a strong desire for reaching out to the unreached groups, especially Muslims. This could be because of a lifelong tension between Christians and Muslims, and social oppressions toward minority Christians by majority Muslims. Livingstone describes the situation in the Arab world with an example of a Muslim-background believer in Egypt, and gives a challenge for both missionaries and the local Arab churches to confidently engage in missions to Muslims:

> Cultural blindness, historical enmity, and fear of government oppression are among the reasons why many otherwise vital churches do not own the goal of ministry among Muslims. It is not the task of the expatiate to scold them, but to demonstrate that it is possible for Muslims to be genuinely converted and become fully productive members of the church.[39]

There should be an ongoing cooperative effort between multiple Arab Christian organizations and churches. Equipping young medical mission leaders involves demonstrating the reality of the kingdom of God in every sphere of life and medical ministries. An incarnational, integrated approach is at the heart of the mission call, so medical ministries in which they are serving should be whole and integrated. The whole medical mission community should hold different dimensions together as God's given community, such as word, personal life, professional medical skills, and contribution to building the church.

Partnership with Local Church and Christian Organizations

The twenty-first century has brought massive changes in the circumstances of Christian medical mission. The responsibility of world mission is being taken up by the global church as well as the local church. Bendor-Samuel writes:

> Mission in the twenty-first century will increasingly focus on the empowering of local churches for mission. A whole raft of factors will make this not only desirable but inevitable.[40]

However, there is a tendency in professional Christian missions, including medical missions, to build their own institutions to provide compassionate care for the lost who would come to faith through their mission works, while neglecting the important place of the church. Ireland seriously warns:

> The social activism in which they engaged, once divorced from the local church, resulted in a deformed understanding of missions. Believers largely lost sight of participation in *missio Dei* as a cross-cultural endeavor. Instead, they tended to see everything the

---

39. Livingstone, *Planting Churches in Muslim Cities*, 203.
40. Bendor-Samuel, "Discipleship," 112.

church does as mission. It was in this context that Stephen Neill responded saying, "if everything is mission, nothing is mission."[41]

He suggests a two-fold solution to overcome this issue: Christian cross-cultural workers must understand the local church as a compassionate community and should direct their efforts toward the strengthening of this capacity among local churches and local believers.[42] John Stringer also points out the same issue with mission agencies:

> For many mission agencies, Church planting is the keyword. We see individuals and groups who negate the realities of existent Churches and who, with enthusiasm, decide to start their own "Church." When they are able to get a good group of people together, it is clear that they are mostly sheep stealing.[43]

He asserts that this tendency is not only from each individual mission agency or professional mission, but also from the whole culture of Christianity and the evangelical mission community.[44] Nevertheless, Christian mission rejoices together in the reality that God advances his kingdom through the global church and seeks effective partnerships in new mission contexts. Modern Christian mission is committed to the development of local churches and the facilitation of those churches into cross-cultural mission and intra-cultural mission such as the Arabs to Arabs movement. For more effective transformational changes through Christian medical mission, medical and health issues must be viewed from the indigenous perspective. Proper partnerships formed with the local believers and churches for biblical contextualization of the issues will develop better solutions for the issues. Corbett and Fikkert rightly indicate the importance of local participation for poverty alleviation by saying: "Participation is not just the means to an end but rather a legitimate end in its own right."[45] This principle which should also be applied carefully to Christian medical mission in the Arab world. The Arabs to Arabs movement gives a vision of what Christian mission can do now to serve the felt needs in the Arab world. This movement recognizes the potential of the Arab churches and nurtures the development of ministry that is long-term and sustainable by local churches.

41. Ireland, *For the Love of God*.
42. Ireland, *For the Love of God*.
43. Stringer, "Two for a Tango," 19.
44. Stringer, "Two for a Tango," 20.
45. Corbett and Fikkert, *When Helping Hurts*, 136.

Shalom: God's Ultimate Purpose for the World

This new beginning also brings many challenges in areas like funding and partnership. While global ideologies antagonistic to mission are spreading throughout the world, at the same time, it is greatly encouraging to see that the growing global church is pursuing mission.

At this point, the fact that Christian medical mission has a different goal in its practice from local churches should be acknowledged very clearly, although both of them ultimately have the same goal for the mission of God. Johnson gives the example of the Apostle Paul's missionary team, which functioned very differently from the local churches that he planted and nurtured.[46] In this sense, understanding the different roles that Christian medical missions and local churches play is critical, and this will set a clear goal of each in their contexts and lead them to effective partnership. Increasing the effectiveness of partnerships in the ministry of establishing and strengthening the medical ministries and churches in the Arab world is an important goal. Those doing ministries in the Arab world have identified the enormous potential for Christian workers from one country to another in the Arab world, and in this instance, Arab Christians, particularly from Egypt and Lebanon, have been playing a very important role. This is something that should be endorsed and supported, because it is believed that this movement would maximize the effectiveness of medical ministries in the Arab world, too. In the Arab world there are particular needs in medical projects, and Arab Christian medical professionals can meet these needs. There also has been a desire among Christian medical professionals in Egypt and Lebanon to reach out to the rest of the countries in the Arab world. It is essential to more actively seek ways to encourage the growth of this type of indigenous movement to bear long term fruit.

The medical mission network among Christian medical professionals should try to meet each other's needs according to their positions, responsibilities, situations, gifts, and stages in their life and ministry. This network aims to grow all Christian medical professionals as disciples within the context of relationship and community. The desire of the network is to enable individuals to fulfill God's call by using their gifts. Being discipled and discipling others should be practiced intentionally in the network, and all of members of the network should be considered as one family, bound together by relationships of mutual accountability. Everyone should celebrate individuality whilst honoring the responsibilities of belonging to community, being committed to pray for, care for and respect one another. For

---

46. Johnson, "Missions and Compassion."

Principles and Strategies of Christian Medical Mission in the Arab World

last two hundred years, the Christian cross-cultural mission force has been the major human instrument to advance God's mission. In recent decades, parachurch organizations and Christian mission agencies have played a very important role in advancing the gospel to unreached people groups and nurturing local churches all over the world although sometimes there were conflicts between local churches and these organizations.

Almost all countries around the world have visible or invisible indigenous local churches, and there are numerous churches in the Arab world as well, especially in Egypt and Lebanon. Yet, as mentioned above, most Arab churches have been existing without proper understanding of the mission of God for a long time. However, recently, the number of believers in the Arab world who have begun taking part in God's mission has been increasing, which is a great blessing to the global church. Whenever Christian medical mission performs its missions, it should build partnerships with local churches if they exist. Johnson illustrates three common compassion ministry scenarios in the contexts of:

1. where the church exists,
2. where a church-planting team works to start indigenous church, and
3. where a compassion ministry serves as the entry platform.[47]

These scenarios are relevant to the Arab world, and Christian medical mission has to consider the circumstances regarding the nature of local churches where it serves very carefully in order to make its strategies relevant in the context. Phil Bourne suggests three practical reasons that Christian mission has to work with local churches in the Arab world:

1. Christ's mandate was to the Church,
2. the Arab churches can interpret their cultures well, and
3. the majority population, including Muslims, can be reached more effectively.[48]

It is a critical time to consider the challenges and the opportunities of a strong partnership with local churches more prudently so that Christian medical mission in the Arab world can envision a fruitful ministry in the near future. Bourne recognizes a current distinctive feature of the Arab

---

47. Johnson, "Missions and Compassion."
48. Bourne, "The Hand cannot say to the Eye," 199–201.

Shalom: God's Ultimate Purpose for the World

churches, and encourages that Christian mission to the Arab world should commit itself to building an intimate partnership with Arab churches:

> We have much to learn from Middle East Christians and their understanding of Muslims. They have a much better understanding of how Muslims think than we do. Nor is it true any longer that Arab Christians have not invested in reaching out to their Muslim neighbors. If you look at the Evangelical Churches in the Middle East today there is plenty of vision, plenty of enthusiasm and many of individuals who are prepared to answer God's call to serve.[49]

A commitment to the development of local churches and to facilitation of those churches into mission is at the heart of the mission call. As a matter of fact, mission agencies and Christian organizations have neglected the importance of working with local churches, because some of them think that the Arab churches have closed minds toward mission and sometimes have regarded them as an obstacle to accomplishing their task. Some conservative Arab churches try to hold tightly to what they have built in the face of hostile conditions against Christianity. These churches do not want to take any risks to possibly damage their reputation, knowing that involvement in mission may bring serious conflicts with Muslim communities. However, a spiritual revival that has been stirring Arab Christians has been changing the story. More churches have come to realize what they are supposed to do as God's people and are trying to learn how to be involved in God's mission more actively. Muslim-background believers also desire to go to another Arab country for their ministry with assistance of mission agencies. Many of these believers are already in different Arab countries for their jobs and lives, and they are encouraged to share the gospel there.

Christian medical missions should strive for excellence and integrity in every aspect of life and seek consistency between participants' public and private lives. Every Christian medical professional is in the process of being transformed into the likeness of Christ through learning and growing together. All the endeavors to pursue these values in medical missions will bring spiritual maturity to those who are willing to serve the Arab world. God has a special plan for his churches in the Arab world that remain in silence and remain afraid of going out to fulfill God's calling. The Arab churches are awakening and responding to God's calling as they begin to see the needs of the lost in the Arab world through the work of the Holy Spirit. One of the most important strategies at this stage is to raise young leaders

---

49. Bourne, "The Hand cannot say to the Eye," 203.

who are professionally equipped and spiritually influential. Various spiritual and medical training programs are offered for young leaders to be prepared in order to participate in God's mission, and international networks put forth efforts to prepare them in their professions and cross-cultural proficiency in the region. The global church exercises services to facilitate ministries with prayer and pastoral care. Everyone in the community must commit to cooperation in reaching common goals through shared vision and values. Partnerships take place at every level of the ministry and define all relationships with churches in both sending and receiving roles.

In conclusion, Christian medical missions should play a part in God's mission by encouraging and facilitating churches and individuals to respond to God's call to mission. Therefore, Christian medical missions should never work alone, but together with the church as it seeks to determine where and how God determines to use those who become part of his mission. This requires attitudes of humility, openness, and sharing vulnerability. In different contexts, it is obvious that the role of the missionary can be different. Johnson rightly distinguishes missionaries' role in situations where the local church does not exist or is very small versus where it exists or is larger in size.[50] The former situation requires missionaries to focus more on evangelism and church-planting, while the latter urges them to closely work with local churches to grow and grasp the mission of God. However, this categorization does not mean one after the other, as both can always be applied in every situation as ministry grows.

Partnership with Local Secular or Government Healthcare System

Although Christian mission clinics and hospitals face interference by local authorities, especially in the CANs, there are more feasible ways of building up a healthy collaboration with local secular or government healthcare systems. This takes a long time and requires enormous effort, but once it is well established, it will be very influential in local communities and also self-sustainable with locally available assets and resources. Humble attitudes are necessary to build up an intimate relationship with local authorities, even if all the efforts of assisting the underdeveloped local medical and healthcare system are neither appreciated nor recognized in the beginning. Without ignoring the local cultural contexts or criticizing any underdeveloped

50. Johnson, "Missions and Compassion."

medical practices disrespectfully, mutual confidence and dependence must be gained.

Not only should a trustworthy relationship with the local authorities be well established, but also various ministry structures accomplishing the goals according to the contexts should be developed. Luke S. Moon, current professional missionary as a dentist in the Central Asia Region (CAR), shares his strategy of comprehensive disciple-making in the workplace.[51] Through his ministry structure based on community development projects—an "NGO that is fully dependent from foreign funds," "partially self-sustainable," and a "fully self-sustainable business platform"—he has been able to develop a disciple-making professional mission structure that has brought a long-term intimate relationship with his local staff and patients.[52] These various programs have allowed him and his team to disciple the local staff and to serve many patients over the years. Importantly, the local staff came to play a very essential role to develop its sustainability. His community development project with a dental prevention program in a Muslim-dominant village opened doors for the expatriate team and the local believers to reach out to people in this village. In addition, under an international NGO, a dental training program for local dental specialists was developed. Then, with a necessity of a self-sustainable plan, a local NGO was inaugurated. Furthermore, to provide long-term sustainability and development with the local professionals, a business structure was added as a model of business as mission (BAM).[53] This development of professional mission throughout his service over twenty years is impressive and displays important principles and strategies that certainly stimulate Christian medical mission to overcome current challenges. This approach suggests more feasible operations of Christian medical missions. Moon focuses on professional training with discipleship, which transforms the whole life of local professionals throughout the training program. Moreover, this structure provides meaningful personal benefits like finance and professional reputation for the local staff to sufficiently support their families and communities. PRISM emphasizes the importance of training programs as ways of transforming local medical professionals and their society, and concludes in this way:

---

51. Moon, "Cases of Comprehensive Disciple-Making," 192–207.
52. Moon, "Cases of Comprehensive Disciple-Making," 200–207.
53. Moon, "Cases of Comprehensive Disciple-Making," 200–207.

> The purpose of medical missions needs to be re-imagined and clarified, as medical missionaries are increasingly called on to add unique value, engage in more training of national coworkers, and model ingenious and evidence-based strategies of care, not just for individuals but for whole populations and health care delivery systems.[54]

There are certainly some advantages to establishing Christian mission clinics and hospitals to train local medical and health professionals by Christian leadership with the biblical values in a more controlled environment without serious intervention from the local religious and political authorities. However, this strategy of Christian mission clinics and hospitals may possibly separate them from the local medical and healthcare system if they are dependent on expatriate medical professionals to run the institutions. By understanding the possible pitfall of being isolated from the fundamental medical and health issues of local communities, Christian medical mission clinics and hospitals have to set a goal to engage in training the local staff, including medical professionals, actively from their establishment. This active engagement of Christian medical missions in the local medical and healthcare system will be able to challenge entire local communities through various health awareness and professional training programs for long-term transformational changes.

It is time for Christian medical missions to seek more actively for collaboration with the secular and government organizations not only because they can be used as ministry platforms, but also because they need transformation by the biblical values which will continually serve their own people. Even if the government of local health systems have more control over Christian missions or strict restriction of religious activities, Christian medical missions should acknowledge that transformational changes do not come only from religious activities like evangelism, but from holistic integral missions that demonstrate the gospel and kingdom values.

Practical Principles and Plans

As members of a church in the North American context, Corbett and Fikkert suggest an "Action Plan and the Principles of Asset-Based, Participatory Development," utilizing the following stages:

---

54. Strand, "Medical Missions in Transition," 32.

Shalom: God's Ultimate Purpose for the World

1. Foster Triggers for Human Change,
2. Mobilize Supportive People,
3. Look for an Early, Recognizable Success,
4. Learn the Context as You Go, and
5. Start with the People Most Receptive to Change.[55]

These principles are relevant to many contexts of cross-cultural Christian medical missions, too, and based on their wealth of experience, this suggested plan of action and principles may richly contribute to Christian medical mission. As transformational development is never a simple short-term project, but a complicated lifelong journey that turns out as a messy process both in people and in communities, it ultimately depends on the reconciling work of Jesus Christ through the power of the Holy Spirit.

Start Small and Remain Small, but Multiply

If the trend seen in the past twenty years continues, fewer expatriates will be willing and able to serve in mission fields with a long-term commitment. The fate of Christian medical missions in the Arab world is not optimistic when considering its current status of dependence on external resources. The needs will be greater as aggravated by never-ending wars, unrest, religious fanaticism and persecution, and the resulting humanitarian disasters coupled with the corresponding spiritual catastrophe and hopelessness. However, in the same circumstances, a force of dedicated and well-equipped local healthcare workers will be able to minister to their own people more effectively with assistance from expatriate individuals, groups, and organizations. There are still attempts to start medical missions with big plans of clinics, hospitals, or medical schools using a large foreign funds, reasoning that it might help resource-poor communities or underdeveloped local healthcare systems as a means of reaching out to the unreached. As medicine itself is a complex system and is growing more expensive to be well-equipped and maintained, this plan takes a long time to see successful progress, and may produce many undesirable consequences to the local healthcare system. An important suggestion was made by Corbett and Fikkert, that missions should seek for "an early, recognizable

---

55. Corbett and Fikkert, *When Helping Hurts*, 223–32.

success" which may bring joy and encouragement to both project providers and local participants:

> To motivate people, participation typically must be accompanied by something else: early and recognizable success toward the goals that the participants deem to be important.[56]

To achieve this early recognizable success, it is important to start small, according to their suggestion, which also reduces a burden of management and makes the project easily sustainable with local assets.[57] When medical missions become big and complicated, their leadership tends to spend more energy on management of the missions by trying to bring large funds into the missions from outside which will lose a vision of intimate relationship with its participants and communities nearby. From the beginning of the missions' planning stage, sustainability should also be discussed and considered. Hurst rightly says, "Sustainability needs to be discussed during the initial phases of project development and not viewed as a latent goal to be addressed towards the end of implementation."[58] To make this sustainable development of missions more feasible, Christian medical mission leaders should consider the strategy of "start small, remain small, but multiply."

Specialized clinics or hospitals are most able to sustain themselves because their specialized medical services will attract more people to come even with higher medical fees to pay. The more important fact to consider for Christian medical mission clinics or hospitals is to prioritize having highly qualified medical doctors and nurses more than hospital buildings, equipment, or organizations. A model of building general clinics or hospitals may require too much capital to sustain long-term medical and healthcare provision. Therefore, to keep the size of missions small, small-sized specialized clinics should be an alternative model. Small-size specialized clinics have many advantages above a general clinic or hospital. Certainly, they can start with a smaller capital fund and require lower costs to manage. An empathetic investor would be looking to invest their money for a small return and be willing to continue to support these clinics as a platform of medical mission. They can be managed more easily because of the smaller staff, which enables them to provide both better medical services and spiritual influence on their patients. More patients will be attracted because of

---

56. Corbett and Fikkert, *When Helping Hurts*, 214.
57. Corbett and Fikkert, *When Helping Hurts*, 214.
58. Hurst, "Best Practices in Compassionate Mission."

higher quality equipment and facilities providing comfortable treatment, which will generate more income to be self-sustainable. Furthermore, these specialized clinics will be great training platforms for local medical professionals, especially for the younger generation who are often seeking advanced medical training to become specialized physicians. In addition, with an advanced communication system, they can have a strong network with specialized hospitals in other countries to continue to develop and grow academically. In this way, the global network of mission will be able to participate more actively and practically in Christian medical missions within medically underprivileged countries.

Always Place Relationships as the Top Priority and Focus on Community

There is no biblical Christian mission if there is no endeavor to build up intimate relationships with people, because without these deep relationships, the gospel will not be shared suitably. People will never listen with their hearts to what a person says unless there is trust in the interpersonal relationship. Especially in cross-cultural contexts, there will not be any transformational changes through Christian mission without first building intimate relationships with local people. Missiologist Duane Elmer emphasizes: "Most people do not change a lifetime of patterns because someone new comes into their culture and announces that they ought to change their ways."[59] Corbett and Fikkert assert the fact that there are people who are most receptive to change and have developed "the Continuum of Receptivity to Change."[60] Although there are people who are double-minded for materialistic benefits or try to take advantage of Christian mission, through the service of faithful Christians, people will be willing to change their lifelong behaviors and worldviews by the power of the Holy Spirit. Christian medical missions must have wisdom and prudence which keep the ultimate purpose in mind by avoiding mindless generosity and paternalistic offers. It participates in God's mission by living out the relationship with Jesus Christ and helping in the formation of the relationship with local people that it serves. Bendor-Samuel asserts the gravity of relationship in terms of discipleship as a core of Christian mission:

---

59. Elmer, *Cross-Cultural Connections*, 98.

60. Corbett and Fikkert, *When Helping Hurts*, 216–18. "The Continuum of Receptivity to Change" is adapted from Srinivasan, *Tools for Community Participation*, 161.

> The focus of relationship in discipleship is a powerful antidote to the reductionism of mission-by-management, with its language of target groups, strategies, and techniques. It is a powerful antidote to the seduction of transformation by policy and program. At the heart of God's project for renewal are people in living relationship to him, growing in their experience of his Lordship as they learn to obey all that Jesus taught.[61]

Shalom is always based on the relationship restored by God's redemptive mission through Jesus Christ; therefore, without building up a long-term intimate relationship with people, there will be neither discipleship nor Christian mission. God invites his people and church to experience an intimate relationship with him and to be part of his mission, which will bring *shalom* in the heart of his people.

The Church is never individual, but always communal. Transformational change leads people from being individuals who respond to the message of the gospel and experience transformation of their worldview and belief system, to effect change in the community that those individuals influence through their lives. Personal spiritual formation by the Holy Spirit based on an intimate relationship with Jesus Christ should always lead to the desire to reach out to the lost who are still in darkness and bound by the enemy. Christian medical mission influenced by the Western medical education system tends to focus only on personal medical issues and diseases that should be treated and remain individualistic regarding personal encounter of the gospel. If personal changes do not grow into the level of changes in their community, these cannot be considered as genuine transformational changes by the gospel. For instance, changes in personal hygienic behavior through health awareness programs may not see effective results when the surrounding environment continues to be filthy. In this sense, Christian medical mission has to approach both individuals and communities together with proper strategies to bring about widespread sustainable transformation.

Chapter Summary

Human history is proceeding with a divinely-planned trajectory of the Creator, the loving God, who is longing to gather his people for eternal fellowship with himself in the ultimate nature of *shalom*. God is actively at

---

61. Bendor-Samuel, "Discipleship," 105.

Shalom: God's Ultimate Purpose for the World

work in all humanity as well as his creatures, yet sinful and fallen as they are, to be the ones within all of creation which may be labeled as moral, just, and righteous. He is working to draw each human being within every culture to himself, prodding them to seek him so that they may find him. He has instituted a divine plan through Christ Jesus and established the global church to fulfill his promise despite the enemy who incessantly takes mankind away from him. Christian medical missions are called to participate in God's mission, the process by which God is reconciling the world to himself. and to reach out to the suffering in the Arab world. Christian medical mission must reflect on the peculiar features of its part in God's mission, and deeply consider the interrogation that Johnson raises:

> Perhaps we disguise our present-day paternalism with words like poverty alleviation, compassion, holism, human flourishing, social justice, interdependence, global unity, and Christian expansion.[62]

To send missionaries, there should be several practical steps: finding a professional mission agency and a main sending church, collecting financial and prayer supporters as a mission community, and discovering a right platform to perform their ministry. This could be a complicated process, but certainly enables the sent individuals to accomplish the mission without any risk of serious failure. Dietrich Bonhoeffer issued the following challenge before his execution by the Nazis:

> God is not ashamed of the lowliness of human beings. God marches right in. He chooses people as his instruments and performs his wonders where one would least expect them. God is near to lowliness; he loves the lost, the neglected, the unseemly, the excluded, the weak and broken.[63]

Undoubtedly, Christian medical missions have carried out their momentous role in God's mission by humbly taking a position of lowliness while being with the sick and the marginalized, and through which many of the lost have been reached and churches established. Nevertheless, at this moment in history, Christian medical missions should humbly reflect what they have done well and poorly, and with deeper understanding of the current situations, they have to make a more biblical and concrete ways to bring *shalom* to individuals and communities through holistic care and gospel proclamation.

62. Johnson, "Missions and Compassion."
63. Bonhoeffer, *God is in the Manger*, 22.

Conclusion

IN THIS BOOK, GOD's ultimate desire of granting *shalom* to all human beings as well as to the whole creation through the Lord Jesus Christ has been presented. Christian mission work is to respond to God's invitation to his mission that brings forth new creations reconciled through the person of Christ. The context wherein the global church resides has been highly influenced by individualism and primitive tribalism with the pursuit of scientific development, which drives people to hide their pain in consumerism. Moreover, the global church has been facing enormous challenges in sharing God's *shalom* with people in desperate need. People in the violent and despair-filled Arab world need to experience God's compassionate healing power over their brokenness through Christian mission and indigenous churches. Christian missionaries are called to create a place inviting people to experience the grace and forgiveness of God and to have a family where they can find healing for their wounded bodies and souls. His loving and righteous reign will certainly restore his original purpose of *shalom* for the world, and he chooses to do this in partnership with his people. God yearns to make the nations as well as the whole creation reconciled with himself and invites his people to be part of his mission to proclaim this message to the lost. Christian missions should clearly understand its ultimate purpose: that the lost would experience *shalom* through the restoration in all aspects of their lives by the person of Christ. In the same vein, Christian medical missions should strive to fulfill the vision of *shalom* in the embodiment of God's love and justice.

The Arab world is dominated by Islam, and its culture permeates people's everyday lives and sense of values. Narrowing down to the pursuit of health, Islamic teaching, mixed with folk practices for healing, has extended far and wide in the region. Christian medical mission professionals should make every effort to deeply understand the underlying worldviews of these practices so that they may present the power of the gospel in culturally relevant ways. A biblical understanding of divine healing is critically important when confronting Muslims' belief in healing as taught by the Qur'an and traditional Islamic teachings. God's divine power of healing did not fade away after the early church, but has continued playing an important role in his mission to bring the lost into his kingdom throughout history. No one can deny that a power encounter often marks a significant turning point in the evangelization to Muslims, and the following truth encounter transforms the full aspects of their lives as they acknowledge of Christ's Lordship over all creation. In the process of bringing the gospel to Muslims affected by the folk Islam, Christian medical missions may have to engage in power encounters against the spiritual forces of the enemy and has to know how to deal with the pertinent issues in biblically appropriate ways. This, of course, is in collaboration with serving people with the modern, scientific-based medicine. Almighty God, *Jehovah Rapha*,[1] the only true Healer, longs to heal all resentfulness and bitterness in the lives alienated from his love and truth. He is invariably trusted in every endeavor that Christian medical missions make for the lost suffering from the fear of death.

Christian medical missions serve people as an important part of cross-cultural mission as well as evangelism of the global church. The concept of "Integral Mission" has enormously influenced Christian medical mission for defining its role in Christian cross-cultural mission and for applying the principles of holistic care to Christian medical missions in biblically healthier ways. Without biblical insight about the current missions in their cross-cultural contexts, Christian medical mission may face undesirable consequences after all efforts and exhaustion of valuable resources given by the Lord. By critiquing the conventional view of development and setting out alternative biblical approaches of holistic care, Christian medical mission will become a better instrument of God's mission, sharing his compassionate care consistently. Although there are obvious perplexities of implementing the principles within various contexts, Christian medical mission must commit itself to prayerfully search for the best ways based on biblical principles. The principles of the "Integral Mission" studied in this research should be drawn out for practical application in a variety of contexts.

---

1. Jehovah Rapha: "The Lord that healeth" (Exod 15:26). That this refers to physical healing is shown by the context, but the deeper healing of soul malady is implied (Scofield, ed., *The Scofield Reference Bible*).

Conclusion

In considering Christian medical mission endeavors in the Arab world, this research reflects how Christian medical missions have impacted local communities and what challenges they have been facing in recent decades. Because the context of Christian medical missions varies, more specified purposes and goals of the missions are essential for each mission according to their circumstances. Leaders of Christian medical missions should choose the right methods to have clear missiological implications in their contexts. According to the survey included in this research, many Christian medical missions sadly lack clear and shared vision and purpose shared among the leadership and the staff. Without sharing the precise understandable purpose and goals of Christian medical missions amidst staff and leadership, the missions may go astray and lose their ability to accomplish their goals. In spite of the belief that God undoubtedly uses even the weaknesses of mission forces, Christian medical mission must prayerfully reflect on what it has been doing poorly and well in order to pursue the excellency of the gospel.

This book, reflecting my personal experiences of Christian medical missions in very different contexts in two different countries, provides useful insights for development of Christian medical missions in different contexts. One of the most serious challenges that Christian medical mission faces is the sustainability of its missions. The issue of sustainability involves the full spectrum of Christian mission principles and strategies because indigenous leadership development, ownership of missions, the asset-based approach of ministries, and independence with strong partnership must be strategically planed and implemented throughout missions. Christian medical missions should commit themselves to empowering the local health system and to building intimate relationships with local health authorities and professionals, which would help the missions sustain themselves for long-term impact. Because the cost of medical care is getting more expensive, the global Christian church carries the burden to continually support large Christian mission clinics and hospitals which, unlike several decades ago, may not be able to influence people any more with biblical values. Therefore, establishing and running large general hospitals or clinics as a platform of Christian medical mission should not be considered any longer unless there is a definite long-term sustainable plan that fits with Christian mission principles and values. In addition, Christian medical missions must reflect on its biblical characteristics of its every activity and must not allow any illegal or unlawful practices toward the

Shalom: God's Ultimate Purpose for the World

local society with justification of serving the marginalized or sharing the gospel with people, which is frequently found in many short-term medical missions. Christian medical missions should acknowledge that the ultimate responsibility of medical care should lay on local churches as well as the local medical society, and its role should be as a facilitator for development of an indigenous healthcare system. Many current challenges that Christian medical mission faces are certainly difficult to overcome, yet they open many opportunities to explore alternative paths for serving people in biblical ways. Christian medical mission must strive for humble introspection about what it has done and see what God leads it to become.

God has called the global church to courageously represent the kingdom of God through witness and service to the lost, and his people have faithfully engaged in his mission to reach out to Muslims in the Arab world. By yielding to the power of the Holy Spirit blowing through all faithful endeavors of his faithful servants and allowing it to transform the global church into the image of Christ Jesus and to experience *shalom* in his loving community, Christian medical missions will humbly continue serving people in desperate physical and spiritual need and taking them out from the captivity of fear and hatred of being alienated from the loving God. It would definitely be interesting to pursue discussions focusing on how to develop principles and strategies of Christian medical mission in the Arab world on the basis of the issues raised by this book. To be faithful stewards and instruments of God's mission as medical professionals, Christian medical mission leaders should evaluate their methods of missions more carefully. Such evaluation demands further objective studies concerning advantages and disadvantages of various missions such as mission hospitals, clinics, medical training programs, community development projects, and emergency medical relief efforts for both spiritual and physical transformational long-term impact through the gospel message on individuals and communities. These further endeavors will certainly nurture Christian medical mission to grasp better principles and strategies based on the biblical truth, which help it serve people in need more effectively.

Bibliography

Adamu, Umar F. *Medicine in the Qur'an and Sunnah: An Intellectual Reappraisal of the Legacy and Future of Islamic Medicine and Its Representation in the Language of Science and Modernity*. Ibadan, Nigeria: Safari, 2006.

Algul, Hussein. "Islam is a Religion of Love and Peace." http://www.peaceandislam.com.

Al-Jeraisy, Khaled. "Self-Ruqya Treatment: Do It Yourself Treat Your Family." http://www.muslim-library.com/dl/books/english_Self_Ruqya_Treatment.pdf.

Al-Najdi, Muhammad Al-Humoud. "Ash-Shaafee (The One Who Cures): Allah's Names and Attributes." http://www.4theseekeroftruth.com/index.php/ash-shaafee-the-one-who-cures/.

Altemeyer, Bob, and Bruce Hunsberger. "Authoritarianism, Religious Fundamentalism, Quest, and Prejudice." *The International Journal for the Psychology of Religion* 2, 2 (November 2009): 113–33.

Anderson, John E. "A Biblical and Economic Analysis of Jubilee Property Provisions." *Faith and Economics* 46 (Fall 2005): 25–41. https://pdfs.semanticscholar.org/8e0f/1f37009dbf571b680c193d0063432ed46f17.pdf.

Andrews, David. "Integral Mission, Relief and Development." http://www.daveandrews.com.au/articles/Integral%20Mission%20in%20Relief%20and%20Development.pdf.

Ansari, Ali. "The Principles and Importance of Spiritual Healing in Islam." http://www.surrenderworks.com/library/abidance/inislam.html

Arrahim, Bismillah A. "Ruqya: Qur'anic Treatment for Jadoo, Jinn, and Zazar." https://alruqya.wordpress.com.

Asar, Adam. *Peace of Mind and Healing of Broken Lives: Spiritual Healing for Body, Mind and Spirit through Qur'an—Diagnosis, Treatment Methods and Protection from Psychic Attack*. Chicago: Universal Mercy, 2010.

"Ash-Shaafee: The One Who Cures." http://understandquran.com/19384.html.

Ateeq, Mohammad, Shazia Jehan, and Riffat Mehmmod. "Faith Healing: Modern Health Care." *The Professional Medical Journal* 21, 2 (2014): 295–301. http://applications.emro.who.int/imemrf/Professional_Med_J_Q/Professional_Med_J_Q_2014_21_2_295_301.pdf.

Babcock, B. C. (2016). "Year of Jubilee." In *The Lexham Bible Dictionary*. Edited by J. D. Barry et al. Bellingham: Lexham Press, 2016.

Bailey, Kenneth E. *Jesus Through Middle Eastern Eyes: Cultural Studies in the Gospels*. Downers Grove: IVP Academic, Logos Edition, 2008.

Balmer, Randall. "Wheaton Declaration." In *Encyclopedia of Evangelicalism*. London: Westminster John Knox, 2002.

Bibliography

Barry, John D., et al. "Peace." In *The Lexham Bible Dictionary*. Bellingham: Lexham, Logos Edition, 2016.

Bendor-Samuel, Paul. "Discipleship: Center of Mission." In *Discipleship: Reclaiming Mission's Strategic Focus*. Edited by Melanie McNeal, 98–115. Kuala Lumpur: Grassroots Mission, 2014.

———. "Holistic Ministry in an Islamic Context: Initial Reflections." In *Doing Mission in the Arab World*. Edited by John Stringer, 1–18. Kuala Lumpur: Grassroots Mission, 2008.

Bernstein, Mark. "Fatalism." In *The Oxford Handbook of Free Will*. Edited by Robert H. Kane, 65–83. New York: Oxford University Press, 2002.

Bido, Jennifer, et al. "Sustainability Assessment of a Short-Term International Medical Mission." *The Journal of Bone and Joint Surgery* 97, 11 (June 2015): 944–49. https://www.ncbi.nlm.nih.gov/pmc/articles/PMC4449340.

Bonhoeffer, Dietrich. *God is in the Manger: Reflections on Advent and Christmas*. Louisville: Westminster John Knox, 2012.

Booth, Beverley E. "Sustainability of Christian Mission Hospitals in India and Nepal: Impact of History." https://www.cmf.org.uk/resources/publications/content/?context=article&id=2627.

Bourne, Phil. "The Hand cannot say to the Eye: 'I have no need of You': The Importance of the Local Church." In *Ministry of Reconciliation*. Edited by John Stringer, 197–203. Bangalore: Grassroots Mission, 2009.

Brand, Chad O., et al. "Peace." In *Holman Illustrated Bible Dictionary*. Nashville: Holman Bible Publishers, Logos Edition, 2003.

Brocker, Mark S. *Coming Home to Earth*. Eugene: Cascade, 2016.

Brown, Rick. "Contextualization without Syncretism." *International Journal of Frontier Missions* 23, 3 (Fall 2006): 127–33.

Brueggemann, Walter. *Peace: Understanding Biblical Themes Series*. St. Louis: Chalice, 2001.

Buenting, Debra. "Evangelicals and Social Action: YWAM's Adoption of Kingdom Mission, Thy Kingdom Come: Proceedings of the 2008 ISFM Conference, Part II." *International Journal of Frontier Missiology* 26, 1 (2009): 15–19.

Bunn, Alex, and David Randall, "Health Benefits of Christian Faith." *CMF Files* 44 (Easter 2010). http://admin.cmf.org.uk/pdf/cmffiles/44_faith_benefits.pdf.

Butrin, JoAnn, and A. Chadwick Thornhill. "Defining Poverty and Need." In *For the Love of God: Principles and Practices of Compassion in Missions*. Edited by Jerry M. Ireland. Eugene: Wipf and Stock, Kindle Edition, 2017.

Calmet, Augustin. *Calmet's Great Dictionary of the Holy Bible: Historical, Critical, Geographical, and Etymological*. Charlestown: Samuel Etheridge, 1812.

Cambridge Dictionary. "Medical Ministry." http://dictionary.cambridge.org/dictionary/english/medical.

Carpenter, Eugene E., and Philip W. Comfort. "Kingdom." In *Holman Treasury of Key Bible Words: 200 Greek and 200 Hebrew Words Defined and Explained*. Nashville: Broadman & Holman, Logos Edition, 2000.

———. "Peace." *Holman Treasury of Key Bible Words: 200 Greek and 200 Hebrew Words Defined and Explained*. Nashville: Broadman & Holman, Logos Edition, 2003.

Carver, William O. "Keys, Power of." In *The International Standard Bible Encyclopaedia*, Volumes 1–5. Edited by James Orr, et al. Chicago: Howard-Severance, Logos Edition, 1915.

Bibliography

CHE Global Network. "Community Health Evangelism (CHE)." *CHENetwork.org*. 2021. https://www.chenetwork.org/what.php.

Chedid, Bassam M. *Islam: What Every Christian Should Know*. Webster: Evangelical USA, 2004.

Christians for Social Action. "Chicago Declaration of Evangelical Social Concern (1973)." http://www.evangelicalsforsocialaction.org/about-esa/history/chicago-declaration-of-evangelical-social-concern/.

Clammer, John, Sylvie Poirier, and Eric Schwimmer. *Figured Worlds: Ontological Obstacles in Intercultural Relations*. Toronto, Canada: University of Toronto Press, 2004.

Claxton, Robert. *A Christian Doctor Speaks on Healing*. Homebush West, Australia: Lancer, 1987.

Cohen-Mor, Dalya. *A Matter of Fate: The Concept of Fate in the Arab World as Reflected Modern Arabic Literature*. New York: Oxford University Press, 2001.

Corbett, Steve, and Brian Fikkert. *When Helping Hurts: How to Alleviate Poverty without Hurting the Poor and Yourself*. Chicago: Moody, 2012.

Coulson, Noel J. "Shariah: Islamic Law." https://www.britannica.com/topic/Shariah.

"Creative Access Nations." http://www.ibmglobal.org/ministry/creative-access-nations/.

Creswell, John W. *Qualitative Inquiry and Research Design: Choosing Among Five Approaches*. Thousand Oaks: SAGE, 2007.

Department of Halal Certification EU. "Islamic Method of Slaughtering," http://halalcertification.ie/islamic-method-of-slaughtering/.

DeYoung, Kevin, and Greg D. Gilbert. *What Is the Mission of the Church? Making Sense of Social Justice, Shalom, and the Great Commission*. Wheaton: Crossway, 2011.

Dockery, David S. "Isaiah 9:1–7." In *Holman Concise Bible Commentary*. Nashville: Broadman & Holman, Logos Edition, 1998.

———. "Peace Offering." In *Holman Concise Bible Commentary*. Nashville, TN: Broadman & Holman Publishers, Logos Edition, 1998.

Dodge, Huda. "*Shirk*: Associating Others with Allah." https://www.thoughtco.com/shirk-2004293.

———. "The Meaning of Da'wah in Islam." https://www.thoughtco.com/the-meaning-of-dawah-in-islam-2004196.

Dyer, Charles H. "Ezekiel." In *The Bible Knowledge Commentary: An Exposition of the Scriptures*. Edited by J. F. Walvoord & R. B. Zuck. Wheaton: Victor Books, Logos Edition, 1985.

Elmer, Duane. *Cross-Cultural Connections: Stepping Out and Fitting in Around the World*. Downers Grove: InterVarsity, 2002.

Elwell, Walter A. *Evangelical Commentary on the Bible, Vol. 3*. Grand Rapids: Baker, Logos Edition, 1995.

Encyclopaedia Britannica. "Dhikr." https://www.britannica.com/topic/dhikr

———. "Mi'raj." https://www.britannica.com/event/Miraj-Islam.

———. "Sufism: Islam." https://www.britannica.com/topic/Sufism.

Encyclopedia of Protestantism. "Three-Self Principles." http://protestantism.enacademic.com/594/three-self_principles.

Encyclopaedia Judaica. "Shalom Aleikhem." https://www.encyclopedia.com/religion/encyclopedias-almanacs-transcripts-and-maps/shalom-aleikhem.

English Oxford Living Dictionaries.

English Living Oxford Dictionary. "Bismillah." https://en.oxforddictionaries.com/definition/bismillah.

Bibliography

———. "Islam." https://en.oxforddictionaries.com/definition/islam.
———. "Ministry." https://en.oxforddictionaries.com/definition/ministry.
———. "Peace." https://en.oxforddictionaries.com/definition/peace.
Erickson, Millard J. *Introducing Christian Doctrine*. Grand Rapids: Baker, 2006.
Esposito, John L. "Islam and Political Violence." In *Religion*, edited by Peter Iver Kaufman. Washington, DC: Prince Alwaleed Bin Talal Center for Muslim-Christian Understanding, Georgetown University, 2015. 1067–81.
Evans, Christopher H. *The Social Gospel in American Religion: A History*. New York: New York University Press, 2017.
Evans, C. Stephen. "Liberation Theology." In *Pocket Dictionary of Apologetics & Philosophy of Religion*. Downers Grove: InterVarsity Press, Logos Edition, 2002.
———. "Relativism." In *Pocket Dictionary of Apologetics and Philosophy of Religion*. Downers Grove: InterVarsity, Logos Edition, 2002.
Evans. C. Stephen, and Christopher L. Flanders. *About Face: Rethinking Face for 21st-Century Mission*. Eugene: Pickwick, 2011.
Faris, Mohammed, "The Healing Power of Prayer." http://productivemuslim.com/the-healing-power-of-prayer/.
Flemming, Dean, *Contextualization in the New Testament: Patterns for Theology and Mission*. Downers Grove: InterVarsity, 2005.
Freeman, James M. *The New Manners and Customs of the Bible*. North Brunswick: Bridge-Logos, Logos Edition, 1998.
Gabriel, Mark A. *Islam and Terrorism: The Truth about ISIS, the Middle East, and Islamic Jihad*. Lake Mary: Frontline, 2002.
Gaiser, Frederick J. *Healing in the Bible: Theological Insight for Christian Ministry*. Grand Rapids: Baker Academic, 2010.
Geisler, Norman L. "Miracle." In *Baker Encyclopedia of Christian Apologetics*. Grand Rapids: Baker, 1999, Logos Edition.
Gholipour, Bahar. "Supernatural 'Jinn' Seen as Cause of Mental Illness Among Muslims." https://www.livescience.com/47394-supernatural-jinn-mental-illness-islam.html.
Gilliland, Dean S. "Chapter 28: The Incarnation as Matrix for Appropriate Theologies." In *Appropriate Christianity*. Edited by Charles H. Kraft. Pasadena: William Carey Library, 2005.
Gillum, Joshua. "Is Islam Peaceful or Violent: Comparing Islam and Christianity to Reveal the Propaganda of Terrorism." http://www.culturaldiplomacy.org/academy/content/pdf/participant-papers/2010www/Is_Islam_Peaceful_or_Violent_-_Comparing_Islam_&_Christianity_to_Reveal_the_Propaganda_of_Terrorism.pdf.
Goheen, Michael W. "Gospel, Culture, and Cultures: Lesslie Newbigin's Missionary Contribution." In *Cultures and Christianity A.D. 2000*. International Symposium of the Association for Reformational Philosophy 2000. http://missionworldview.com/wp-content/uploads/2011/06/Gospel-and-Culture-in-Newbigin.pdf.
Gomes, Gabriel J. *Discovering World Religions: A Guide for the Inquiring Reader*. Bloomington: iUniverse, 2012.
Gornik, Mark R. *To Live in Peace: Biblical Faith and the Changing Inner City*. Grand Rapids: Eerdmans, 2002.
Gorske, Arnold. "Harm from Drugs in Short-Term Mission: Review of the Medical Literature." http://www.csthmbestpractices.org/resources/Harm+From+Drugs+in+Short-term+Missions.pdf.

Bibliography

Goss, Leonard G. "What is the Occult?" In *The Apologetics Study Bible: Real Questions, Straight Answers, Stronger Faith*. Nashville: Holman, Logos Edition, 2007.

Greenall, John. "What is the Future of Medical Mission?" *Nucleus* 46, 2 (May 2016): 6–10.

Greever, Joshua M. "Peace." In *The Lexham Bible Dictionary*. Bellingham: Lexham, Logos Edition, 2016.

Grenz, Stanley J., and John R. Franke. *Beyond Fundamentalism: Shaping Theology in a Postmodern Context*. Louisville: Westminster John Knox, 2001.

Grudem, Wayne. *Systematic Theology: An Introduction to Biblical Doctrine*. Leicester: IVP, 1994.

Gruenler, Royce G. "Romans." In *Evangelical Commentary on the Bible, Vol. 3*. Edited by Walter A. Elwell. Grand Rapids: Baker, Logos Edition, 1995.

Gumprecht, Jane D. *Holistic Health: A Medical and Biblical Critique of New Age Deception*. Moscow, ID: Ransom, 1986.

Haafiz Wasim Ismail. "How to Do *Istinja*—Part 2." http://www.myislaam.com/fiqh/how-to-do-istinja-part2/.

Hardiman, David, ed. *Healing Bodies, Saving Souls: Medical Missions in Asia and Africa*. New York: Rodopi, 2006.

Hart, Henry C. *The Animals Mentioned in the Bible*. London: The Religious Tract Society, Logos Edition, 1888.

"Hasanat Ruqya: Services of Spiritual Healing." 2021. http://hasanatruqya.com.

"Health Outreach to the Middle East (HOME)." https://www.homeforhim.org.

Hesselgrave, David J. "Contextualization that is Authentic and Relevant." *International Journal of Frontier Missions* 12, 3 (1995): 115–19.

———. "Great Commission Contextualization." *International Journal of Frontier Mission* 12, 3 (1995): 139–44.

Hiebert, Paul G. "The Flaw of the Excluded Middle." *Missiology* 10, 1 (1982): 35–47.

———. *Anthropological Insights for Missionaries*. Grand Rapids: Baker, 1985.

———. *Anthropological Reflections on Missiological Issues*. Grand Rapids: Baker, 1994.

Hiebert, Paul G., R. Daniel Shaw, and Tite Tienou. "Responding to Split-Level Christianity and Folk Religion." *International Journal of Frontier Mission* 16, 4 (1999/2000): 173–82.

Hoehner, Harold W. "Ephesians." In *The Bible Knowledge Commentary: An Exposition of the Scripture*. Edited by J. F. Walvoord and R. B. Zuck. Wheaton: Victor Books, Logos Edition, 1985.

Hurst, Suzanne. "Best Practices in Compassionate Mission." In *For the Love of God: Principles and Practices of Compassion in Missions*. Edited by Jerry M. Ireland. Eugene: Wipf and Stock, Kindle Edition, 2017.

Hussain, Musharraf. *The Five Pillars of Islam: Laying the Foundations of Divine Love and Service to Humanity*. Leicestershire: KUBE, 2012.

Hussnayn, Abu Ibraheem, "Ruqya-QA: The Official Ruqyah Website of Abu Ibraheem Hussnayn: Ruqya QA." http://www.ruqya-qa.co.uk/the-ruqya-plan/.

Inchley, Valerie. "Medical Mission: What's the Future?" https://www.cmf.org.uk/resources/publications/content/?context=article&id=1084.

Institute for Economics & Peace. "Global Peace Index 2017: Measuring Peace in a Complex World." http://visionofhumanity.org/app/uploads/2017/06/GPI-2017-Highlights-1.pdf.

Ireland, Jerry M., ed. *For the Love of God: Principles and Practice of Compassion in Missions*. Eugene: Wipf and Stock, Kindle Edition, 2017.

Bibliography

———. *Evangelism and Social Concerns in the Theology of Carl F. H. Henry*. Eugene: Wipf and Stock, 2015.

Jamieson, Robert, A.R. Fausset, and David Brown. *Commentary Critical and Explanatory on the Whole Bible*. Oak Harbor: Logos, 1997.

Johnson, Alan R. "Missions and Compassion." In *For the Love of God: Principles and Practices of Compassion in Missions*. Edited by Jerry M. Ireland. Eugene: Wipf and Stock, Kindle Edition, 2017.

Johnson, Jean. "Counterintuitive Missions in a McDonald's Age: Recovering the Apostolic, Incarnational Model to Integrating Gospel-as-Mission and Gospel-as-Deed." In *For the Love of God: Principles and Practice of Compassion in Missions*. Edited by Jerry M. Ireland. Eugene: Wipf and Stock, Kindle Edition, 2017.

Jones, Francis P. "The Christian Church in Communist China." *Far Eastern Survey* 24, 12 (December 1955). http://www.jstor.org/stable/3023787.

Joshua Project. "Affinity Bloc: Arab World." https://joshuaproject.net/affinity_blocs.

Kabbani, Hisham M. "Spiritual Healing in the Islamic Tradition." http://www.nurmuhammad.com/Dwnlds/harvardhealinglecture.pdf.

Kabbani, Shaykh Muhammad Hisham and Shayk Seraj Hendricks. "Jihad, A Misunderstood Concept from Islam—What Jihad is, and is not." http://islamicsupremecouncil.org/understanding-islam/legal-rulings/5-jihad-a-misunderstood-concept-from-islam.html?start=9.

Kaltner, John. *Introducing the Qur'an: For Today's Reader*. Minneapolis: Fortress, 2011.

Keene, Michael. *This is Islam*. Cheltenham: Stanley Thornes, 1999.

Keener, Craig S. *Miracles: The Credibility of the New Testament Accounts*. Grand Rapids: Baker, 2011.

Kennard, Douglas W. *The Gospel*. Eugene: Wipf and Stock, 2017.

Kennedy, D. James. *Led by the Carpenter: Finding God's Purpose for Your Life*. Nashville: Thomas Nelson, 1999.

Khan, Maulana W. "The Concept of Peace in Islam." *CPS International Center of Peace and Spirituality* 2005. http://cpsglobal.org/content/concept-peace-islam.

Kim, Hark Yoo. "What Sort of Relationship Does the Sending Church Want with the Receiving Church?" In *Church and Mission: Partnership in Mutual Dependence*. Edited by John Stringer, 81–98. Groningen, Netherlands: Grassroots Mission, 2011.

Kim, Min Chul. "Missionary Medicine in a Changing World." https://missionexus.org/missionary-medicine-in-a-changing-world/.

Kim, Sophia. "*Sufism* in Egypt: The Shrine Culture of Cairo." In *Doing Mission in the Arab World*. Edited by John Stringer, 105–17. Kuala Lumpur: Grassroots Mission, 2008.

Kittel, Gerhard, and Gerhard Friedrich, ed. *Theological Dictionary of the New Testament: Abridged in One Volume*. Grand Rapids: Eerdmans, 1985.

Kotze, Zacharias. "The Evil Eye of Sumerian Deities." *Asian and African Studies* 26, 1 (2017): 102–15.

Kraft, Charles H., ed., *Appropriate Christianity*. Pasadena: William Carey Library, 2005.

Kraft, Charles H. *Power Encounter in Spiritual Warfare*. Eugene: Wipf and Stock, 2017.

Landa, Apolos. "How Short-Term Missions Can Go Wrong." *International Journal of Frontier Missions* 20, 4 (Winter 2003): 104–18.

Lazich, Michael C. *Seeking Souls through the Eyes of the Blind: The Birth of the Medical Missionary Society in Nineteenth-Century China*. Edited by David Hardiman, 59–86. New York: Rodopi B.V., 2006.

Bibliography

Langston, Scott, and E. Ray Clendenen, "Sacrifice and Offering." In *Holman Illustrated Bible Dictionary*. Nashville: Broadman & Holman, Logos Edition, 2003.

Lausanne Movement. "Evangelism and Social Responsibility." https://lausanne.org/content/lop/lop-21.

———. "Integral Mission." https://www.lausanne.org/networks/issues/poverty-and-wealth.

———. "The Legacy of the Lausanne Movement: The Beginnings of the Lausanne Movement." https://www.lausanne.org/our-legacy.

———. "The Lausanne Covenant." https://www.lausanne.org/content/covenant/lausanne-covenant.

Lemaire, Andre. "Who or What Was Yahweh's Ashera?" *BAR* 10, 6 (November–December 1984). http://cojs.org/who-or-what-was-yahwehs-asherah.

Linthicum, Robert C. "Why Build a Justice Interpretation Around 'Shalom'?" http://www.rclinthicum.org/fullset/RCL_Cycles_ABC_Chapter_4.pdf.

Livermore, David A. *Serving with Eyes Wide Open: Doing Short-Term Missions with Cultural Intelligence*. Grand Rapids: Baker, 2006.

Livingstone, Greg. *Planting Churches in Muslim Cities: A Team Approach*. Grand Rapids: Baker, 1993.

Longman, T. Ill, et al., ed. "Sacrifice and Offering." In *The Baker Illustrated Bible Dictionary*. Grand Rapids: Baker, 2003.

Love, Richard D. "Church Planting Among Folk Muslims." *International Journal of Frontier Missions*, 11, 2 (April, 1994): 87–91.

Love, Rick. *Muslims, Magic, and the Kingdom of God: Church Planting among Folk Muslims*. Pasadena: William Carey Library, 2000.

Maclean, Ruth. "Crisis Engulfs Gabon Hospital Founded to Atone for Colonial Crimes: Institution Launched by Novel Prize Winner Dr. Albert Schweitzer on Brink of Closure as Funding Woes and Racism Dispute Take Toll." https://www.theguardian.com/world/2016/sep/07/gabon-hospital-albert-schweitzer-atone-colonial-crimes-funding-racism-allegations.

Manser, Martin H. *Dictionary of Bible Themes: The Accessible and Comprehensive Tool for Topical Studies*. London: Logos Edition, 2017.

Martin, John A. "Isaiah." In *The Bible Knowledge Commentary: An Exposition of the Scriptures*. Edited by John F. Walvoord and Roy B. Zuck. Wheaton: Victor, 1985.

Mathews, Ed. "History of Mission Methods: A Brief Survey." *Journal of Applied Missiology* 1, 1. http://web.ovc.edu/missions/jam/histmeth.htm.

McGonigal, Terry. "If You Only Knew What Would Bring Peace: Shalom Theology as the Biblical Foundation for Diversity." https://www.cccu.org/filefolder/2009_CMD_Shalom_theology.pdf.

McNeal, Melanie. "Mission Paradigms: Is Discipleship Important?" In *Discipleship: Reclaiming Mission's Strategic Focus*. Edited by Melanie McNeal, 48–97. Kuala Lumpur: Grassroots Mission, 2014.

Medical Ambassadors International. "Community Health Evangelism (CHE)." https://www.medicalambassadors.org.

Melby, Melissa K., et al. "Beyond Medical 'Missions' to Impact-Driven Short-Term Experiences in Global Health (STEGHs): Ethical Principles to Optimize Community Benefit and Learner Experience." *Academic Medicine* 1–6 (2016). https://www.nafsa.org/_/File/_/2016colloquia/2016_health_missions.pdf.

Bibliography

Merriam-Webster's Collegiate Dictionary, 11th ed. "Folk Medicine." Springfield: Merriam-Webster, 2003.

Merriam-Webster Online Dictionary. "Bait and Switch." https://www.merriam-webster.com/dictionary/bait%20and%20switch.

———. "Evil Eye." https://www.merriam-webster.com/dictionary/evil%20eye.

Micah Network Global. "Declaration on Integral Mission." http://www.micahnetwork.org/sites/default/files/doc/page/mn_integral_mission_declaration_en.pdf.

Migliore, Sam. *Mal'uocchiu: Ambiguity, Evil Eye, and the Language of Distress*. Toronto, Canada: University of Toronto Press, 1997.

Miller, Darrow L. *Discipling Nations: The Power of Truth to Transform Cultures*. Seattle: Youth with a Mission, 2001.

Mish, Frederick C. "Peace." In *Merriam-Webster's Collegiate Dictionary*, 11th ed. Springfield: Merriam-Webster, 2003.

Moon, Luke S. "Cases of Comprehensive Disciple-Making (Discipling) in the Workplace of CAR Muslim Context." In *Discipleship: Reclaiming Mission's Strategic Focus*. Edited by Melanie McNeal, 192–207. Kuala Lumpur: Grassroots Mission, 2014.

Moreau, A. Scott. *Contextualization in World Missions: Mapping and Assessing Evangelical Models*. Grand Rapids: Kregel, 2012.

Moreau, A. Scott, Evvy Hay Campbell, and Susan Greener. *Effective Intercultural Communication: A Christian Perspective*. Grand Rapids: Baker, 2014.

Moreau, A. Scott, Gary R. Corwin, and Gary B. McGee. *Introducing World Missions: A Biblical, Historical, and Practical Survey*. Grand Rapids: Baker, 2004.

Muhaiyaddeen, M. R. Bawa. *Islam and World Peace: Explanations of a SUFI*. Philadelphia: Fellowship, 1987.

Munson, Robert H. "Changing Priorities and Practices in Christian Missions: Case Study of Medical Missions." https://www.slideshare.net/bmunson3/changing-priorities-in-christian-missions.

———. "Healthy Medical Missions: Principles for the Church's Role in Effective Community Outreach in the Philippines." Quezon City: Asia Baptist Graduate Theological Seminary, 2012.

Muslimah, "The Healing Powers of the Names of Allah." https://amuslimsistermaria200327.wordpress.com/2010/05/14/the-healing-powers-of-the-names-of-allah/.

Musk, Bill. *The Unseen Face of Islam: Sharing the Gospel with Ordinary Muslims at Street Level*. Grand Rapids: Monarch, 2003.

Myers, Bryant L. *Walking with the Poor: Principles and Practices of Transformational Development*. Maryknoll: Orbis Books, 1999.

Newbigin, Lesslie. *Foolishness to the Greeks: The Gospel and Western Culture*. Grand Rapids: Eerdmans, 1986.

Newell, James. "Asherah, Asherim or Ashera." In *Holman Illustrated Bible Dictionary*. Nashville: Holman, Logos Edition, 2003.

Odeh, Lemuel Ekedegwa. "A Comparative Analysis of Global North and Global South Economies." *Journal of Sustainable Development in Africa* 12, 3 (2010): 338–48.

"One Race, One Gospel, One Task." http://www2.wheaton.edu/bgc/archives/berlin66.htm.

Oyewole, Yahya. "Healing in Islam, Continuity + Change: Perspectives on Science and Religion." http://irfi.org/articles3/articles_4201_4300/healing%20in%20islamhtml.htm.

Bibliography

Padilla, Rene. "Integral Mission and Its Historical Development." http://formacaoredefale.pbworks.com/f/Integral+Mission+and+its+Historical+Development_Ren%C3%A9+Padilla.doc.

Palmer, Jeff, and Lynda Hausfeld, "Compassion and Unreached People Groups." In *For the Love of God: Principles and Practice of Compassion in Missions*. Edited by Jerry M. Ireland. Eugene: Wipf and Stock, Kindle Edition, 2017.

Parshall, Phil. *Bridges to Islam: A Christian Perspective on Folk Islam*. Grand Rapids: Baker, 1983.

———. *The Cross and the Crescent: Understanding the Muslim Heart and Mind*. Waynesboro: Authentic, 2002.

———. *Muslim Evangelism: Contemporary Approaches to Contextualization*. Downers Grove: InterVarsity, 2003.

Pew Research Center. "Mapping the Global Muslim Population." http://www.pewforum.org/2009/10/07/mapping-the-global-muslim-population/.

Pelaia, Ariela. "Learn About the Hamsa Hand and What It Represents: Find out About This Protective Talisman Guarding Against Evil." https://www.thoughtco.com/what-is-a-hamsa-2076780.

Qamar, Azher H. "Belief in the Evil Eye and Early Childcare in Rural Punjab, Pakistan." *Asian Ethnology* 75, 2 (2016): 397–418.

"Observance of *Salat*—Daily Prayers." https://free-islamic-course.org/stageone/stageone-module-2/observance-salat-daily-prayers.html.

Qureshi, Nabeel. *No God But One: Allah or Jesus?* Grand Rapids: Zondervan, 2016.

Reimer, Johannes and Zuze Banda. "Doing Mission Inclusively." *Herv.teol.stud* 72, 1 (2016). http://www.scielo.org.za/scielo.php?script=sci_arttext&pid=S0259-94222016000100016.

Ritzer, George. *The McDonaldization of Society: 20th Anniversary Edition*. Thousand Oaks: SAGE, 2013.

Saeed, Abdullah. "Jihad and Violence: Changing Understandings of Jihad Among Muslims." In *Terrorism and Justice: Moral Argument in a Threatened World*. Edited by Tony Coady and Michael O'Keefe. Victoria, Australia: Melbourne University Press, 2002.

Sahih Bukhari. "Book 55: Prophets, Hadith Number 549, Volume 4." *Gowister* 2021. http://www.gowister.com/sahihbukhari-4-549.html.

Said, Chrystal. *Muslim Southern Belle Guide for Teens*. Houston: Pink Hijab, 2017.

Sanders, Fred. "The Kingdom in Person." http://scriptoriumdaily.com/the-kingdom-in-person/.

Schwartz, Glenn. "Short-Term Medical Missions: A Summary of Experiences." *Latin American Theology* 2, 2 (2006): 27–34.

Scofield, C. I., ed. *The Scofield Reference Bible: The Holy Bible Containing the Old and New Testaments*. New York: Oxford University Press, Logos Edition, 1917.

Shah, Niaz A. "The Use of Force under Islamic Law." *European Journal of International Law* 24, 1 (February 2013): 343–65.

Sherali, Hanif D. *Spiritual Discourses*. Bloomington: AuthorHouse, 2014.

Sider, Ronald J. *Rich Christians in an Age of Hunger: Moving from Affluence to Generosity*. Nashville: Thomas Nelson, 2015.

Snodderly, Beth. "Shalom: The Goal of the Kingdom and of International Development." In *International Development from a Kingdom Perspective*. Edited by James Butare-Kiyovu. Pasadena: WCIU, 2010.

Sourdel, Dominique and Janine Sourdel-Thomine. *A Glossary of Islam*. Edinburgh: Edinburgh University Press, 2007.
Srinivasan, Lysa. *Tools for Community Participation: A Manual for Training Trainers in Participatory Techniques*. Washington, DC: PROWWNESS/UNDP, 1990.
Stanford Encyclopedia of Philosophy. "Fatalism." https://plato.stanford.edu/entries/fatalism/.
———. "Miracles." https://plato.stanford.edu/entries/miracles/#ConDef.
Steyne, Philip M. *In Step with the God of the Nations*. Columbia: Impact International, 1999.
Stockwell, Clinton. "Fundamentalisms and the Shalom of God: An Analysis of Contemporary Expressions of Fundamentalism in Christianity, Judaism and Islam." *ERT* 36, 3 (2012): 266–79.
Stringer, John. "Two for a Tango: The Delicate Relationship Between Church and Mission." In *Church and Mission: Partnership in Mutual Dependence*. Edited by John Stringer, 15–24. Groningen, Netherlands: Grassroots Mission, 2011.
Strong, James. *The New Strong's Concise Dictionary of Bible Words*. Nashville: Thomas Nelson, 2000.
Stott, John R. W., ed. *Making Christ Known: Historic Mission Documents from the Lausanne Movement, 1974–1989*. Grand Rapids: Eerdmans, 1997.
Strand, Mark A. "Medical Missions in Transition: Taking to Heart the Results of the PRISM Survey." https://www.cmda.org/library/doclib/Prism-Survey-2011.pdf.
Swanson, James A. *Dictionary of Biblical Languages with Semantic Domains: Aramic, Old Testament*. Oak Harbor: Logos, 1997.
———. *Dictionary of Biblical Languages with Semantic Domains: Hebrew, Old Testament*. Oak Harbor: Logos, 1997.
Swartley, Keith E., ed. *Encountering the World of Islam*. Colorado Springs: Authentic, 2008.
Swartley, Willard M. *Covenant of Peace: The Missing Peace in New Testament Theology and Ethics*. Grand Rapids: Eerdmans, 2006.
Swing, William E. "The Etymology of Salam: An Insight Into the Arabic Word for Peace." http://www.uri.org/the_latest/2010/10/the_etymology_of_salam__an_insight_into_the_arabic_word_for_peace.
"TB Treatment—TB cure, how is TB cured, TB drugs, treatment duration." https://www.tbfacts.org/tb-treatment/.
Teague, David P. "Integral Mission: A Truer Theological Foundation." In *Ministry of Reconciliation*. Edited by John Stringer, 13–26. Groningen, Netherlands: Grassroots Mission, 2009.
Tennent, Timothy C. *Invitation to World Missions: A Trinitarian Missiology for the Twenty-first Century*. Grand Rapids: Kregel, 2010.
"The Theology of Medical Mission." https://www.cmf.org.uk/doctors/miscellaneous/working-overseas/rsl-2002-medical-mission/.
The Religion of Peace. "What Makes Islam So Different: What Does Islam Teach About Violence." https://www.thereligionofpeace.com/pages/quran/violence.aspx.
"The World of *Jinn*: A Brief Introduction about the Existence and Abilities of *Jinn*." https://www.islamreligion.com/articles/669/viewall/world-of-jinn/.
"Three Self Church: China's Three Self Church." http://www.billionbibles.com/china/three-self-church.html.
Travis, John. "C1–C6 Spectrum." *Evangelical Missions Quarterly* (October, 1998): 407–408. https://www.thepeopleofthebook.org/about/strategy/c1-c6-spectrum/.

Bibliography

Tripathi, Mayank. *Salvadora Persica L.*"*Miswak*: An Endangered Multipurpose Tree of India.*" Indian Journal of Plant Sciences* 5, 3 (July–September, 2016): 24–29. https://www.researchgate.net/profile/Mayank_Tripathi5/publication/308951379_SALVADORA_PERSICA_L_MISWAK_AN_ENDANGERED_MULTIPURPOSE_TREE_OF_INDIA/links/57f9bb9f08ae8da3ce5a15b8/SALVADORA-PERSICA-L-MISWAK-AN-ENDANGERED-MULTIPURPOSE-TREE-OF-INDIA.pdf.

Turner, David L. "Whom Does God Approve: The Context, Structure, Purpose, and Exegesis of Matthew's Beatitudes." https://faculty.gordon.edu/hu/bi/ted_hildebrandt/ntesources/ntarticles/ctr-nt/turner-beatitudes-ctr.htm.

Tursunova, Zulfiya, et al. "Cultural Patterns of Health Care Beliefs and Practices among Muslim Women in Uzbekistan." *Health, Culture and Society* 6, 1 (2014): 47–61.

United Nations High Commissioner for Refugees. "UNHCR: Figures at a Glance." http://www.unhcr.org/figures-at-a-glance.html.

———. "UNHCR: Syria: Internally Displaced People." http://www.unhcr.org/sy/29-internally-displaced-people.html.

———. "UNHCR: Syria Regional Refugee Response: Inter-Agency Information Sharing Portal." http://data.unhcr.org/syrianrefugees/country.php?id=122.

———. "UNHCR: Syria Regional Refugee Response, Operational Portal: Refugee Situations." https://data2.unhcr.org/en/situations/syria.

United Lutheran Church in America. *Anointing and Healing*. Philadelphia: United Lutheran Church Board of Publication, 1962.

United Nations. "Millennium Development Goals." http://www.undp.org/content/undp/en/home/sdgoverview/mdg_goals.html.

———. "Sustainable Development Goals." https://sustainabledevelopment.un.org/?menu=1300.

———. "Sustainable Development Knowledge Platform: Multi-stakeholder partnerships and voluntary commitments." https://sustainabledevelopment.un.org/sdinaction.

"Urban CHE Overview: Community Health Evangelism." http://www.medicalambassadors.org/wp-content/uploads/2016/01/Urban-CHE-Overview-09-2013.pdf.

Van Rheenen, Gailyn. *Communicating Christ in Animistic Context*. Pasadena: William Carey Library, 1991.

Varner, Gary R. "The History & Use of Amulets, Charms and Talismans." https://www.academia.edu/27209097/The_History_and_Use_of_Amulets_Charms_and_Talismans.

Vocabulary.com. "Reductionism." https://www.vocabulary.com/dictionary/reductionism.

Walter, Suzan. "Holistic Health." https://ahha.org/selfhelp-articles/holistic-health/.

Walker, W. L. "Peace." In *The International Standard Bible Encyclopaedia*. Edited by James Orr, et al. Chicago: Howard-Severance, 1915.

Wang, Chuanxin. "Holistic Health Definition: The Essential Elements." http://www.amcollege.edu/blog/the-essential-elements-that-define-holistic-health.

Weddle, David L. *Miracles: Wonder and Meaning in World Religions*. New York: New York University Press, 2010.

Wehr, Hans. *A Dictionary of Modern Written Arabic*, 4th ed. Wiesbaden, Germany: Otto Harrassowitz GmbH & Co., 1979.

"What are *Hadith*?" https://www.whyislam.org/prophet-muhammad/hadith/.

"What is Haram?" http://www.halalcs.org/halal-explained/what-is-haram.html.

"Wheaton Declaration: The Congress on the Church's Worldwide Mission." *International Review of Mission* 55, 220 (October 1966): 458–76.

Bibliography

WHO. "Constitution of the World Health Organization, WHO Basic Documents. 45th ed., Supplement." http://www.who.int/governance/eb/who_constitution_en.pdf.

"Who was Edgar Cayce?" https://www.edgarcayce.org/edgar-cayce/his-life/.

Wiersbe, Warren W. *The Bible Exposition Commentary, Vol. 1*. Wheaton: Victor, 1996.

Wilkinson, John. "Making Men Whole: The Theology of Medical Missions." The Maxwell Memorial Lecture for 1989. London: Christian Medical Fellowship, 1990.

Winter, Ralph. "The Two Structures of God's Redemptive Mission." *Missiology: An International Review* 2, 1 (January 1974): 121–39

Woodberry, J. Dudley. *Muslims & Christians on the Emmaus Road: Crucial Issues in Witness among Muslims*. Monrovia: MARC, 1989.

Woodward, Kenneth L. *The Book of Miracles: The Meaning of the Miracle Stories in Christianity, Judaism, Buddhism Hinduism, and Islam*. New York: Simon & Schuster, 2000.

World Council of Churches. "Lebanon." https://www.oikoumene.org/en/member-churches/middle-east/lebanon.

Wright, Christopher J. H. *The Mission of God: Unlocking the Bible's Grand Narrative*. Downers Grove: IVP Academic, 2006.

"*Wudu* Steps—How should a Muslim Perform *Wudu* or Ablution?" http://www.iqrasense.com/salat-prayers/how-should-a-muslim-perform-wudu-or-ablution.html.

Yamamori, Tetsunao. "Christian Health Care and Holistic Mission." *International Journal of Frontier Missions* 18, 2 (Summer 2001): 98–103.

Yassin, Nasser. *101 Facts & Figures on the Syrian Refugee Crisis*. Beirut, Lebanon: Issam Fares Institute for Public Policy and International Affairs, American University of Beirut, 2018.

Yoder, Perry B. *Shalom: The Bible's Word for Salvation, Justice, and Peace*. Eugene: Wipf and Stock, 1997.

Yucel, Salih, *Prayer and Healing in Islam*. Clifton: Tughra Books, 2010.

Zaharna, R. S. "An Associative Approach to Intercultural Communication Competence in the Arab World." In *Intercultural Communication Competence*. New York: SAGE, 2009. https://www.researchgate.net/publication/278157448_An_Associative_Approach_to_Intercultural_Communication_Competence_in_the_Arab_World.

www.ingramcontent.com/pod-product-compliance
Lightning Source LLC
Chambersburg PA
CBHW062041220426
43662CB00010B/1598